ADVANCE PRAISE FOR

Possibilities in Practice

"A powerful collection of case studies, *Possibilities in Practice: Social Justice Teaching in the Disciplines*, is a serious engagement with social justice pedagogy as an approach to teaching and its application in everyday practice. With tangible examples of teaching from P–12 and across disciplines, this book shows us social justice pedagogy in action."
—Luis Urrieta, Susan and John Adams Professor of Education, University of Texas at Austin

"A real strength of this book is its scope. It offers images of students ranging from pre–K to high school, in language arts, math, science, social studies, and arts-based classrooms. It delves into topics including gender and sexuality, anti-racism, immigration, ethnicity, linguistic diversity, among others. And instead of providing a chapter for everyone, it provides a kaleidoscope of possibilities for teachers committed to the ongoing, increasingly difficult, work of social justice in their classrooms."
—Mollie Blackburn, Professor, School of Teaching and Learning, College of Education and Human Ecology, The Ohio State University

"Teachers, and teacher educators, agree that meaningful education must be oriented toward equity and justice. These terms and concepts are ubiquitous in educational texts, but are rarely illustrated in action. This text fills that gap, providing much-needed real-world models of justice-oriented teaching practices. Spanning a wide range of grade levels, disciplines, and pedagogical approaches, authors present methods, projects and materials based on classroom experiences. The editors have collected narrations of practice that will inspire educators in their efforts to apply critical approaches to interdisciplinary, liberatory instruction in ways that will benefit all learners."
—Julie Gorlewski, Associate Professor of Teaching and Learning, Virginia Commonwealth University

Possibilities in Practice

This book is part of the Peter Lang Education list.
Every volume is peer reviewed and meets
the highest quality standards for content and production.

PETER LANG
New York • Bern • Frankfurt • Berlin
Brussels • Vienna • Oxford • Warsaw

Possibilities in Practice

Social Justice Teaching in the Disciplines

Summer Melody Pennell, Ashley S. Boyd,
Hillary Parkhouse, Alison LaGarry
EDITORS

PETER LANG
New York • Bern • Frankfurt • Berlin
Brussels • Vienna • Oxford • Warsaw

Library of Congress Cataloging-in-Publication Data

Names: Pennell, Summer Melody, editor.
Title: Possibilities in practice: social justice teaching in the disciplines /
edited by Summer Melody Pennell, Ashley S. Boyd, Hillary Parkhouse, Alison LaGarry.
Description: New York, NY: Peter Lang Publishing, Inc., 2017.
Includes bibliographical references and index.
Identifiers: LCCN 2017023020 | ISBN 978-1-4331-4609-1 (hardcover: alk. paper)
ISBN 978-1-4331-4602-2 (pbk: alk. paper) | ISBN 978-1-4331-4610-7 (ebook pdf)
ISBN 978-1-4331-4611-4 (epub) | ISBN 978-1-4331-4612-1 (mobi)
Subjects: LCSH: Education—Social aspects—United States.
Social justice—Study and teaching—United States.
Interdisciplinary approach in education—United States.
Classification: LCC LC191.4 .P667 2017 | DDC 370.11/5—dc23
LC record available at https://lccn.loc.gov/2017023020
DOI 10.3726/b11431

Bibliographic information published by **Die Deutsche Nationalbibliothek.**
Die Deutsche Nationalbibliothek lists this publication in the "Deutsche
Nationalbibliografie"; detailed bibliographic data are available
on the Internet at http://dnb.d-nb.de/.

© 2017 Peter Lang Publishing, Inc., New York
29 Broadway, 18th floor, New York, NY 10006
www.peterlang.com

Table OF Contents

Acknowledgments ix

Part One: Contexts of Social Justice Teaching 1
Chapter One: Possibilities in Practice: Introduction and Contextual Background 3
    Summer Melody Pennell and Ashley S. Boyd
Chapter Two: Theoretical and Historical Foundations of
    Social Justice Teaching 15
    Hillary Parkhouse, Ashley S. Boyd, and Summer Melody Pennell

Part Two: Pre-K–Elementary: Social Justice and Primary
    Students: How Early Is Too Early? 25
Chapter Three: Re-drawing the Line: Queering Our Pedagogy in the
    Early Childhood Classroom 27
    Pre-Kindergarten
    Laura Bower-Phipps, Jessica S. Powell, Marissa Bivona, Rebecca
    Harmon, and Anne Olcott
Chapter Four: *we are*: Exploring an Anti-Racist Summer Program for
    Elementary Students 41
    Kindergarten–3rd Grade
    Ronda Taylor Bullock, Cherish Williams, Daniel Kelvin·Bullock,
    and Stef Bernal-Martinez

Chapter Five: Immigration Today: Perspectives from Primary Classrooms 53
2nd Grade
Sunghee Shin and Beverly Milner (Lee) Bisland
Chapter Six: "Act Like a Girl!": Preservice Elementary Teacher
Perspectives of Gender Identity Development........................... 65
4th–5th Grade
Elizabeth E. Saylor
Chapter Seven: One Social Justice Music Educator: Working Within and
Beyond Disciplinary Expectations.. 79
Kindergarten–5th Grade
Alison LaGarry

**Part Three: Middle Grades: Investigating Equity with Middle Grades
Youth: Personalizing Justice for Students and Teachers 91**
Chapter Eight: Reading the Math on Marriage Equality: Social Justice
Lessons in Middle School... 93
5th–7th Grade
Summer Melody Pennell and Bryan Fede
Chapter Nine: Cultivating Communities of Care: Story Circles as Social
Justice Practice.. 107
6th–7th Grade
Courtney B. Cook and Celina Martínez Nichols
Chapter Ten: Fixing the World: Social Justice in World History.................. 121
7th Grade
Jeff A. Greiner
Chapter Eleven: Technology Integration in Urban Middle School
Classrooms: How Does Culturally Relevant Pedagogy Support 1:1
Technology Implementation? 133
6th–8th Grade
Lana M. Minshew, Martinette Horner, and Janice L. Anderson
Chapter Twelve: What's Science Got To Do with It? Possibilities for
Social Justice in Science Classroom Teaching and Learning 145
8th–9th Grade
Alexis Patterson, Deb Morrison, and Alexandra Schindel

**Part Four: High School Grades: Justice and Teens: Curricular
Approaches to Equity in High School 159**
Chapter Thirteen: "Project Read Freely": Using Young Adult Literature
to Engender Student Choice in an English Language Arts Classroom 161
9th Grade
Ashley S. Boyd, Alyssa Bauermeister, and Holly Matteson

Chapter Fourteen: Geography Matters: Face-to-Face Contact Pedagogies
   to Humanize Unfamiliar Ethnocultural Differences 175
   9th Grade
   Joanne M. Pattison-Meek
Chapter Fifteen: "I, Too, Sing America": Operationalizing #WeAreNotThis and
   #BlackLivesMatter in an English Classroom 187
   9th Grade
   Jeanne Dyches
Chapter Sixteen: Teaching Columbus to Newcomer Students:
   Social Justice in the Classroom and Across the Urban Landscape 201
   9th–10th Grade
   Jay M. Shuttleworth and Josef Donnelly
Chapter Seventeen: "Couch the Oppression in Resistance":
   Teaching Strategies for Social Change Through U.S. History 213
   11th Grade
   Hillary Parkhouse
Chapter Eighteen: "It's Like We Were Slow-Roasted … But in a Really
   Good Way": Embedded Y-PAR in a U.S. History Course 225
   11th Grade
   Brian Gibbs
Chapter Nineteen: Students as Researchers: A Co-teaching Narrative
   from a Social Justice-Oriented U.S. Government Class 237
   12th Grade
   Linsay DeMartino and Sara Rusk

Notes on Contributors 251
Index 257

Acknowledgments

This book would not exist without our chapter authors and the teachers and classrooms in which they studied to document and analyze social justice. We are ever-grateful to our contributors for sharing their insights and their work. To the teachers whose practices are reported within these pages, we also extend our gratitude. Allowing a researcher into your space can be disconcerting, and to open up what is essentially (for a teacher) your heart to them, is sometimes a challenge. We thank you and those like you for your passion and commitment to equity.

We are also indebted to Silvia Bettez, who, many years ago, put us on this path to social justice education and to examining the myriad ways justice can appear in classrooms. As our teacher, Silvia embodied what it meant to teach social justice with love and critical care and led us through a consideration of many of the texts and topics that appear here in our work. We are grateful to the professors who inspired us at UNC-Chapel Hill: Jocelyn Glazier, Lynda Stone, Cheryl Bolick, Xue Rong, and Jim Trier. Each of you were central to our development as scholars and we thank you for supporting us. We are especially grateful to George Noblit, not only for his encouragement in creating this collection, but for his unwavering dedication to each of us in our graduate studies, his commitment to justice-oriented education, and his example of researching and teaching with values intact. George, you have invigorated so many, and we are honored to be among them.

Many thanks also goes to each of our support systems—the families, friends, and furry companions who sacrifice so that we can pursue our research agendas, write, and edit at all times of the day and night. The Critical Carpool, the four of us who are not only co-editors but friends, feel so fortunate to have had the opportunity to work together on this project.

I, Summer, thank Morgan and the students at The Anchor School for allowing me to collaborate with you in Math for a Cause. Many thanks are owed to Bryan Fede, my research partner. My parents, Dennis and Diana, taught me to be critical and always pointed out power structures, creating a future social justice educator. I am grateful for the support of my partner, Susan, my sister Tegan, and my many extended kin and chosen family members. Lastly, thank you to my wonderful colleagues and students at Truman State University.

I, Ashley, would like to thank my family—my parents, Michael and Christy, and Brian and Ginger—for keeping me grounded and supporting my work, even when it takes me far from home. Especially to my mom, thank you for your endless patience and encouragement. To Avery, Lillian, Ellis, Wren, and Ember, my nieces, I am so grateful for the joy you bring to my life and am so proud of the strong young women you are becoming. I hope for a future filled with possibilities and justice for each of you. To Keith, thank you for your love, encouragement, and fortitude over this past year. To my WSU colleagues, especially Todd Butler, Bill Condon, Victor Villanueva, Leeann Hunter, and Roger Whitson, many thanks for your support and mentorship as I have navigated academia.

I, Hillary, would like to thank my mother, Nancy, for being my earliest social justice teacher. You helped me understand how the playing field is not even, and you modeled how those with privilege can do their part for a better world. I thank my father, Keith, for being an example of unwavering belief that all youth, even (and especially) those in the criminal justice system, deserve support and second chances. I thank Thomas for listening to my rambling without ever tuning out, and Felix for bringing me constant joy. And finally, to Gabriel Reich, Kurt Stemhagen, Philip Gnilka, Christine Bae, Jason Chow, and my other new friends at VCU, thank you for making work feel like play and colleagues feel like family.

I, Alison would like to thank my former students who encouraged me to see past the traditional boundaries of music education. Specifically, my students at Westlake High School in Waldorf, Maryland helped me to see that there was more to learn about arts, equity, and justice. I am thankful for the ongoing support of my family, colleagues, and friends as I pursue this work. Special thanks to my parents—Mary and Phil, my brother—Tim, and my partner James. Also, to my colleagues in cultural studies at the University of North Carolina at Chapel Hill— thanks for your mentoring and friendship in this first year of my academic career!

In these uncertain times in which we find ourselves, teaching for social justice is more crucial than ever. We agree with Urrieta (2009) that, "activism needs to be rethought by viewing daily 'moments' of agency in practice as activism. Agency and activism … are tools embedded in the mundane details of daily interactions"

(p. 14). The work teachers do, on the ground and in schools, holds vast potential for justice and for making a difference. We must recognize and harness the potential in those small moments, as the teachers in this book illustrate.

REFERENCE

Urrieta, L. (2009). *Working from within: Chicana and Chicano activist educators in whitestream schools.* Tucson, AZ: University of Arizona Press.

PART ONE

Contexts of Social Justice Teaching

CHAPTER ONE

Possibilities IN Practice

Introduction and Contextual Background

SUMMER MELODY PENNELL AND ASHLEY S. BOYD

Social justice evokes images of activism, of protests and marches advocating for marginalized peoples. Social justice in pedagogy and education also connotes working toward equity for all students, thus maintaining the focus on action for the betterment of society. Social justice pedagogy is, like all critical pedagogies, a way of thinking and framing an approach to teaching rather than a set of pre-scribed practices. It is versatile and differs depending upon contextual factors such as student background and experiences (Darder, Baltodano, & Torres, 2009). Social justice pedagogy does not have to mean leading students in a march or beginning a revolution; rather, it can be a part of everyday teaching practices (e.g., North, 2009). What, then, might these practices look like? How can classroom teachers—who are under local and societal pressures to increase test scores and meet varied standards and accountability measures—incorporate social justice teaching into their curriculum while meeting those expectations and mandates? This volume seeks to answer those questions by demonstrating examples of social justice teaching from actual PK–12 contexts.

As editors, we collectively felt the need for a book like this one as we worked through our individual research studies on social justice education in different school disciplines. We currently teach our pre-service teachers about injustices and equity at our respective universities and wanted a collection for our students. Pennell (2016) completed a study on a social justice-based interdisciplinary math and literacy course in a middle school and continues to research social justice practices in English Language Arts. Boyd (2014, 2016) studies the social justice practices of in-service secondary English Language Arts teachers and works with pre-service teachers to develop their critical literacies. Parkhouse (2016) investigates how high school social studies teachers develop students' critical consciousness. And LaGarry (2016) researches social justice-oriented music educators as well as arts integration. The four of us presented on a panel together at the 2015 annual conference of the American Educational Studies Association, sharing the discipline-specific work we have done to document social justice practices. We were approached after our presentation by pre-service teachers who were eager for more material on incorporating equity-oriented teaching in the classroom. They, like many of our own teacher candidates, believe in social justice and seek to implement related pedagogies in their classrooms, but they felt they lacked real-world examples of methods and ideas for projects and materials. Since then, we have connected with teacher educators and in-service teachers who are also yearning for more models of justice-oriented teaching practices. They acknowledge that equity work sounds great in theory, but they wonder what it looks like on the ground, amidst lively children, bustling hallways, watchful administrators, and skeptical colleagues.

While we know that teachers and researchers are doing social justice work in the classroom, documentation of these efforts is sparse. It may be that practicing teachers are too busy to write about their lessons because—in addition to their regular teaching duties—such teachers are committed to connecting their students to the local, national, and global communities beyond their classrooms. With these multiple and complex pedagogical goals, it is not surprising that many lack the time to write about their teaching. It may also be that dissemination is not at the forefront of teachers' minds who place their priorities of practice on their students. While the literature on social justice abounds with research on students in teacher education programs, there is a significant dearth of studies that focus on—or even merely include—PK–12 classroom and teaching practices. It is this gap which we aim to fill in the pages that follow.

This volume presents chapters from researchers and teachers on empirical studies of social justice-oriented teaching practices from a variety of subjects and grade levels. We hope that this can serve as a starting point for in-service teachers who need tangible take-aways and who seek methods they can adapt for their own spaces. We also aspire to demonstrate the effectiveness of social justice teaching to those who doubt that it is research-based, grounded in sound methodology, and present in findings that emerge from careful observation and study (Cochran-Smith, Barnatt, Lahann, Shakman, & Terrell, 2009). Additionally, we feel the work documented here can be a model for teacher educators to share with pre-service teachers, again to provide concrete examples of social justice in action, which is especially important both for students who have the desire to implement such practices as well as those who are doubtful that social justice has a place in the classroom.

DEFINING SOCIAL JUSTICE EDUCATION

Few renderings of social justice education include a focus on PK–12 students, as the enactment of social justice depends on the local context and thus any definition needs to be open to various applications. Social justice pedagogy comes from a variety of anti-oppressive movements, such as the Civil Rights Movement and the Women's Movement, as well as from a number of critical theories (e.g. Althusser, 1971; Delgado & Stefancic, 2012; Gramsci, 1971; Hall, 1980; Marx & Engels, 1848) that have in turn led to a host of critical pedagogies (e.g. Applebaum, 2010; Freire, 1968/1970; Janks, 2000; Ladson-Billings, 1995; McLaren, 2003; Morrell, Dueñas, Garcia, & López, 2013). Given this background, social justice education is inclusive of areas of race, ethnicity, socioeconomic status, gender, gender identity and expression, sexual orientation, disability, religion, and nationality. The next chapter highlights details of these influential movements and pedagogies.

Social justice pedagogy was largely informed by the work of Paulo Freire (1968/1970), particularly his concepts of "reading the word and the world" and "conscientization." At the heart of these notions is the idea that oppression in society is pervasive on every level, in the materiality of our everyday lives. Practitioners want to instill in students a recognition of the presence of privilege and oppression and to cultivate their critical consciousness, which begins as "an awareness that our ideas come from a particular set of life experiences" and acknowledges that "others have equally valid, if different, life experiences and ideas" (Hinchey, 2004, p. 25). The hope is that students will go beyond recognizing and caring about injustices by actually taking action against them. Common approaches to help students become more discerning are incorporating culturally-relevant pedagogy (Ladson-Billings, 1995, 2006) and acknowledging students' funds of knowledge (Moll, Amanti, Neff, & Gonzalez, 1992). These strategies emphasize utilizing students' strengths and diverse cultural backgrounds in the classroom. In this way, students who differ from the majority are seen as having cultural assets, rather than deficits viewed from the dominant perspective. Social justice also involves reflexivity, both for the teacher and learner. When teaching is approached critically, teachers must reflect not only on their own responses but on how their teaching practices relate to their local context and community (Pennell & Cain, 2016), in turn considering how they can use these for personal growth and to drive their curriculum forward.

CURRENT PRACTICES

Overall, practices in social justice education hold the students at the center. As social justice is based on classroom and community contexts and can incorporate a host of different critical approaches or foci, there is no "one size fits all" approach. Thus, there is much variability in what this type of teaching might look like. Each teacher (or preferably teachers and students together) must decide what will work best for the students. In many cases, this includes explicitly teaching students of color and from working class backgrounds the culture of power (Delpit, 1995) so that they can appropriate these norms and codes in order to gain access to grades, standardized test scores, and extracurricular activities that will give them a better chance at college admission (Bender-Slack, 2010; North, 2009). In other instances, teachers ask students to critically respond to written texts, including those on topics such as race in the United States (Camangian, 2009) or global labor issues (Bigelow, 1998). Other forms of social justice teaching include hip-hop based education (Hill & Petchauer, 2013; Stovall, 2006) and critical media literacy (Leard & Lashua, 2006). Another common thread in social justice teaching is using interdisciplinary units and co-teaching. Beyond these tangible methods, researchers who focus on what social justice pedagogy looks like in PK–12 classrooms suggest the following as pedagogic goals: (a) helping students gain critical consciousness and awareness (Cammarota & Romero, 2011; Greene, 1998; Hayden-Benn, 2011); (b) teaching students to navigate obstacles, oppressions, and injustices (Ayers, 1998; Cammarota & Romero, 2011; Swalwell, 2013); (c) giving students practical knowledge to accomplish these goals (North, 2009; Skerrett, 2010); and (d) enabling students to produce their own knowledge and texts (Cammarota & Romero, 2011; Yang, 2009).

SOCIAL JUSTICE EDUCATION AND STUDENT OUTCOMES

Across the existing scholarship on social justice education in classrooms, the main categories for research-supported student outcomes from social justice education are: (a) problem solving skills, (b) evaluation and analysis skills, (c) collaboration and community building, (d) critical literacy, and (e) social action. These outcomes are not discrete: many times they intersect.

Classroom-Based Skills

Problem solving is a necessary skill for students engaging in social justice. As Westheimer and Kahne (1998) asserted, "students must learn how to respond to social problems and also how certain problems come to the fore while others remain unnamed" (p. 18). An example with high school students comes from Bigelow's (1998) classroom, in which students examined corporate policy and marketing materials from Nike for loopholes that allowed the company to exploit their workers and the environment. Students then contacted the company to encourage them to change these policies.

Evaluation and analysis skills go hand-in-hand with problem solving. When analyzing a social problem, students can investigate the complex roots of inequities (Swalwell, 2013). By increasing skills in analysis and evaluation, students deepen their critical thinking skills, learn to dissect complex texts, consider differing points of view, and recognize hidden curriculums.

Evaluation and analysis can lead to collaborations. Because of the types of group discussions and reflections many teachers use, students are able to bond as a class and create a collaborative community (Christensen, 1998; Hutchinson & Romano, 1998; Stern, 1998; Westheimer & Kahne, 1998). Johnson, Oppenheim, and Suh (2009) noted that one teacher in their study facilitated this community building and collaboration through her community circle activity, which she used for group discussions where students were encouraged to respectfully share and listen to each other.

Students in social justice classrooms gain and improve a wide variety of literacy skills: writing, creating films, researching, and learning to critically approach a variety of texts (Akom, 2009; Bigelow, 1998; Johnson et al., 2009; Pescatore, 2007). Some teachers enabled students to create their own knowledge through these literacy practices. For example, Yang (2009) worked with students to create public texts, such as films, research reports, and websites to report on social justice issues.

Skills Beyond the Classroom

Beyond these classroom-based skills, a more abstract outcome is gaining a critical mindset that students then take outside of their school walls. This can be traced directly from the teaching practices enabling students to critically reflect on their own experiences as well as on contemporary and historical events. Forging interpersonal connections, where students learn to see others in new light and to understand more fully our intimate human connections, is crucial to fostering critical and social justice mindsets. These relationships also help move students from seeing inequality as an individual issue to beginning to see the systemic connections between issues (Boyd, LaGarry, & Cain, 2016). Rather than perceiving, for example, discrimination solely as an act one person commits against another, they can begin to see how oppression operates on a broader level, such as in government policies (Barry, 2005). This relates to another skill needed for students' critical mindsets: the recognition of social problems. While this may seem simple, awareness must include knowledge of systemic oppression (Christensen, 1998).

Action is the ultimate goal of social justice education. This includes action from all parties involved—students and teachers—and applies across the board to students of all demographics. As Swalwell (2013) noted in her study of privileged students engaged in social justice,

> rather than committing individual random acts of kindness or being involved in leadership roles divorced from root causes of social problems, privileged students educated in social justice pedagogy mobilize their privilege on behalf of and act in alliance with marginalized people. (p. 3)

Action can be taken in the local level of the school or community, for a national cause, or even on a global scale to lobby for a particular issue. As such, it could take the form of student presentations at events (Hayden-Benn, 2011; Stern, 1998; Westheimer & Kahne, 1998; Yang, 2009), dissemination of student-created materials on social justice issues (Akom, 2009; Hayden-Benn, 2011; Yang, 2009), or discussing unfair treatment with administrators to encourage policy changes (Cammarota & Romero, 2011).

CHALLENGES TO SOCIAL JUSTICE EDUCATION IN PK–12 SCHOOLS

Social justice pedagogy, despite the advantages it provides for student learning, is not without its challenges. First and foremost, school administrators and districts, like many who question social justice education, may be resistant to any curriculum that is seen as promoting a progressive agenda (Cochran-Smith et al., 2009; Westheimer & Kahne, 1998). Often, politicians and other individuals involved in analyzing social policies issue the harshest critiques of social justice and in turn affect popular opinion as well educational policy. For instance, conservative political commentator George Will's (2006) harangue in *Newsweek* mocked schools of education for their focus on cultivating teachers as change agents and lamented the tendency toward progressivism which allegedly ignores teaching basic knowledge. Suggesting that we return to teacher-centered classrooms, Will proposed the return to a diluted curriculum that ultimately preserves the status quo.

Will (2006) claimed a social justice approach ignores "real" or "serious" knowledge (hooks, 2000) for the sake of preparing teachers to be what others have labeled being "nice" and "making children feel good" (Cochran-Smith et al., 2009, p. 627). From this perspective, social justice teaching is celebratory and superficial. Nothing could be further from the truth. In the words of renowned social justice educator Linda Christensen, who has worked tirelessly in secondary English classrooms, "It's academically rigorous; we don't do social justice at the expense of students' gaining the kind of skills that they need to be able to traverse the world" (Golden, 2008, p. 60). Her work demonstrates the writing, reading, and social skills students gain while simultaneously working toward social justice.

The sentiment, however, that social justice work is not rigorous or that it is biased is a challenge to the field because it hinders practitioners from fulfilling equity-oriented goals. Many worry that standards cannot be met if the focus in the classroom is too heavily slanted toward justice-related curriculum, although researchers such as Dover (2015) have proven how the two go hand-in-hand. Dover's (2015) study illustrated how twenty-four teachers across thirteen states "conceptualized teaching for social justice and how they reconciled that vision with the demands of teaching amid restrictive curricular mandates," (p. 519), mainly the Common Core State Standards. The lessons she analyzed contained a range of social justice topics including racism, religious oppression, sexism, classism, sexual orientation, and general oppression. She correlated these lessons with specific objectives met, such as those that required students to "draw inferences, or cite specific textual evidence" (p. 521) or engage in "writing informative/explanatory texts ... research projects ... and written, evidence-based literary analysis" (p. 522).

Despite such evidence, however, many teachers retain a real fear of losing jobs or facing student and parent resistance and avoid social justice in the classroom (Bender-Slack, 2010). This is likely why so many schools where teachers practice social justice are private (e.g. Swalwell, 2013) or otherwise non-traditional public schools (e.g. Hines & Johnson, 2007), or already have a school-wide social justice focus (e.g. North, 2009). Additionally, Beliveau, Holzer, and Schmidt (2008) fear that in some spaces social justice may be equated to political correctness and that students and teachers both will censor themselves for fear of offending.

Researchers have pointed out that sometimes awareness of injustice may be emotionally painful for students (Bigelow, 1998; Hayden-Benn, 2011), but that this pain is necessary for growth (Leonardo, 2009). As Camangian (2009) wrote, sometimes pain "is essential to move students' analyses from the personal to the interpersonal, and to address cross-cultural and gendered differences" (p. 505), even though sometimes it can cause students to shut down (Brion-Meisels, 2009). Social justice education is an emotional process, and negative emotions can help spur students to work for positive social change. By engaging students in questioning, reflection, and critical thinking, teachers and students can collaboratively create new knowledge from socially-engaged emotional depths. Teachers can also balance lessons on inequity by including lessons on positive outcomes from social movements, such as how different groups in the United States gained voting rights.

POSSIBILITIES IN PRACTICE

In order to speak to a dire need for more models of equity-oriented teaching practices from the field, this book aims to show real-life examples of social justice pedagogy in action in PK–12 teaching from a variety of grade levels and disciplines. The authors use myriad theories to talk about subjects ranging from music (LaGarry), science (Patterson, Morrison, & Schindel), math (Pennell & Fede), English Language Arts and literacy (Boyd, Bauermeister, & Matteson; Dyches; Pennell & Fede), and social studies (DeMartino & Rusk; Gibbs; Greiner; Parkhouse; Pattison-Meek; Saylor; Shuttleworth & Donnelly). There are also interdisciplinary examples (Cook & Martinez-Nichols; Pennell & Fede) as well as chapters focused on specific populations of students, such as immigrant students (Pattison-Meek; Shin & Bisland; Shuttleworth & Donnelly) and English Language Learners (DeMartino & Rusk). The chapters span a variety of grade levels, ranging from PK–5 (Bower-Phipps, Powell, Bivona, Harmon, & Anne Olcott; Bullock, Williams, Bullock, & Bernal-Martinez; LaGarry; Saylor; Shin & Bisland), to middle school (Cook & Martinez-Nichols; Greiner; Minshew, Anderson, Horner; Patterson, Morrison, & Schindel; Pennell & Fede), to high school (Boyd, Bauermeister, & Matteson; Dyches; Gibbs; Parkhouse; Pattison-Meek; Shuttleworth & Donnelly). For the ease of readers, the book is organized into three sections by grade level: (1) Pre-kindergarten and elementary, (2) middle grades, and (3) high school. With this variety of disciplines, grade levels, and student populations, we hope to provide a nuanced portrait of the possibilities for social justice in practice, one from which all teachers can find inspiration for their own classrooms.

Since we started working on this collection, there has been a major political shift in the United States that has struck fear in the hearts of many students, families, and teachers. With the Southern Poverty Law Center documenting a marked increase in hate crimes and bullying in schools since the 2016 presidential election it is vital that teachers are prepared to not only create welcoming and safe environments in their classrooms, but to face adversity head on. One way to do this is by employing social justice pedagogy to give students the tools they need to think critically, gain empathy, and learn to problem solve and discuss difficult subjects. This volume offers examples for teachers to practice social justice teaching across grade levels and disciplines, and to use these research-based practices to maintain a sense of critical hope (Duncan-Andrade, 2009) in uncertain times.

REFERENCES

Akom, A. A. (2009). Critical hip hop pedagogy as a form of liberatory praxis. *Equity & Excellence in Education, 42*(1), 52–66.

Althusser, L. (1971). Ideology and ideological state apparatuses. In B. Brewster (Trans.), *Lenin and philosophy and other essays*. New York, NY: Monthly Review Press.

Applebaum, B. (2010). *Being white, being good: White complicity, white moral responsibility, and social justice pedagogy*. Lanham, MD: Lexington Books.

Ayers, W. (1998). Foreword: Popular education – Teaching for social justice. In W. Ayers, J. A. Hunt, & T. Quinn (Eds.), *Teaching for social justice: A democracy and education reader* (pp. xvii–xxv). New York, NY: W. W. Norton.

Barry, B. (2005). *Why social justice matters*. Malden, MA: Polity Press.

Beliveau, L. B., Holzer, K. O., & Schmidt, S. (2008). It's in the telling and the sharing: Becoming conscious of social justice through communal exploration. *Counterpoints, 332*, 23–44.

Bender-Slack, D. (2010). Texts, talk … and fear? English language arts teachers negotiate social justice teaching. *English Education, 42*(2), 181–203.

Bigelow, B. (1998). The human lives behind the labels: The global sweatshop, Nike, and the race to the bottom. In W. Ayers, J. A. Hunt, & T. Quinn (Eds.), *Teaching for social justice: A democracy and education reader* (pp. 21–38). New York, NY: Teachers College Press, The New Press.

Boyd, A. (2014). *Contradictions in teaching: A collective case study of teachers' social justice literacies in middle and secondary English Classrooms* (Doctoral dissertation). The University of North Carolina at Chapel Hill, Chapel Hill, NC.

Boyd, A. (2016). Deconstructing a new teacher savior: Paladins and politics in *Won't Back Down*. In M. Schoffner (Ed.), *Saviors, scapegoats and schoolmarms: Examining the classroom teacher in fiction and film for teacher education* (pp. 160–170). New York, NY: Routledge.

Boyd, A., LaGarry, A., & Cain, J. (2016). Moving from self to system: A framework for social justice centered on issues and action. *International Journal of Critical Pedagogy, 7*(2), 171–197.

Brion-Meisels, G. (2009). Playing in the light: Experiential learning and white identity development. In D. Stovall, T. Quinn, & W. Ayers (Eds.), *Handbook of social justice in education* (pp. 661–667). New York, NY: Routledge.

Camangian, P. (2009). Real talk: Transformative English teaching and urban youth. In D. Stovall, T. Quinn, & W. Ayers (Eds.), *Handbook of social justice in education* [electronic version] (pp. 437–507). New York, NY: Routledge.

Cammarota, J., & Romero, A. (2011). Participatory action research for high school students: Transforming policy, practice, and the personal with social justice education. *Educational Policy, 25*(3), 488–506.

Christensen, L. (1998). Writing the word and the world. In W. Ayers, J. A. Hunt, & T. Quinn (Eds.), *Teaching for social justice: A democracy and education reader* (pp. 39–47). New York, NY: Teachers College Press, The New Press.

Cochran-Smith, M., Barnatt, J., Lahann, R., Shakman, K., & Terrell, D. (2009). Teacher education for social justice: Critiquing the critiques. In W. Ayres, T. Quinn, & D. Stovell (Eds.), *The handbook for social justice in education* (pp. 625–639). New York, NY: Routledge.

Darder, A., Baltodano, M., & Torres, R. D. (Eds.). (2009). *The critical pedagogy reader* (2nd ed.). New York, NY: Routledge.

Delgado, R., & Stefancic, J. (2012). *Critical race theory: An introduction*. New York, NY: New York University Press.

Delpit, L. (1995). *Other people's children: Cultural conflict in the classroom*. New York, NY: The New Press.

Dover, A. (2015). Teaching for social justice and the common core: Justice-oriented curriculum for language arts and literacy. *Journal of Adolescent and Adult Literacy, 59*(5), 517–527.

Duncan-Andrade, J. (2009). Note to educators: Hope required when growing roses in concrete. *Harvard Educational Review, 79*(2), 181–194.

Freire, P. (1968/1970). *Pedagogy of the oppressed.* (M. B. Ramos, Trans.). New York, NY: Bloomsbury. (Original work published 1968).

Golden, J. (2008). A conversation with Linda Christensen on social justice education. *English Journal, 97*(6), 59–64.

Gramsci, A. (1971). Hegemony, intellectuals and the state. In J. Storey (Ed.), *Cultural theory and popular culture: A reader* (pp. 215–221). New York, NY: Harvester Wheatsheaf.

Greene, M. (1998). Introduction: Teaching for social justice. In W. Ayers, J. A. Hunt, & T. Quinn (Eds.), *Teaching for social justice: A democracy and education reader* (pp. xvii–xivi). New York, NY: W. W. Norton.

Hall, S. (1980). Encoding/decoding. In S. Hall, D. Hobson, A. Love, & P. Willis (Eds.), *Culture, media, language* (pp. 128–138). London: Hutchinson.

Hayden-Benn, J. (2011). Creating critical activists rather than robots of hegemony: A grade six social justice club. *Radical Teacher, 91*(1), 50–58.

Hill, M. L., & Petchauer, E. (Eds.). (2013). *Schooling hip-hop: Expanding hip-hop based education across the curriculum.* New York, NY: Teachers College Press.

Hinchey, P. H. (2004). *Becoming a critical educator: Defining a classroom identity, designing a critical pedagogy.* New York, NY: Peter Lang.

Hines, M. B., & Johnson, J. (2007). Teachers and students as agents of change: Toward a taxonomy of the literacies of social justice. In D. Rowe, R. Jimenez, D. Compton, D. Dickinson, Y. Kim, K. Leander, & V. Risko (Eds.), *2007 Yearbook of the National Reading Conference* (Vol. 56, pp. 281–292). Oak Creek, WI: National Reading Conference.

hooks, b. (2000). *Feminist theory: From margin to center* (2nd ed.). Boston, MA: South End Press.

Hutchinson, J. N., & Romano, R. M. (1998). A story for social justice. In W. Ayers, J. A. Hunt, & T. Quinn (Eds.), *Teaching for social justice: A democracy and education reader* (pp. 254–269). New York, NY: Teachers College Press, The New Press.

Janks, H. (2000). Domination, access, diversity, and design: A synthesis for critical literacy education. *Educational Review, 52*(2), 175–186.

Johnson, E., Oppenheim, R., & Suh, Y. (2009). "Would that be social justice?" A conceptual constellation of social justice curriculum in action. *New Educator, 5*(4), 293–310.

Ladson-Billings, G. (1995). Toward a theory of culturally relevant pedagogy. *American Educational Research Journal, 32*(3), 465–491. doi:10.3102/00028312032003465

Ladson-Billings, G. (2006). "Yes, but how do we do it": Practicing culturally relevant pedagogy. In J. Landsman & C. Lewis (Eds.), *White teachers/diverse classrooms: A guide to building inclusive schools, promoting high expectations, and eliminating racism* (pp. 29–41). Herndon, VA: Stylus Publishing.

LaGarry, A. E. (2016). *Narratives of note: The dynamics of socially just music education* (Doctoral dissertation). The University of North Carolina at Chapel Hill, Chapel Hill, NC.

Leard, D. W., & Lashua, B. (2006). Popular media, critical pedagogy, and inner city youth. *Canadian Journal of Education/Revue canadienne de l'*éducation, *29*(1), 244–264.

Leonardo, Z. (2009). Reading whiteness: Antiracist pedagogy against white racial knowledge. In D. Stovall, T. Quinn, & W. Ayers (Eds.), *Handbook of social justice in education* [electronic version] (pp. 231–248). New York, NY: Routledge.

Marx, K., & Engels, F. (1848). *The communist manifesto.* In S. Moore (Trans.). *Marx/Engels selected works* (pp. 98–137). Moscow: Progress Publishers. (Original work published 1848).

McLaren, P. (2003). Critical pedagogy: A look at the major concepts. In A. Darder, M. Baltodano, & R. D. Torres (Eds.), *The critical pedagogy reader* (pp. 69–96). New York, NY: Routledge.

Moll, L. C., Amanti, C., Neff, D., & Gonzalez, N. (1992). Funds of knowledge for teaching: Using a qualitative approach to connect homes and classrooms. *Theory into Practice, 31*(2), 132–141.

Morrell, E., Dueñas, R., Garcia, V., & López, J. (2013). *Critical media pedagogy: Teaching for achievement in city schools.* New York, NY: Teachers College.

North, C. E. (2009). *Teaching for social justice? Voices from the front lines.* Boulder, CO: Paradigm Publishers.

Parkhouse, H. (2016). *Critical pedagogy in U.S. history classrooms: Conscientization and contradictory consciousness* (Doctoral dissertation). The University of North Carolina at Chapel Hill, Chapel Hill, NC.

Pennell, S. M. (2016). *Queering the curriculum: Critical literacy and numeracy for social justice* (Doctoral dissertation). The University of North Carolina at Chapel Hill, Chapel Hill, NC.

Pennell, S. M., & Cain, J. M. (2016). Adorned: Moving from decoration to disposition in social justice. In J. Diem (Ed.), *The social and cultural foundations of education: A reader* (pp. 148–165). San Diego, CA: Cognella Academic Publishing.

Pescatore, C. (2007). Current events as empowering literacy: For English and social studies teachers. *Journal of Adolescent & Adult Literacy, 51*(4), 326–339.

Skerrett, A. (2010). Teaching critical literacy for social justice. *Action in Teacher Education, 31*(4), 54–65.

Stern, D. (1998). Teaching for change. In W. Ayers, J. A. Hunt, & T. Quinn (Eds.), *Teaching for social justice: A democracy and education reader* (pp. 276–284). New York, NY: Teachers College Press, The New Press.

Stovall, D. (2006). We can relate: Hip-hop culture, critical pedagogy, and the secondary classroom. *Urban Education, 41*(6), 585–602.

Swalwell, K. (2013). "With great power comes great responsibility:" Privileged students' conceptions of justice-oriented citizenship. *Democracy & Education, 21*(1), 1–11.

Westheimer, J., & Kahne, J. (1998). Education for action: Preparing youth for participatory democracy. In W. Ayers, J. A. Hunt, & T. Quinn (Eds.), *Teaching for social justice: A democracy and education reader* (pp. 1–20). New York, NY: Teachers College Press, The New Press.

Will, G. (2006, January 16). Ed schools vs. education: Prospective teachers are expected to have the correct 'disposition,' proof of which is espousing 'progressive' political beliefs. *Newsweek.* Retrieved from faculty.tamu commerce.edu/slstewart/EdSchoolsGeorgeWill.doc

Yang, K. W. (2009). For and against: The school-education dialect in social justice. In D. Stovall, T. Quinn, & W. Ayers (Eds.), *Handbook of social justice in education* [electronic version] (pp. 455–464). New York, NY: Routledge.

CHAPTER TWO

Theoretical AND Historical Foundations OF Social Justice Teaching

HILLARY PARKHOUSE, ASHLEY S. BOYD, AND
SUMMER MELODY PENNELL

HISTORY: RAPID GROWTH, SETBACKS, AND THE BUZZWORD PROBLEM

Although the field of social justice education—by that title—is relatively new, teaching for social justice is not new at all. Early 20th century education scholars such as George Counts, John Dewey, and Carter G. Woodson advocated for similar ideas, such as participatory democracy and the expansion of literacy to create a more equitable society. Moreover, many fields emerging within education over the second half of the 20th century share similar aims and underlying tenets with social justice education. These fields include ethnic studies, multicultural education, culturally relevant pedagogies, critical pedagogy, anti-colonial education, feminist pedagogy, and queer pedagogy.

Since the emergence of *social justice education* as a distinct field in the 1990s, its popularity has spread rapidly among educational researchers, practitioners, publishing outlets and others (North, 2008). According to Adams, Bell, and Griffin (2007), by the 2006 annual conference of the American Education Research Association (AERA), there were 112 sessions on this topic, and "AERA now has a director of social justice, a Social Justice Action Committee, a special interest group (SIG) on Educators for Social Justice, and another newly formed SIG on Leadership for Social Justice" (p. xvii). Schools of education and other programs are increasingly using the term in their stated aims and curricula.

Even within this short history, however, there has already been some backlash against the term and backpedaling in response to its ideological position. The National Council for Accreditation of Teacher Education (now the Council for Accreditation of Educator Preparation) removed social justice language from its accrediting standards as a result of the term's politically charged and controversial nature (Hytten & Bettez, 2011). Another impact of the rapid expansion of the term into all arenas of education is that some feel it has already been reduced to a mere buzzword. Worried it will follow one of its predecessors, multicultural education, which initially contained a critical focus but was eventually diluted to a more celebratory "heroes and holidays" approach, advocates of social justice fear that its entry into public discourse will lead to a detraction of its emphasis on activism and social change. Teachers in some schools are charged to use social justice teaching, but are given little explanation of what that means or how to do it. It seems Adams' and colleagues' (2007) fear that the term would become a buzzword is already becoming a reality in some places.

The future of social justice in education may be even more in peril with the election of Donald Trump, whose intentions to use public funds to pay for private school vouchers (Education: Donald Trump's Vision, 2016) would undermine public education, which has long been held as a vital institution for democratic societies (Dewey, 1916/1980). At the time of writing, Trump had also pledged to scale back the Department of Education's civil rights office, which could affect social justice issues like protections for transgender students and redressing racial disparities in school disciplinary actions (Ujifusa, 2016).

RENEWING COMMITMENT TO SOCIAL JUSTICE THROUGH ILLUSTRATING POSSIBILITIES IN PRACTICE

In compiling this book of researched, concrete, and classroom-tested social justice teaching practices and their impacts on students, we hope to address this problem and center the deeper meanings and implications of social justice so as to obviate its becoming widely dismissed as just another education fad. The chapters here illustrate how social justice should not be thought of as one more burden placed on teachers, but rather as the foundation for what many teachers are already doing: working toward a more equitable society and disrupting systems of oppression and privilege. Furthermore, the chapters exemplify how social justice aims can be incorporated at any grade level and in any subject area, and how they can complement standards and curriculum teachers are already using. Thus, the examples in these chapters serve two purposes: (a) to help practicing teachers and teacher candidates—who may hear the phrase "social justice" without an explanation of it—to understand what it looks like in practice, specifically in their own grade level and content area; and (b) to help teachers see how they may already be acting on some of the underlying premises of social justice education without realizing it.

THEORETICAL FOUNDATIONS

Social justice in education rests upon several theoretical assumptions, including the necessity of democracy and the universality of human rights, the focus on equity and attention to structural barriers that inhibit equitable opportunities, and the sustaining of cultural diversity. Each of these theoretical bases is addressed in the following sections.

Participatory Democracy and Human Rights

Most conceptualizations of social justice education rest on the social liberalist view that all humans have certain rights and that protection of these rights should be guaranteed to all. These rights may include freedom from harm—physical and emotional—and the right to participate in one's governance. These are also under-lying tenets of democracy. Particularly relevant to social justice is the perspective that democracy is not an endpoint that has already been achieved or can eventually be reached, but rather an ongoing process and a tradition that individuals make together (Parker, 1996). What distinguishes a social justice view from other views of participatory democracy is that the former specifically entails "a vision of society in which the distribution of resources is equitable and all members are physically and psychologically safe and secure" (Bell, 2007, p. 1).

Importantly, the process for achieving this vision must be "democratic and participatory, inclusive and affirming of human agency and human capacities for working collaboratively to create change" (Bell, 2007, p. 2). Thus, both the goals of social justice and the process for achieving those goals are founded upon democratic principles. Some have also argued that the reverse is also true: that democratic principles such as concern about the welfare of others and the common good arise from the pursuit of social justice (Beane & Apple, 2007).

However, terms like *democracy* and *social justice* are essentially contested concepts (Parker, 1996). A central issue of debate for both terms is the appropriate balance of unity and diversity among individuals in a society. Virtually all modern nation-states must continually determine how to maintain a cohesive society while respecting differences among cultures. This affects questions such as how many refugees should be permitted into a country, whether Muslim women in western societies should be able to wear burkas in public, and—of particular relevance for this book—what should be taught in public schools (e.g., ethnic studies, bilingual education, various forms of citizenship education).

Equity and Diversity

Two defining features of social justice teaching are its focus on equity and its valuing of cultural diversity. Advocates are careful to distinguish between *equality*—that each student receives the same instruction—and *equity*—that each student receives what he or she needs, which may or may not be what other students are receiving. A social justice view of equity also opposes the meritocratic position that equity is achieved through each person getting what they deserve based on how hard the person works (Oakes, Lipton, Anderson, & Stillman, 2015). By contrast, social justice advocates argue that people are playing on an uneven field, which means that for those who begin on the downhill end of the field, their hard work will not yield the same results as will the hard work of those on the uphill end of the field. The social justice view of equity thus entails efforts to make the playing field more even, by addressing the structural factors that constrain individuals' abilities to flourish—factors related to race, class, gender, disability, sexuality, and other dimensions of identity that marginalize some while privileging others.

Related to these identity dimensions is the question of diversity: Can democracy sustain unlimited diversity or is there a point at which individuals are too different to live peacefully with one another? Conservatives tend to express concern over the latter possibility, particularly regarding diversity along lines of race, ethnicity, gender, sexual orientation, and disability (Haidt, 2012). Social justice advocates point to multicultural education, ethnic studies, culturally relevant pedagogy, and other areas as evidence that youth can develop positive cultural, racial, and ethnic identities while still acting cross-culturally in service of the betterment of American society as a whole. In fact, many argue that it is just this positive cultural identity development which *enhances* civic participation for the common good (Parkhouse & Freeman, 2017; Rubin, 2007; Westheimer & Kahne, 2004). To the charge that curriculum centered around a particular ethnic identity is divisive or unpatriotic, Asante (1991) countered that the purpose of promoting ethnic identity development "is not to divide America, it is to make America flourish as it ought to flourish" (p. 179).

FIELDS INFLUENCING AND INFLUENCED BY SOCIAL JUSTICE TEACHING

Social justice education refers both to validating students' cultures and backgrounds as well as to having students question and critique society (Dyches & Boyd, 2017). A number of fields align with this sort of teaching and provide a foundation from which to draw upon with regard to pedagogic approaches and classroom resources. These areas have similarly advocated for centering students' voices and developing students' proclivities for disrupting oppression. A brief overview of those avenues of influence follows.

Afrocentric Education, Ethnic Studies, and Multicultural Education

One important component of social justice teaching is combating the tendency for schools to reproduce current social hierarchies in society. This is accomplished in part through recentering the curriculum around groups who have historically been left out, or minimized, within it. Ethnic studies and Afrocentric education similarly share an emphasis on ensuring that *all* students see themselves reflected in the curriculum and learn the historical contributions made by members of all races and ethnicities. As early as 1933, Carter G. Woodson made the case in *The Miseducation of the Negro* that African American youth need to learn about their long history both in the United States and in Africa to counteract dominant narratives that European culture and histories are the only ones of import (Asante, 1991). More recently, Critical Race Theory has contributed to the argument for Afrocentric education in asserting that schools are one institution through which the white supremacist view becomes universalized (Ladson-Billings & Tate, 2006).

Ethnic studies courses are also geared toward questioning dominant views of what counts as knowledge and teaching students from historically marginalized populations about the history and contributions of these groups. One high-profile example is the Tucson Unified School District's Mexican American Studies program, which Arizona banned in 2010. This program pursued social justice by teaching indigenous epistemologies, literature, and other curriculum centered around Chicana/o culture, and resulted in significant academic gains for the students (Acosta, 2014). Multicultural education shares similar aims, but without a specific focus on one cultural group. There has been some disagreement amongst scholars as to whether multicultural education has empowered marginalized groups or if it merely tacked minority perspectives onto the existing curriculum. Nonetheless, many of the conceptual components of multicultural education, such as analysis of institutional power and discrimination, form part of the foundation for contemporary social justice teaching practices (Banks, 1995; Nieto, 2004).

Culturally Relevant and Responsive Pedagogies

Bearing some overlaps with multicultural education, but making even more explicit the commitment to collective empowerment and social justice, are culturally responsive teaching and culturally relevant pedagogy. Both focus on emancipatory practices, high expectations, educating the whole child, and validating students' cultures (Gay, 2002; Ladson-Billings, 1995). Whereas culturally responsive teaching focuses more on specific practices (Gay, 2002), culturally relevant pedagogy emphasizes the dispositions and mindset of the teacher (Aronson & Laughter, 2016; Ladson-Billings, 1995). Culturally responsive teaching advocates using students' cultures in affirming ways as vehicles for teaching, and culturally relevant pedagogy notes the necessity of developing sociopolitical consciousness in marginalized student populations, particularly African American students, thereby raising their awareness of social injustices.

Critical Pedagogy

Another theoretical strand that has influenced social justice teaching and echoes the idea of raising students' sociocultural awareness is critical pedagogy. Most often associated with Paulo Freire's (1970/2000) book *Pedagogy of the Oppressed*, critical pedagogy is concerned with education for liberation. An important component is conscientization or critical consciousness, which is "the process by which students, as empowered subjects, achieve a deepening awareness of the social realities which shape their lives and discover their own capacities to recreate them" (Darder, Baltodano, & Torres, 2009, p. 14). Students and teachers develop an acumen for reading and questioning the world around them and then combine this critical awareness with action, an integrative concept Freire termed *praxis*. An additional feature of critical pedagogy is a focus on dialogue and students-as-teachers/teachers-as-students thereby shifting traditional power dynamics in schools. Traces of all of these features can be seen in social justice teaching frameworks and practices.

Anti-Colonial Education

Emerging from postcolonial scholarship and critical pedagogy, anti-colonial and decolonizing pedagogies act to counter the hegemony of Western epistemology and Eurocentric education (Andreotti, 2011). Scholars in this field argue that, while the age of imperialism via conquest and colonization may have officially ended, we continue to see the global dominance of Euro-American cultural and political institutions. This plays out not only through the ongoing influence of Euro-American culture in African, Latin-American, and Asian countries, but also through *internal colonialism*. Among populations residing within the same borders, particularly in the United States, "there continues to be a structured relationship of cultural, political, and economic domination and subordination between European whites on the one hand, and indigenous and non-white peoples on the other" (Tejeda, Espinoza, & Gutiérrez, 2003, p. 11). Thus the concept of internal colonialism is helpful in raising consciousness of how racism and nativism have taken new forms in our postcolonial context, having shifted from overt acts such as enslavement and forced removal, toward the more invisible work of cultural and ideological domination.

Feminism

In its first wave in the late 19th and early 20th centuries, feminism represented a response to patriarchal society and a call for equal rights for women in terms of property ownership, access to employment, and suffrage. Traditional gender expectations and roles, such as the woman's supposed place in the sphere of the home and the man's in the public sphere, or workforce, were called into question. The social movements of the 1960s gave way to second wave feminism, characterized by its focus on women's reproductive rights and social equality. More radical than its predecessor, second wave feminism made famous the expression "the personal is political," which denoted the inextricable aspects of womanhood and rights to participatory self-government. Finally, third wave feminism began in the 1990s and exhibited a marked shift in attention to Women of Color who were often excluded in previous iterations and was characterized by an explosion of boundaries related to gender, sexuality, and femininity.

Third wave feminists argued for the recognition of intersections of race, class, and gender and for the right to self-identification. Black feminists in particular advocated for attention to intersectionality (Crenshaw, 1991), or an understanding of how categories of identity such as being a woman and being African American overlap and do not exist independently. Feminist pedagogies, connected to these various histories, emphasize "women's experiences, feelings, ideas, and actions" and strive "to understand and challenge oppressive power relations" while centering "dialogue, reflection and problem solving" in classroom practices (Villaverde, 2008, p. 122). Much like critical pedagogies, feminist pedagogies task students with calling into question the structures that subjugate groups in society and developing ways to act on those systems.

Queer Theory and Pedagogy

Queer theory, like social justice, is a relatively new term, having gained popularity in the 1990s. At its heart, queer theory is about questioning norms and limits, particularly those surrounding heteronormativity, the concept that heterosexuality is the norm in our society and the base for judging behavior (Turner, 2000). Queer theory uses queer as both a noun—meaning people who are lesbian, gay, bisexual, pansexual, transgender, or otherwise do not identify as heterosexual and cisgender (LBGTQ+)—and a verb—meaning to challenge, question, and stretch norms and boundaries. *Queer pedagogy* is the questioning and challenging of norms related to education.

Britzman's (1995) influential article discussed queer pedagogy as challenging norms, limits, reading habits, and ignorance. While Britzman's work was theoretical in nature and more about queering conceptions of teaching and learning, scholars have applied these ideas to classroom practices (DePalma, 2010; Krywanczyk, 2007; Pennell, 2016) and demonstrated that curriculum can be queered through such activities as blurring lines between students and teachers (similar to ideas in critical pedagogy), allowing students to grapple with uncomfortable topics, favoring student-led work, and directly challenging heteronormativity. Further, queer pedagogy scholars point out that it is not enough to include LGBTQ+ people and experiences in the curriculum, arguing that this may serve only to flatten differences under a guise of equality (i.e., phrases like "we are all the same under our skin"). Instead, inquiry should be centered around celebrating differences and questioning norms (Goldstein, Russell, & Daley, 2007; Loutzenheiser & MacIntosh, 2004).

CONCLUSION

All of these fields of study and pedagogical traditions have at their core both questioning the institutions that oppress on the basis of factors such as gender, race, or class and approaching students in affirming ways. Achieving equity, or removing structural barriers and providing for individuals what they need in a specific context, permeates the theoretical frameworks that support social justice. These theories and approaches have thus both influenced social justice education and been influenced by it. As a result, social justice teachers have a long and rich history of concepts to draw upon for ideas and inspiration. The work of the teachers described in this volume represents just a few of the many possibilities and each provides the theoretical basis from which it draws. While the chapters in this volume offer varying takes on how social justice tenets can shape classroom instruction, they all share the goal of advancing equity both in classrooms and in society.

REFERENCES

Acosta, C. (2014). Dangerous minds in Tucson: The banning of Mexican American studies and critical thinking in Arizona. *Journal of Educational Controversy, 8*(1), 9.

Adams, M., Bell, L. A., & Griffin, P. (Eds.). (2007). *Teaching for diversity and social justice* (2nd ed.). New York, NY: Routledge.

Andreotti, V. (2011). *Actionable postcolonial theory in education: Postcolonial studies in education.* New York, NY: Palgrave Macmillan.

Aronson, B., & Laughter, J. (2016). The theory and practice of culturally relevant education: A synthesis of research across content areas. *Review of Educational Research, 86*(1), 163–206.

Asante, M. K. (1991). The Afrocentric idea in education. *The Journal of Negro Education, 60*(2), 170–180.

Banks, J. A. (1995). Multicultural education and curriculum transformation. *Journal of Negro Education, 64*(4), 390–400.

Beane, J. A., & Apple, M. W. (2007). The case for democratic schools. In M. W. Apple & J. A. Beane (Eds.), *Democratic schools: Lessons in powerful education*. Portsmouth, NH: Heinemann.

Bell, L. A. (2007). Theoretical foundations for social justice education. In M. Adams, L. Bell, & P. Griffin (Eds.), *Teaching for diversity and social justice: A sourcebook* (2nd ed., pp. 3–15). New York, NY: Routledge.

Britzman, D. P. (1995). Is there a queer pedagogy? Or, stop reading straight. *Educational Theory, 45*(2), 151–165.

Crenshaw, K. (1991). Mapping the margins: Intersectionality, identity politics, and violence against women of color. *Stanford Law Review, 43*(6), 1241–1299.

Darder, A., Baltodano, M., & Torres, R. D. (Eds.). (2009). *The critical pedagogy reader* (2nd ed.). New York, NY: Routledge.

DePalma, R. (2010). The no outsiders project: In search of queer primary pedagogies. *Transformations: The Journal of Inclusive Scholarship & Pedagogy, 21*(2), 47–58.

Dewey, J. (1916/1980). The need of an industrial education in an industrial democracy. In J. A. Boydston (Ed.), *John Dewey. The Middle Works, 1899–1924* (Vol. 10, pp. 137–143). Carbondale, IL; Edwardsville, IL: Southern Illinois University Press. (Original work published 1916).

Dyches, J. & Boyd, A. (2017). Foregrounding equity in teacher education: Toward a model of social justice pedagogical and content knowledge (SJPACK). *Journal of Teacher Education,* DOI: 10.1177/0022487117705097.

Education: Donald Trump's Vision. (2016). Retrieved from https://www.donaldjtrump.com/policies/education

Freire, P. (1970/2000). *Pedagogy of the oppressed, 30ᵗʰ anniversary edition* (M. B. Ramos, Trans.). New York, NY: Continuum. (Original work published 1970).

Gay, G. (2002). Preparing for culturally responsive teaching. *Journal of Teacher Education, 53*(2), 106–116.

Goldstein, T., Russell, V., & Daley, A. (2007). Safe, positive and queering moments in teaching education and schooling: A conceptual framework. *Teaching Education, 18*(3), 183–199.

Haidt, J. (2012). *The righteous mind: Why good people are divided by politics and religion*. New York, NY: Pantheon.

Hytten, K., & Bettez, S. C. (2011). Understanding education for social justice. *Educational Foundations, 25*(1–2), 7–24.

Krywanczyk, L. (2007). Queering public school pedagogy as a first-year teacher. *Radical Teacher, 79*, 27–34.

Ladson-Billings, G. (1995). Toward a theory of culturally relevant pedagogy. *American Educational Research Journal, 32*(3), 465–491. doi:10.3102/00028312032003465

Ladson-Billings, G. J., & Tate, W. F. (2006). Toward a critical race theory of education. In A. D. Dixon & C. K. Rousseau (Eds.), *Critical race theory in education: All God's children got a song* (pp. 11–30). New York, NY: Routledge.

Loutzenheiser, L. W., & MacIntosh, L. B. (2004). Citizenships, sexualities, and education. *Theory into Practice, 43*(2), 151–158.

Nieto, S. (2004). *Affirming diversity: The sociopolitical context of multicultural education* (4th ed.). New York, NY: Longman.

North, C. E. (2008). What is all this talk about. *Teachers College Record, 110*(6), 1182–1206.

Oakes, J., Lipton, M., Anderson, L., & Stillman, J. (2015). *Teaching to change the world*. New York, NY: Routledge.

Parker, W. (1996). "Advanced" ideas about democracy: Toward a pluralist conception of citizenship education. *The Teachers College Record, 98*(1), 104–125.

Parkhouse, H., & Freeman, E. (2017). Embodying citizenship: A case study of undocumented youth fighting for in-state tuition policy. In X. L. Rong & J. Hilburn (Eds.), *Immigration and education in North Carolina: The challenges and responses in a new gateway state* (pp. 125–148). Rotterdam: Sense.

Pennell, S. M. (2016). *Queering the curriculum: Critical literacy and numeracy for social justice* (Doctoral dissertation). The University of North Carolina, Chapel Hill, NC.

Rubin, B. (2007). "There's still not justice": Youth civic identity development amid distinct school and community contexts. *The Teachers College Record, 109*(2), 449–481.

Tejeda, C., Espinoza, M., & Gutiérrez, K. (2003). Toward a decolonizing pedagogy: Social justice reconsidered. In P. P. Trifonas (Ed.), *Pedagogies of difference: Rethinking education for social change* (pp. 9–38). New York, NY: Routledge.

Turner, W. B. (2000). *A genealogy of queer theory*. Philadelphia, PA: Temple University Press.

Ujifusa, A. (2016, November 9). Trump set to shift gears on civil rights, ESSA, says a K–12 transition-team leader. *Education Week Blogs*. Retrieved 2016, December 11 from http://blogs.edweek.org/edweek/campaign-12/2016/11/trump_ESSA_civil_rights_transition_education.html

Villaverde, L. (2008). Feminist pedagogy and activism. In L. Villaverde (Ed.), *Feminist theories and education* (pp. 119–142). New York, NY: Peter Lang.

Westheimer, J., & Kahne, J. (2004). What kind of citizen? The politics of educating for democracy. *American Educational Research Journal, 41*(2), 237–269.

PART TWO

Pre-K–Elementary

Social Justice and Primary Students: How Early Is Too Early?

Often when considering the potential of social justice education, concerns about appropriateness and age arise. How early is too early? This is a question many pre-service and practicing teachers often ask. Suitability based on age is a myth that scholars have debunked over time (Greenbaum, 1997), noting that stage theories, which normalize age expectations, and developmental progressions are not generalizable across or within cultures (Lesko, 1996). Nevertheless, much apprehension continues to exist with regard to bringing up sensitive topics with children. However, it is absolutely necessary that we begin in early childhood if we hope to make change and to work against forces of oppression that operate during these key socialization years. If primary teachers do not address issues of racism, gender inequity, or social class distinctions, for example, our younger students run the risk of maintaining the status quo and—either willfully or unknowingly—the injustices of our systems.

The authors in this section show us that, with sensitivity and conscientiousness, it is never too early to talk with children about culturally relevant topics and to pay close attention to the spaces in which we construct their learning. In Chapter 3, Bower-Phipps, Powell, Bivona, Harmon, and Olcott describe their work in a teacher inquiry group to consider the prevalence of gender norms in early childhood settings and to work against complicity in upholding the gender binary. Bullock, Williams, Bullock, and Bernal-Martinez describe in Chapter 4 a program for elementary students they specifically designed using anti-racist pedagogies to engage children in discussions on race and their worlds. From examples in a second grade classroom, Shin and Bisland depict through Chapter 5 how elementary students become knowledge producers, studying immigration on a local level and engaging in their own research in their community. In Chapter 6, Saylor shares examples from elementary student teachers social studies lessons after they considered their own knowledge and perceptions of feminism. Finally, employing methods of narrative inquiry in Chapter 7, LaGarry shows an elementary teacher perspective by sharing the story of a music educator whose personal critical reflection prompts her to push beyond the conventional boundaries of her discipline and into culturally responsive, inclusive, and engaging practices. Taken together, these chapters provide powerful portraits of how the seeds of social justice can be planted with even the youngest of our students so that they can begin to consider the cultural topics that will be a part of their growth.

REFERENCES

Greenbaum, V. (1997, February). Censorship and the myth of appropriateness: Reflections on teaching reading in high school. *English Journal, 86*(2), 16–20.

Lesko, N. (1996). Past, present, and future conceptions of adolescence. *Educational Theory, 46*(4), 453–472.

CHAPTER THREE

Re-drawing THE Line

Queering Our Pedagogy in the Early Childhood Classroom
Pre-Kindergarten

LAURA BOWER-PHIPPS, JESSICA S. POWELL, MARISSA BIVONA, REBECCA HARMON, AND ANNE OLCOTT

The National Association for the Education of Young Children (NAEYC) has a code of ethics that all early childhood programs must follow. The single most important principle, taking precedence over all others, states, "Above all, we shall not harm children. We shall not participate in practices that are emotionally damaging, physically harmful, disrespectful, degrading, dangerous, exploitative, or intimidating to children" (2005, P-1.1). As three early childhood educators and two university teacher educators, our conception of social justice is intertwined with ethical practice and queer theory. Social justice, ethical practice, and queer theory serve as political calls to action, urging us as educators to identify and challenge educational inequities. William Ayers (2010) described teaching as a profoundly ethical act. He argued that to teach for justice means "working the gap" (p. 137): teaching beyond what is, toward what should be. Such teaching requires educators to navigate the space between the inequities and challenges of reality and the world—free from oppression—which we are working to create. Building on social justice teaching as ethical practice, queer theory provides a lens to understand how institutions normalize certain identities and performances while pathologizing others (Foucault, 1978). Queer theory empowers us to envision and engage with ethical, anti-oppressive practices that challenge systems and policies that harm children who do not fit constructed concepts of normal.

In our schools today, there are an increasing number of children whose performances of gender extend beyond society's narrow definitions of what it means to be a boy or girl (Slesaransky-Poe & García, 2009). By the age of three, children begin to understand socially constructed gender norms (Weinraub et al., 1984). In preschools, children are exposed to what Reay (2001) described as the hidden curriculum of gender, which teaches that boys and girls act and think differently and have separate interests. This curriculum is reinforced through seemingly innocuous practices such as lining up boys and girls separately, gendered dress codes, and sex-specific bathrooms (Carrera, DePalma, & Lameiras, 2012). Reinforcing the gender binary through classroom practices and curricula communicates the message that "gender divisions are natural, innate, and normal. And conversely, that gender non-conformity is abnormal, deviant, and symptomatic of illness and pathology" (Slesaransky-Poe & García, 2009, p. 205).

Creating more inclusive, open minded, self-aware citizens must begin in the early childhood classroom; however, many teachers are still learning what it means to bring gender-fluid teaching into their practice (Smith & Payne, 2016). When our curriculum and pedagogy in the early childhood classroom do not honor gender fluidity and a multiplicity of gender expressions and identities, our children are harmed and the code of ethics has been violated. In contrast, our study explores ways early childhood educators conceptualize gender and take pedagogical actions to create gender fluid experiences in the classroom, or in other terms, *queer their pedagogy.*

Although a growing body of literature on queer pedagogy has emerged over the past two decades, the research has largely addressed middle, secondary, or higher education (e.g. Britzman, 1995; Luhmann, 1998; Macintosh, 2007; Zacko-Smith & Smith, 2013). While some scholars have begun to address this gap (e.g. Blaise & Taylor, 2012; Taylor & Richardson, 2005), there remains a dearth of research on queering the early childhood classroom. Our research responds to this gap by exploring the experiences of three preschool teachers who challenged themselves and each other to embody a queer pedagogy in their classrooms. Using an action research methodology, three teacher-researchers,[1] who are also co-authors of this chapter, engaged in cycles of reflection and action to move through discomfort, risks, and subversive actions to take an ethical stance for equity in their classrooms. Through these cycles of reflection and exploration, the teacher-researchers are drawing a new line in the sand: a line that is fluid and changeable. This shift in threshold represents the teacher-researchers' willingness to push the boundaries of discomfort, ethical stances, and pedagogical actions. A new line is drawn that opens space for new possibilities.

DEVELOPING A QUEER EYE

Queer theory (Butler, 1990; Foucault, 1978; Pinar, 1998; Sedgwick, 1990; Warner, 1999) informs our understanding of gender and facilitates our identification of classroom practices that normalize certain performances of gender and pathologize others. Within queer theory, "queer" can be understood as a verb that "makes strange" assumptions that we hold about gender and sexuality. In terms of gender, queer theory destabilizes fixed categories of gender (Piontek, 2006). Girl and boy are no longer monolithic, opposing categories with singular meanings. Rather, there are many ways to be a boy or a girl, and there are genders that exist between and beyond the categories of girl and boy. Gender can be understood as a performance: "Gender ought not to be constructed as a stable identity or locus of agency from which various acts follow; rather gender is an identity tenuously constituted in time, instituted in an exterior space through a stylized repetition of acts" (Butler, 1990, p. 179). These performances are inextricably tied to heterosexual norms for what it means to be male or female (Butler, 1990) and shaped by heteronormativity, the assumption that everyone is or should be heterosexual (Warner, 1993). What is troubling to us as teachers is that institutional discourses, as communicated through curricula and classroom practices, normalize certain performances of gender and pathologize others (Foucault, 1978; Warner, 1999). As Butler (1990) observed, "we regularly punish those who fail to do their gender right" (p. 178). In turning a "queer eye" to our practice, "we become aware of how the children behave in agreement with dominant gender discourses, negotiate the power relations of these discourses, and at the same time behave in accordance with the overarching discourse of heterosexuality" (Blaise & Taylor, 2012, p. 91). Queer theory provides us with a framework for critiquing, destabilizing and subverting heteronormative gender norms with our students. Such practices benefit all students through expanding their notions of gender beyond boy/girl binaries. Most importantly, in queering our practices, we create spaces for children whose gender expression and identities exist outside of rigid heteronormative expectations of what it means to be a boy or a girl.

RESEARCH METHODOLOGY

Action research, which "changes people's practices, their understandings of their practices, and the conditions under which they practice" (Kemmis, 2009, p. 463), provided a methodology for taking an ethical stance and queering pedagogy. Accordingly, the teacher-researchers, as guided by the university researchers, collaboratively engaged in cycles of reflection, planning, action, and observation (Carr & Kemmis, 1986).

We met biweekly over the course of three months for teacher-researchers to reflect upon their classrooms and experiences and make plans for queering their pedagogy. In early meetings, we completed a shared reading to initiate an explicit dialogue on queer pedagogy and how it related to our experiences in the early childhood classroom (Blaise & Taylor, 2012). Following the meetings where we interrogated gender in our lives and classrooms, teacher-researchers developed plans for specific actions to queer their pedagogy. Later meetings included reflection upon the implementation and outcomes of the actions.

This inquiry was initially driven by the following questions, co-developed by the university and teacher researchers: (1) What are our understandings of gender in the early childhood classroom? (2) In what ways can we queer our pedagogy around gender? (3) What are the barriers to queering our pedagogy?

Context

This research project occurred in early childhood classrooms situated in Southern New England. The following provides a description of each teacher-researcher's classroom setting:

Anne is a full-time teacher at a private, non-profit, nationally accredited nursery school. She has a mixed age classroom with 31 students, ages three-to-five. The school is in a medium-sized urban city. One-third of the students receive state-funded tuition support, allowing for economic diversity. The majority of students are white, but the school also serves racially and linguistically diverse children and families. It is a play-based program that teachers describe as socially and politically progressive. Anne has been teaching for 19 years.

Marissa is a full time teacher at a private, non-profit, university-affiliated, nationally accredited early childhood center, serving three-to-six year-olds. The school is located in a medium-sized city which includes both urban and suburban neighborhoods. The school offers sliding scale tuition to promote economic diversity. The demographics are evenly split between white, middle and upper-middle class families and racially and linguistically diverse children and families. The program offers a play-based curriculum that is driven by children's interests and development. Marissa has taught for six years.

Rebecca teaches at a private, for-profit, childcare center in a suburban community. The school serves infants through five year-olds. Rebecca teaches in the four-year-olds' classroom with a co-teacher. The school primarily serves white, middle-class families. The curriculum is unit-driven with elements of play. Rebecca has taught for two years.

Our own identities and positionalities impacted our teaching practices and our interpretation of the findings. All of us, including the two university researchers, identify as white, cisgender women. We are all native English speakers. Some of us identify as heterosexual; others as lesbian or queer.

Data Sources and Analysis

Our research meetings were audio-recorded and transcribed. As the teacher-researchers completed cycles of reflection, planning, acting, and observing, the university researchers used qualitative analysis to identify emergent themes within the transcripts. Following a process of comparing and contrasting emergent themes with the data and revising themes accordingly (Creswell, 1994), resulting themes were member-checked with the teacher-researchers. Our findings include the following themes: (1) gender is open for discussion; (2) some pieces feel harder; and (3) the importance of taking a stance. Additionally, each teacher-researcher developed a narrative to describe actions taken to queer her pedagogy. Abbreviated narratives and a description of the qualitative themes follows.

QUEERING OUR TEACHING

While we, as teacher-researchers, engaged in many actions to queer our pedagogy, we each chose to highlight a particular action that stood out in our minds as representative of our process of developing a queer eye and taking that new sensibility to queer our own teaching.

The teacher-researchers' actions are written in narrative form, without interruptions or interpretation. Our intention is for their stories to invite readers to interact with these actions, interjecting their own experiences and making their own interpretations (Ellis, 1993; Powell, 2016). The section following the narratives provides a thematic analysis of these actions and others shared in our bi-weekly meetings.

Anne: Queering Literacy Practices

I have long relied on books in my teaching as a means to approach meaningful or challenging topics with young children. So when I became part of this research group and began to discuss gender issues, my mind naturally turned to books as a resource for considering gender identity with preschoolers.

I have used some existing books in our classroom library to introduce gender non-conforming and/or queer characters. I researched and added additional books to our classroom library to promote sexual and gender diversity. (See Appendix for examples.) However, the most rewarding action I have taken relating to books is to intentionally use a "queered" lens when I comment and encourage group discussion. For example, I was reading the book *Mighty Dads* (Holub, 2014) to a small group of children who already knew the story well. As I read, I realized that all the construction machines depicted are given male pronouns and referred to as dads. This is totally irrelevant to their function or the story, so I interjected on the cement mixer page, "Hey I just realized that the author chose only dads for this book. I wish this page talked about a mom, because I'm a mom and my favorite trucks are cement mixers." All pairs of eyes really looked at me and the book. Two girls at the table smiled broadly, leading me to think that perhaps I had addressed an inner awareness of theirs. We talked a little, and soon resumed reading. That brief interaction raised some important notions for them and for me that continue to inform our readings: First, that readers can questions authors' and illustrators' choices. Second, that making trucks male leaves some people out and therefore feels unfair.

I am fortunate to work in a fairly progressive setting with colleagues who respect and accept all forms of diversity. The parent body is also generally respectful and accepting. So having these kinds of conversations and reading these books does not feel particularly risky. I recognize that in some classrooms it could be, depending on the personal beliefs of the families and the teaching staff. I do think that issues related to gender and sexuality are the most uncomfortable for adults, teachers or parents, to consider with young children. My primary concern is to present some counter-examples and accurate information that encourage children to do their own critical thinking and come to their own conclusions when they are with me and when they are not. Building habits of listening, thinking, and respecting will establish the strongest foundation for social justice. Maybe building that foundation is the most subversive act of all?

Marissa: Queering Dramatic Play

Early childhood educators often say that children learn by watching, doing, and playing. Learning about gender should be no different. As educators using a queer eye in the classroom, it is our job to support play and exploration around gender, asking questions and guiding the child to come to their own conclusions, not simply impose our own ideas on them. My action was centered in the dramatic play area. Dramatic play (in our school) is a safe space where children can take on and try out different roles. Sometimes the roles conform to traditional ideas about gender, and sometimes they do not. For my action I chose to add dress up clothes to the dramatic play area, including some princess dresses and shoes recently donated to our school. We typically would not put these clothes out, but I wanted to observe how the children would interact with these new props and perhaps start a conversation about gender, using this princess dress—to me a symbol of the heterosexual norm/ princess narrative—as a jumping-off point.

On the morning when I put out the dresses, many children entered the dramatic play area. One boy excitedly put on a dress with help from a teacher and looked at himself in the mirror. Another boy said, "Hey! Dresses are for girls," at which point the teacher pointed out that another boy was in fact wearing a dress and that the dresses were out for whoever would like to wear them. "Why do you think dresses are just for girls?" the teacher asked. The boy wasn't quite sure, and observed from afar before timidly approaching and asking for help to try on a dress himself. This is where the discomfort sometimes occurs for me; I have to resist my knee-jerk reaction to share my ideas, especially if a child says something sexist. Having the child come to the conclusion on their own is far more powerful.

Just creating this safe space for people to "play" with gender is important. Depending on the school community context, asking the child to pause and question her/his/their preconceived notions of gender can be subversive. Sometimes it can feel like our school is a "bubble," and that the real world beyond is harsher when it comes to acknowledging the fluidity of gender expression. It feels uncomfortable to think about a child getting hurt, or taking a risk beyond this space, but at the end of the day we learn and grow by taking these risks.

Sometimes I feel discomfort or don't know how to answer questions about gender, which is why it has been helpful to collaborate with like-minded peers, educate myself, and share strategies. I want to be able to communicate my philosophy on gender and queer theory to families without judging their viewpoint, and be realistic without compromising my morals and the ethical responsibilities I have as a teacher. I do not know the opinions of the families we serve or how they feel about gender fluidity. While it seems that many families accept girls stepping out of gender roles and taking on traditional male roles, there seems to be more resistance to boys taking on female traits or roles. The tension here is between the wishes of families and the need to create a safe environment where *any* expression of gender is accepted and celebrated. It is our job as teachers to provide children with a safe space and acceptance to explore, while providing different models of what gender is.

Rebecca: Queering Teaching in Plain Sight

I find queering our practices as educators to be some of the most important activism we can do in our classrooms and in our schools. When we queer our practices, we not only create a safer, more accepting environment for our students, but we also educate our coworkers. Our individual actions in our classrooms and the hard work we do queering our pedagogy might not be enough, so we need others on board with us. That is why I was so willing to push the limits of my own level of comfort when queering my practices in front of my coworkers.

Even the idea of doing this was discomforting. Those I work closest with have been in the childcare business for most of their lives. When I started working at the school, they loved my outgoing personality, my new ideas, and my young perspective on education and what to do to enhance their programs. However, I observed that they constantly judge our students' and parents' sexualities based on clothing, attitudes, and performances, and none of it is appropriate or accurate. After years of witnessing this behavior, I knew I had no other option than to queer my pedagogy right in front of their eyes.

I began by asking my colleagues, including those in other classrooms at the center, questions in an attempt to figure out their views and opinions on gender and sexuality. I asked if they thought anything was wrong with constantly grouping children by boy and girl, which is something I see occurring daily. Not surprisingly, they did not think anything was wrong with it. Most of them questioned why I would waste my time on having the conversation.

At first, I was a little hesitant to introduce my colleagues to queer theory. I was concerned that I was being too proactive about queering gender roles, norms, and stereotypes, because I knew that I intended eventually to come out as a lesbian to them. I did not want them to think all of my intentions were selfish or out of place. However, I knew that I was only creating a safer, better environment for the students in this school, so I dived right in.

I talked with my co-teacher, who usually runs morning meeting, about not grouping students by boy and girl, especially with our daily routine of morning meeting. She typically gives clues as to who the "morning meeting person" will be beginning with, "Today's morning meeting person is a girl (or boy)." I never felt comfortable with this routine, but when I began working here, it was her classroom (of many years) that I was joining. Still, whenever I got the chance to run morning meeting, I would say "Morning meeting person has [on a red shirt, or brown hair, or blue eyes, or pets at home, or another relevant detail for young children]." I ran morning meeting in front of her a few times, and while she never questioned or critiqued my practice, she never changed her own ways. One day I confronted the topic head on by asking her if she would consider not saying boy or girl. She responded by not using gender designations during that day's meeting, however, directly after morning meeting, called boys to wash their hands, and then girls. Taking this big step and talking to my co-teacher about changing her ways was really uncomfortable, especially because she has been teaching this same way for almost 20 years. It was uncomfortable for me to even approach her with an idea, but I knew I needed to, even if it didn't work (yet). This experience re-structured my priorities. While I will continue to queer my practices, my aims of explicitly influencing my colleagues is secondary.

Taking this stance, and despite my colleagues' resistance, I continued to queer my teaching. This took the form of reading books that challenged the gender binary or introduced queer thinking, such as *Red: A Crayon Story* (Hall, 2015). This is a story of identity: a personified crayon who appears red on the outside, but feels blue on the inside. I kept the story around on my classroom shelves for the students to look at or for us to read in small groups—where we'd actually be able to have deeper conversations about the messages in the story.

I will continue to queer my teaching, whether or not my colleagues agree. It is still a little nerve-wracking to perform this pedagogy in the early childhood classroom, especially when the toughest critics are my coworkers.

REFLECTING ON OUR ACTIONS

The above narratives emphasize how queering the teacher-researchers' pedagogy became ethical work, in light of the complexity and discomfort inherent in the process. In this section, we provide a discussion of the themes the university researchers developed through an analysis of bi-weekly group discussions, which include the actions above.

Gender Is Open for Discussion

Interpreting gender through a queer lens means understanding gender as fluid, with performances of gender based in particular social contexts (Butler, 1990). In early childhood settings, a queer reading of gender not only entails thinking beyond and between the categories of "boy" and "girl;" it also means taking an ethical stance that problematizes and calls into question gender with students and other adults.

The teacher-researchers queered gender with their students through creating and finding existing opportunities in curricula to incite conversations about gender. Anne, for example, queered literature that already existed in her classroom by calling into question why the anthropomorphized trucks were male and suggesting that not only boys like trucks. Marissa created opportunities to try on different performances of gender through adding dresses to her dramatic play center. They moved beyond simple insertion of queer content into their teaching and helped students explore and critique the deployment of gender norms at a developmentally appropriate level (Luhman, 1998).

Owing to the public nature of teaching, particularly in preschools where co-teaching is the norm, opening gender for discussion meant doing so for adults as well as for children. The strategies teacher-researchers used for opening gender for discussion depended largely on context. Because of the resistance Rebecca experienced when she first began questioning binary gender practices in her preschool, she led by example: not grouping students by gender, reading books featuring gender diversity, and inviting all children to play with toys considered by other teachers as "girl toys." Marissa, on the other hand, teaches in a setting she describes as very progressive with co-workers who are advocates of sexual and gender diversity. In one of our research meetings, she explained that she had shared the article we read about queering early childhood teaching with her colleagues. Anne, who works in a similarly progressive setting, responded to children's assertions that boys should not or could not wear make up by sharing a picture of a "Cover Boy," who wore make-up to sell a company's product. She held this conversation in a context in which there were four other teachers and several parents present. The teacher-researchers encouraged their students, and at times their colleagues, to challenge binaries and normative practices through dialogue that was largely led through an exchange of questions.

Some Pieces Feel Harder

The three settings in which the teacher-researchers implemented their actions provided distinct challenges. To engage a queer lens requires not only destabilizing and resisting norms, but also creating something new. Inherent in this process is troubling the comfort zone (Koschoreck, Meek, Campanello, & Mominee, 2010). Thus, safe spaces that allow moments of queering are characterized by discomfort. Each teacher-researcher identified elements where she crossed her line of discomfort, and challenged herself to either simply notice and reflect or, at times, continue to move forward.

For Rebecca, discomfort emerged through vulnerability, where coming out to her colleagues pushed her own identity into the conversation around queering her classroom. Challenging her colleagues to reflect on their own teaching, by asking questions at multiple points throughout the action cycles, complicated the traditional norms of the novice/veteran teacher relationship.

For Anne and Marissa, who identified their work environments as progressive, discomfort appeared spontaneously in the unplanned moments when children engaged gender normative behaviors or ideas, causing Anne and Marissa to think on their feet to queer the conversation. There was, at times, uncertainty as to how to do this, or how it would be received by other adults in the school community, including parents.

As the teacher-researchers began to use a queer eye to examine experiences in the classroom, they noticed the different spaces where discomfort creeped in. Through their observations, and dialoguing with the self and each other, they were able to declare an intention around the discomfort. Often, this intention led them to push through the sense of vulnerability and continue to queer their practices, while at other times their discomfort was strong enough to make them pause and pivot. The teacher-researchers noticed that developing a language to queer heteronormative practice with children and adults is challenging and complicated, and they did not always feel like they got it right. But, as we sit in this discomfort, queer theory provides us with some comfort, reminding us that when we notice the uncomfortable, confuse our understandings, and question power, we are in a sense *getting it right*.

The Importance of Taking a Stance

"Working the gap" in the classroom means existing in a liminal space, between what is and what ought to be (Ayers, 2010). Embodying practices that allow us to strive towards new possibilities requires taking an ethical stance that challenges the way we make meaning of the world (Piontek, 2006), and at times, enlisting subversive practices to transgress normative, oppressive boundaries. Anne, Marissa, and Rebecca view their queered teaching as ethical and political work. Not unlike the public performance of gender identity (Butler, 1990), teaching is a public act. Queering pedagogy involves taking a public stance. In one example, Anne crafted a newsletter to families that called on the NAEYC (2005) code of ethics to remind her school community that their practices to teach for social justice are grounded in the profession's principles. Marissa shared readings on queer pedagogy with her colleagues, inviting them into dialogue. And Rebecca, working with colleagues who were resistant to queer ideas, believed that the consequences of *not* queering her teaching were far too great. So, despite her colleagues' resistance, Rebecca risked vulnerability, and perhaps even her livelihood, for what she believed was ethical and socially-just teaching. While the risks varied for each teacher-researcher, to re-draw the line was to take an important, public, ethical stance.

CONCLUSION

Queering early childhood pedagogy is a necessary and messy process. Despite the teacher-researchers' bold actions and the research team's deep reflection on these actions, we do not claim to be the authorities or to have all of the answers. In the tradition of Kumashiro (2002), we invite the reader to question our interpretation of our stories, just as we would have them question gender. In continually re-drawing the lines of comfort, action, risk, and stance, we ask ourselves and the reader to consider these questions to move forward the dialogue on queering our pedagogy in early childhood education:

- How do we leave gender open for discussion?
- How do we create and find opportunities within our curriculum to queer gender?

- Why do some pieces feel harder?
- How do we identify the risks?
- How do we find the courage to take a stance regardless of the risks?

APPENDIX: CHILDREN'S BOOKS USED IN OUR CLASSROOMS

My Princess Boy (Cheryl Kilo Davis)
Not All Princesses Dress in Pink (Jane Yolen)
And Tango Makes Three (Justin Richardson)
Red: A Crayon's Story (Michael Hall)
Worm Loves Worm (JJ Austrian)
Morris Micklewhite and the Tangerine Dress (Christine Baldacchino)
Gaston (Kelly DiPucchio)
Not Every Princess (Jeffrey and Lisa Bone)
King and King (Linda de Haan and Stern Nijland)
The Different Dragon (Jennifer Bryan)
Who Are You? The Kids Guide to Gender Identity (Brook Pessin-Whedbee)

NOTE

1. In this chapter, teacher-researchers refers to the practicing teachers who participating in this study and co-authored this piece: Anne, Marissa, and Rebecca. University researchers refers to the two principal investigators of the study who facilitated the research project: Laura and Jessica.

REFERENCES

Ayers, W. (2010). *To teach: The journey of a teacher* (3rd ed.). New York, NY: Teachers College Press.
Blaise, M., & Taylor, A. (2012). Using queer theory to rethink gender equity in early childhood education. *YC Young Children, 67*(1), 88–96.
Britzman, D. (1995). Is there a queer pedagogy? Or, stop reading straight. *Educational Theory, 45*(2), 151–165.
Butler, J. (1990). *Gender trouble: Feminism and the subversion of identity.* New York, NY: Routledge.
Carr, W., & Kemmis, S. (1986). *Becoming critical: Education, knowledge and action research.* London: The Falmer Press.
Carrera, M. V., DePalma, R., & Lameiras, M. (2012). Sex/gender identity: Moving beyond fixed and 'natural' categories. *Sexualities, 15*(8), 995–1016.
Creswell, J. (1994). *Research design: Qualitative & quantitative approaches.* Thousand Oaks, CA: Sage.
Ellis, C. (1993). "There are survivors:" Telling a story of sudden death. *The Sociological Quarterly, 34*(4), 711–730.

Foucault, M. (1978). *The history of sexuality* (R. Hurley, Trans., Vol. I). New York, NY: Random House.

Hall, M. (2015). *Red: A crayon story.* New York, NY: Greenwillow Books.

Holub, J. (2014). *Mighty dads.* New York, NY: Scholastic Press.

Kemmis, S. (2009). Action research as a practice-based practice. *Educational Action Research, 17*(3), 463–474.

Koschoreck, J. W., Meek, J. B., Campanello, K., & Mominee, M. (2010). Queer scholarly activism: An exploration of the moral imperative of queering pedagogy and advocating social change. *The International Journal of Critical Pedagogy, 3*(1), 8–25.

Kumashiro, K. K. (2002). *Troubling education: Queer activism and antioppressive pedagogy.* New York, NY: Routledge Falmer.

Luhmann, S. (1998). Queering/querying pedagogy? Or, pedagogy is a pretty queer thing. In W. F. Pinar (Ed.), *Queer theory in education* (pp. 141–155). Mahwah, NJ: Lawrence Erlbaum Associates.

Macintosh, L. (2007). Does anyone have a band-aid? Anti-homophobia discourses and pedagogical impossibilities. *Educational Studies, 41*(1), 33–43.

National Association for the Education of Young Children. (2005). *Code of ethical conduct and statement of commitment.* Retrieved from https://oldweb.naeyc.org/about/positions/PSETH05.asp

Pinar, W. F. (1998). *Queer theory in education.* Mahwah, NJ: Lawrence Erlbaum Associates.

Piontek, T. (2006). *Queering gay and lesbian studies.* Champagne, IL: University of Illinois Press.

Powell, J. S. (2016). "To have better than what I had": The transgenerational family pedagogy of an African American family in the South. *Journal of Family Diversity in Education, 2*(2), 1–18.

Reay, D. (2001). 'Spice Girls','Nice Girls','Girlies', and 'Tomboys': Gender discourses, girls' cultures and femininities in the primary classroom. *Gender and Education, 13*(2), 153–166.

Sedgwick, E. K. (1990). *The epistemology of the closet.* Berkeley, CA: University of California Press.

Slesaransky-Poe, G., & García, A. M. (2009). Boys with gender variant behaviors and interests: From theory to practice. *Sex Education, 9*(2), 201–210.

Smith, M. J., & Payne, E. (2016, January). Binaries and biology: Conversations with elementary education professionals after professional development on supporting transgender students. *The Educational Forum, 80*(1), 34–47.

Taylor, A., & Richardson, C. (2005). Queering home corner. *Contemporary Issues in Early Childhood, 6*(2), 163–174. Retrieved from http://dx.doi.org/1 0.2304/ciec.2005.6

Warner, M. (1993). *Fear of a queer planet: Queer politics and social theory.* Minneapolis, MN: University of Minnesota Press.

Warner, M. (1999). *The trouble with normal: Sex, politics, and the ethics of queer life.* Cambridge, MA: Harvard University Press.

Weinraub, M., Clemens, L. P., Sockloff, A., Ethridge, T., Gracely, E., & Myers, B. (1984). The development of sex role stereotypes in the third year: Relationships to gender labeling, gender identity, sex-types toy preference, and family characteristics. *Child Development, 55*(4), 1493–1503.

Zacko-Smith, J. D., & Smith, G. P. (2013). Recognizing and utilizing queer pedagogy: A call for teacher education to reconsider the knowledge base on sexual orientation for teacher education programs. *Multicultural Education, 20*(3/4), 74–80.

we are

Exploring an Anti-Racist Summer Program for Elementary Students
Kindergarten–3rd Grade

RONDA TAYLOR BULLOCK, CHERISH WILLIAMS, DANIEL KELVIN BULLOCK, AND STEF BERNAL-MARTINEZ

Social justice education is an ongoing process of creating curriculum and learning opportunities geared toward addressing issues of inequity. Curriculum that specifically names inequities or addresses biases related to racism, heterosexism, sexism or religious discrimination, for example, makes these somewhat abstract concepts more concrete for students to grasp. This type of teaching focuses on actions that purposefully seek to create inclusive spaces that build community and validate individual students' identities and cultures.

Anti-racist education, which centers practices that dismantle systemic and ideological racism, falls under the umbrella of social justice teaching. *we are*, which stands for *working to extend anti-racist education*, is an affiliate of the Samuel DuBois Cook Center on Social Equity at Duke University. Its primary purpose is to provide anti-racist educational programs for students, parents and educators. *we are* uses a three-pronged approach to dismantle systemic racism in education and beyond through summer camps for kids, workshops for parents, and professional development for educators.

As a team of both current and former teachers, doctoral students, and passionate parents, *we are* created a curriculum for students in kindergarten through second grade. The first author of this chapter is the cofounder and director of *we are*. During the initial stages of the organization's formation, she reached out to former colleagues, current doctoral classmates, and friends who shared a common interest and desire to use education to dismantle systemic racism in schools. Many of the team members are certified teachers who have taught in both public and private school systems from pre-kindergarten to college. Using each person's expertise, we co-created a curriculum to help children better understand race and racism.

The curriculum was implemented through a five-day pilot summer camp. The goals of the *we are* Summer Camp were to (1) foster healthy racial identities in youth; (2) build a historical understanding of race and racism; and (3) equip families with tools and resources with which to extend anti-racist practices in the home and community.

Team members recruited participants for the summer camp primarily through email and social media. One member created a flyer that was emailed to principals, educators, and community members in surrounding areas. Funding for the camp was provided through student registration fees, monetary support from the Cook Center, and crowdsourcing.

Fifteen students from diverse backgrounds attended the pilot program: seven identified as African American, five White, and three bi-racial. Seven of the students received either a partial or full scholarship to participate. There was one rising kindergarten student, seven rising-first-grade students, six rising-second-grade, and two rising-third-grade students. While the curriculum was intended to stop at the second grade, two interested parents requested special consideration for their children to participate. Because the curriculum was accessible and appropriate for third graders, we did not adjust it; however, we used purposeful grouping at times so that the older students could work together.

Prior to attending the camp, all participating families were invited to attend the Family Orientation. At Orientation, parents and guardians had the opportunity to meet the *we are* planning team, along with the teachers who facilitated the camp. They also received a copy of Tahar Ben Jelloun's (2003) *Racism Explained to My Daughter*, along with a journal to document their experiences and conversations with their children as they came home each day. The book documents conversations parents had with their children addressing issues of discrimination, including but not limited to racism, anti-semitism, and anti-immigration. Parents were encouraged to use the text as a resource to help guide conversations with their children.

THEORETICAL FRAME FOR THE *WE ARE* SUMMER CAMP

The *we are* Summer Camp was grounded in critical race parenting (CRP), a framework stemming from critical race theory (CRT), which engages parents and children in a process of learning about race and ways of combatting racist ideas (Matias, 2016). Research has shown that racist ideologies are passed down to children through family, media, and various systems including both legal and educational (Van Ausdale & Feagin, 2001). Traditionally, families of color are known to have talks with their children in order to prepare them for a society built on structural racism (DePouw & Matias, 2016). These efforts are seen as ways to arm children of color against whiteness; however, largely absent from this type of preparation are discussions about arming White youth against whiteness. Thandeka (1999) wrote, "The first racial victim of the White community is its own child" (p. viii). The *we are* Summer Camp was designed to equip all families, but particularly White families, with the tools and resources to dismantle racism.

CRP utilizes many of the methodologies and tenets that are common to CRT to problematize issues of race and racism. For example, racial realism, the first principle of CRT and also a central component of CRP, is the idea that racism is normal and permanent in American society (Matias, 2016). Delgado and Stefancic (2001) expanded on this idea as they stated that racism in the United States is "the usual way society does business, the common, everyday experience of most people of color in this country" (p. 7). Counterstories, another component of CRT, are vital as a means of validating narratives from historically oppressed groups and challenging master narratives that reinforce ideals of the superiority of one racial group over others (Solórzano & Yosso, 2002). For example, master narratives in American history tend to focus on the experiences of White, privileged, land-owning males, while counterstories would bring to light the thoughts, words, and actions of Black Americans, both enslaved and free. Counterstories are utilized in CRP as parents help children to reconsider historical master narratives that minimize the contributions and stories of people of color and, instead, to learn and create counternarratives.

A third tenet of CRT that is essential in CRP is intersectionality or "the examination of race, sex, class, national origin, and sexual orientation and how their combinations play out in various settings" (Delgado & Stefancic, 2001, p. 51). Intersectionality is important to consider in CRP because it causes parents to question how different facets of identity impact their children's experiences with race and racism.

OVERVIEW OF CAMP

The *we are* Summer Camp was a five-day program intended to foster healthy racial identity development in youth, build historical understandings of race and racism, and equip families with tools and resources to extend anti-racist practices in the home and community. The essential components of the camp are reflected in Table 4.1.

Table 4.1: Overview of Camp.

Camp Component	Description
Family Orientation	• Parents/guardians were introduced to the *we are* team and given additional details about the purpose and structure of the *we are* Summer Camp • Parents/guardians received the text *Racism Explained to My Daughter* by Tahar Ben Jelloun (2003), and a journal to document conversations with their child
Day One of Camp	• Students analyzed texts: *The Name Jar* by Yangsook Choi (2013) and *I Am Mixed* by Garcelle Beauvais and Sebastian A. Jones (2013) • Essential questions included: Who am I? What is culture? Who or what is your community?
Day Two of Camp	• Students analyzed texts: *All the Colors We Are* by Katie Kissinger (2014) and *These Hands* by Margaret H. Mason (2011) • Essential questions included: What is skin color? What is race? How do we build a healthy community?
Day Three of Camp	• Students analyzed texts: *Amazing Grace* by Mary Hoffman (1991) • Essential questions included: What do you know about racism?
Day Four of Camp	• Students analyzed text: *Ruby Bridges Goes to School: My True Story* by Ruby Bridges (2009) • Essential questions included: What are systems in our community? How do systems build a healthy community? How do systems harm a community?
Day Five of Camp	• Students analyzed text: *Say Something* by Peggy Moss (2004) • Essential questions included: How does one become an ally? What are examples of unfairness or discrimination in my community?

The summer camp utilized a co-teacher model in which three facilitators helped students navigate between whole-group readings and small-group activities. The co-teaching model, which typically involves collaboration between a general education teacher and a specialist (Friend, 2008), was utilized to provide additional support to students as they explored novel content. Each day of the camp was grounded in an age-appropriate mentor text coupled with activities that helped the students discuss and process the content of the books. For example, the facilitators used texts such as *Amazing Grace* by Mary Hoffman (1991) and *These Hands* by Margaret H. Mason (2011) to engage students in discussions about fairness, racism, and biases, and their relationship to contributing to healthy or unhealthy communities. Each day the students took home the book or books used during the lesson with the expectation that they would share the book with family members. By the end of the week, each family had a home library of eight books that helped address race and racism.

Other camp activities included, but were not limited to, visual and musical arts lessons, presentations from guest speakers in the community, and a culminating project presentation for parents and community members. The teaching philosophy governing the summer camp was one that valued the use of multiple learning styles and opportunities for students to demonstrate their understanding in a variety of ways. The *we are* Summer Camp incorporated counterstories by having students read and analyze stories from historically oppressed groups and by allowing students to construct their own narratives about race and racism. Additionally, parents and guardians signed a consent form allowing for the use of their child's name, work, and image in future publications. Despite receiving consent, authors of this chapter opted to utilize pseudonyms to ensure anonymity. Some of the camp's social justice teaching moments are described in detail in the following section.

SOCIAL JUSTICE TEACHING IN PRACTICE

Colorism

Each social justice lesson in the *we are* curriculum began with the group of 15 students gathered together on the carpet while listening and sharing their ideas about topics including racism, skin color, culture, and healthy communities. One specific focus on Day 2 of the camp was understanding skin color. Using the book *All the Colors We Are* (Kissinger, 2014), students learned that skin color was the result of the amount of melanin a person has, their family genes, and the sun's impact. As a follow-up activity, each student was provided a palette of paints and instructed to mix different colors in order to recreate and name their own skin color. Several students took pride in naming their complexion, which was evident by names such as Peanut Better, Aloha Beach, and Beautiful Brown. This activity was designed to make students aware of their own skin tone and to allow students the opportunity to name themselves.

During this activity, the co-teachers paid particular attention to the language students used to describe themselves and to the language students used when referencing each other. It was important to note any negative self-talk or negative projections. An incident arose in which one African American student, Imani, attempted to tell another African American student, Chris, which color paint to use. Imani informed Chris that he only needed to use black paint to recreate his skin tone. Imani was making a reference to the darker skin of Chris, implying that lighter paint would not be necessary. It is important to note that Imani had a lighter shade of skin. After hearing the comments, Chris no longer wanted to participate in the activity, and this became a teaching moment for the classroom. As a psychologist in training, one of the co-teachers knew it was imperative to recognize Chris's self-concept and motivation for engagement were at-risk. This moment was addressed in front of the students with the expectation that they would learn how to respond to discrimination. Rather than disapproving of Imani's words, this moment was used as an opportunity for the students to generate ideas about how these words can affect another person, the effects of these words within the community, and how we can respond when this happens. One of the questions we posed repeatedly throughout the camp was, "Do these actions contribute to a healthy community or an unhealthy community?" Using this question helped students reflect on the larger impact of one's thoughts, actions, and words.

After the group reflected on the comments, Chris was discreetly pulled aside to assess his mental health and ensure he was equipped to handle similar situations in the future. In debriefing with Imani, she shared that members of her family described her skin tone in a way that led her to believe her lighter skin was superior. Imani was resistant to changing her beliefs about the value of certain skin colors; however, this particular lesson of disassociating skin color and value was purposefully reinforced throughout the week to change the narrative surrounding skin color with the students, which was important for both Black and White students. As educators, it is important to be aware of the challenges associated with dismantling discriminatory beliefs, especially when the beliefs are reinforced at home. Students may feel conflicted about their inherent trust to listen to their family versus the message they may be receiving from their teacher. Remaining consistent, though, will help students come into their own understanding of which beliefs contribute to healthy or unhealthy community.

Racism and Prejudice

Illustrating the differences between prejudice and racism can be a difficult task with younger students in the concrete stage of their cognitive development. To gather students' understanding of racism as a before-reading strategy, one co-teacher led the students in an activity where she asked, "What do you know about the word racism?" Racism was written on chart paper, and the co-teacher recorded student responses, creating a bubble map. Student responses ranged from recognizing separate water fountains to mistreatment due to skin color to people racing, as in race cars. It was obvious that most students had prior experiences learning about racism.

To illustrate racism at a relevant level, one co-teacher then engaged the class in reading *Amazing Grace* (Hoffman, 1991). The protagonist, Grace, is an African American young girl who wanted to play the part of Peter Pan in the school play. One of her White classmates informed her that she could not play this part because she was Black and Peter Pan was White. The students were charged to think about why Grace was treated unfairly while the teacher read the book. A first-grade student recognized Grace was being treated unfairly because she was Black, and he stated, "Grace should paint her skin White to be Peter Pan." This was a moment to help students think about the actual problem with the scenario in the book: Grace being treated unfairly because of the color of her skin. The co-teacher restated the definition of racism used for the camp—when someone uses their thoughts and actions to treat others unfairly because of the color of their skin—and also reminded students that Grace's skin color was beautiful, and it was not the problem. The beliefs and attitudes held by the children in Grace's class were the problem and did not allow Grace to be a part of a healthy community. It was important to name this form of unfair treatment as racism because it would help students to recognize and name racist acts in the future.

After the book discussion, students were asked to raise their hands if they had experienced racism or ever been treated unfairly because of the color of their skin. Several hands were raised and stories were shared; however, none of the raised hands were those of the Black students. Stories shared by the White students included themes of peers reneging on friendship, not being invited to birthday parties, and being excluded from peer groups. As teachers, we had to be careful to label these stories as acts of prejudice or discrimination and not racism, while also validating the students' experience. The co-teachers realized that based on the definition of racism they shared, what the White students named would be considered racism. However, it was important that students understood that racism is connected to a system of power. Day 4 of the camp focused on systems: legal, law, and school. On this day, the co-teachers revisited how racism works through systems.

In-vivo Practice

As educators, we not only wanted to assess the students' current knowledge of racism and anti-racism, but we also wanted to equip the students with the terminology to respond to racism and advocate for anti-racism outside of the classroom. During the last few days of the camp, the educators encouraged the students to use their problem-solving skills when issues within peer groups arose. Each day the students participated in recess, because social justice can be taught anywhere.

A trend emerged each day as the children raced to the playground to engage with one another on the jungle gym.

There was one popular swing that became a source of conflict for the students. It was shaped like a saucer and could accommodate up to four children: two standing on the side and two sitting in the cup of the saucer. As observers, we noticed the norms and rules of the playground were made by two of the White students, Brittany and Jeffrey. These students managed to stay on the swing the entire recess period, while also dictating their peers' time on the swing. Brittany and Jeffrey stood on opposite sides of the saucer, allowing the other students to only have access to the cup of the saucer. What became more interesting was the number of students who complained about others not sharing the swing, but never questioned Brittany and Jeffrey, who remained on the swing the entire time. In fact, the two White students sent their peersto the teachers to report when others were not following their rules. The students were then told to use the problem-solving skills they were learning in the classroom to ask pertinent questions about the playground, as if it were an unfair system. These questions included who made the rules, why must everyone follow the rules, and who is currently benefitting from these rules? It was astonishing to watch the students work together to restructure the rules of the playground and ensure everyone's play was equitable. This was one example of watching our children apply the anti-racist education to problem-solving.

To further assess the effectiveness of our anti-racist education, the students were divided into groups based upon age, given scenarios, and asked to determine whether each scenario was an example of racism or anti-racism. There was one educator within each group to facilitate the students' discussions and ensure they were reaching accurate conclusions about the scenarios. One scenario asked whether a club encouraging Black girls to run promoted racism or anti-racism:

Madeline, White, 13 years old

Madeline wanted to join the Black Girls Run Club. Madeline really enjoyed running, and she was really good at it. When Madeline asked to join the club, she was told that the club was meant to encourage Black girls to run. Madeline understood that this club was to support Black girls so they could have a healthy community. Is this an example of racism or anti-racism?

With this particular scenario, the co-teachers tried to help students understand how certain groups, such as the Black Girls Run Club, were created to help establish a healthy community for Black girls where one did not exist. Students struggled somewhat, with this particular scenario; however, overall they were able to correctly label the rest as either an example of racism or anti-racism.

IMPLICATIONS

Students Can Develop Deeper Understandings of Race Through Anti-Racist Discussions

Throughout the *we are* Summer Camp, students were constantly challenged to think deeply about their understandings of race and racism. While many of the challenges came to students via planned discussions and activities, some of the learning opportunities came about through organic situations. The common thread in both the planned and unplanned learning opportunities was the preparation and willingness of the teachers to engage students in critical conversations about race.

Many of the planned opportunities for students to learn about race and racism were connected to texts and learning activities. For example, the activity where students utilized paints to recreate their own skin color allowed them to truly reflect on the tone and hue of their skin and to assign a positive, affirming name to it. The name "Chocolate Nice" was generated by a young female of color and was indicative of her positive perception of her brown skin tone. Another planned activity involved students learning the words to the Summer Camp theme song. The lyrics of the song, which was written to the tune of "She'll be Coming 'Round the Mountain," focused on the anti-racist changes that the students would be prepared to make in the world once they completed the camp. Through this activity, students first had to learn the initial verses that were written by one of the camp organizers. Then they created their own verse by incorporating information they learned during the camp. This activity enabled students to learn through kinesthetic and artistic means, while also considering how their camp experiences might impact society at large.

There were also a number of unplanned discussions that helped students develop deeper understandings of race and racism. For example, two scenarios that developed organically were the aforementioned scenarios regarding the students vying for the opportunity to play on the swings during recess and the child who offered the suggestion about only needing the color black to re-create another child's skin color. Teachers did not plan to facilitate discussions in these particular situations. However, due to their preparation to educate students about race and racism in general, they were able to turn these situations into learning experiences. Additionally, students showed evidence of growth as they responded in ways that demonstrated their understanding of the role of race and racism in these unplanned discussions.

Any of these activities, discussions, or lessons could be utilized in traditional elementary classrooms. The challenge lies in the need for educators to develop their own thorough understanding of racism and to construct learning experiences that will enhance students' knowledge of this topic and ways of dismantling it. As educators develop lessons intended to encourage anti-racism in students, they will enhance their own intelligence and be better prepared to effectively navigate unplanned discussions on race with students that will inevitably arise.

Literature Can Be Utilized to Analyze Issues of Race and Racism with Students

Age-appropriate literature was very useful for challenging students to analyze issues of race and racism. Throughout the *we are* Summer Camp, students continuously read and examined texts that included issues of race, racism, prejudice, bullying, etc. to help them gain a better understanding of racism and how it operates. This enabled students to think about how unfair actions were addressed in texts and also how they might handle similar situations in their own lives.

The text *Ruby Bridges Goes to School: My True Story* (Bridges, 2009) was an excellent tool for helping students to learn about a portion of the historical context of race in America. Students were able to read the story of Ruby Bridges, her experience in desegregating a school and the consequences of that action. As students read the story, teachers guided them to analyze the images and photos that were included in the text. There were images of signs that were created to discourage and intimidate African Americans from entering the school. There were images of White people who vehemently opposed the entrance of Ruby Bridges in her school. And, there were images of a White teacher who was in support of Ruby Bridges. Paying close attention to these different images enabled students to see diverse people engaged in racist and anti-racist behavior and to distinguish between the two. The conversation led back to the question that was constantly posed at the camp: how are people contributing to a healthy or unhealthy community in this text?

The book *Say Something* by Peggy Moss (2004) was also helpful for students to consider the impact of action and inaction when it comes to race, prejudice, and bullying. This book was read during the last day of the camp as students thought about ways to continue anti-racist work beyond the summer camp. After reading the examples of action and inaction in the book, students discussed the need to speak up and advocate for others whenever they see people being mistreated. This particular conversation was not limited to issues of racism, but it applied to any type of discrimination that one might observe. Students also discussed the negative effects of inaction that were portrayed in the book and how they might avoid being silent when people are treated unjustly. This text (and others) truly challenged students to think about how they react in different situations and how they might become more proactive in creating healthy communities.

Again, educators should be encouraged to think deeply about how to engage students in analyses of race and racism. The Common Core State Standards for English language arts focuses on students' development of literacy skills. Teachers can help students enhance these skills and develop anti-racist practices by deciphering texts that feature issues of race, prejudice, discrimination, tolerance, and/or anti-racism. When choosing texts, we encourage teachers to look for books that are culturally authentic, meaning the race or ethinicity of the author aligns with the race or ethnicity of the protagonists (Tschida, Ryan, & Ticknor, 2014). Doing so often minimizes the likelihood of a negative or stereotypical portrayal of a marginalized community.

QUESTIONS

There were many questions that were left unresolved and were points of reflection as the camp organizers moved into the planning phase for the next iteration of the *we are* Summer Camp. The teachers noticed that during social times on the playground, there were power dynamics that aligned with children's racial identities and the racial hierarchy that we lived in—the same systems we were studying. Looking towards the future, camp organizers must ask: How do we bring in the interactions of children on the playground as conversation starters and reflection tools? How do we help children connect how these systems impact their everyday lives? How will we utilize the findings from this camp to help educators rethink and incorporate anti-racism in the elementary classroom and on the playground?

CONCLUSION

The purpose of the *we are* Summer Camp was to foster healthy racial identity development in youth, build historical understandings of race and racism, and equip families with tools and resources to extend anti-racist practices in the home and community. Based upon the outcomes of the pilot camp, organizers are excited about the potential for the camp to grow, improve, and provide an even greater opportunity for young people to deeply engage in issues of race and anti-racism as a form of social justice. There are questions to consider as *we are* seeks to enhance the overall experience of participants. But, the outlook is very encouraging as students and parents exhibited greater understanding of race, racism, and steps that can be taken to demonstrate the ideals of anti-racism. What's even more encouraging is that elementary educators can work towards building a socially just curriculum by starting with at least one text that directly addresses race and/or racism.

The commitment to social justice teaching is ongoing. As the saying goes, it is a marathon and not a sprint. One week at camp or one lesson in a classroom will not solve the social ills of the world; however, it is a step in the right direction.

REFERENCES

Beauvais, G., & Jones, S. (2013). *I am mixed.* Los Angeles, CA: Stranger Comics.

Bridges, R. (2009). *Ruby Bridges goes to school: My true story.* New York, NY: Scholastic Incorporated.

Choi, Y. (2013). *The name jar.* New York, NY: Knopf Books for Young Readers.

Delgado, R., & Stefancic, J. (2001). *Critical race theory: An introduction.* New York, NY: New York University Press.

DePouw, C., & Matias, C. (2016). Critical race parenting: Understanding scholarship/activism in parenting our children. *Educational Studies, 52*(3), 237–259.

Friend, M. (2008). Co-teaching: A simple solution that isn't simple after all. *Journal of Curriculum and Instruction, 2*(2), 9–19.

Hoffman, M. (1991). *Amazing grace.* New York, NY: Dial Books.

Jelloun, T. B. (2003). *Racism explained to my daughter.* New York, NY: The New Press.

Kissinger, K. (2014). *All the colors we are: The story of how we get our skin color = Todos los colores de nuestra piel: la historia de por qué tenemos diferentes colores de piel.* St. Paul, MN: Redleaf Press.

Mason, M. H. (2015). *These hands.* Boston, MA: Houghton Mifflin Harcourt.

Matias, C. E. (2016). "Mommy, is being Brown bad?": Critical race parenting in a "post-race" era. *Journal of Race and Pedagogy, 1*(3), Article 1. http://soundideas.pugetsound.edu/rpj/vol1/iss3/1

Moss, P. (2014). *Say something.* Gardiner, Maine: Tilbury House.

Solórzano, D. G., & Yosso, T. J. (2002). Critical race methodology: Counter-storytelling as an analytical framework for education research. *Qualitative Inquiry, 8*(1), 23–44.

Thandeka. (1999). *Learning to be white: Money, race, and God in America.* New York, NY: Bloomsbury.

Tschida, C. M., Ryan, C. L., & Ticknor, A. S. (2014). Building on windows and mirrors: Encouraging the disruption of "single stories" through children's literature. *Journal of Children's Literature, 40*(1), 33.

Van Ausdale, D., & Feagin, J. R. (2001). *The first R: How children learn race and racism.* Lanham, MD: Rowman & Littlefield Publishers.

CHAPTER FIVE

Immigration Today

Perspectives from Primary Classrooms
2nd Grade

SUNGHEE SHIN AND BEVERLY MILNER (LEE) BISLAND

With a new national administration, immigration is in the forefront of the country's news and political discussions. As the new president begins his administration with an executive order barring some individuals and groups from immigrating into the United States (Gonchar & Schulten, 2017), essential questions arise for discussion in the nation's classrooms. Who comes to this country from other countries? Why do they come? How does my community reflect immigration today?

This topic can be explored by young children in the primary grades, and should not only be a topic in U.S. history courses in the upper grades. The concepts of who comes to the United States and why are initial understandings that build a foundation for more critical exploration of challenges facing immigrants as students' progress through the grades. Younger children understand the push and pull of immigration with concrete examples and typically without interpretation. They recognize that immigrants want a better education, better financial opportunities, and a better life than they had in their home countries. Older students are able to investigate with more depth and nuance the conditions in an immigrant's home country that provide the push to leave: wars, famines, and persecution, for example. Also, they can explore more critically the pull of a better life in a new country and how that new life meets the immigrants' expectations.

By applying the essential questions above to their own families or their own communities in a unit of study, the primary students explore the idea that any history is someone's history (Levstik, 1997). Research suggests the importance of integrating assets students bring into the classroom in instruction. Changing pedagogies also emphasize the need for students to participate in community-based inquiries. This asset-based perspective centers students as knowledge producers, instead of knowledge consumers, making them active participants in learning.

The study of personal and community immigration is particularly relevant today because the United States is experiencing what is described as a "tsunami-proportion migratory flow" (Finkelstein, 2013, p. 126) in a world that is increasingly interconnected. In 2013, immigrants comprised 13.1% of the total US population. In 1990, immigrants were just 7.9% of the total U.S. population. The largest group of foreign-born residents in the United States is from Mexico and the second largest group is from China (Camarota & Ziegler, 2014).

A study of immigration today can be difficult since it is a controversial topic that brings out antagonistic feelings. Anti-immigrant sentiments and laws have been demonstrated by rhetoric in the 2016 presidential campaign, recent developments with executive orders from a new president, and outbreaks of violence against immigrants (Rabrenovic, 2007). These sentiments are not exclusive to the United States, as they have also appeared in European countries such as Germany and France (Graff, 2010). In U.S. classrooms, discussions of recent immigration can reach a flashpoint between the isolationist attitudes of some individuals, whose families have lived in the United States for many years, and the needs and attitudes of recent immigrants and children of immigrants. This atmosphere of contentiousness highlights the need to discuss the topic of recent immigration in classrooms as U.S. society is increasingly composed of the foreign born.

Unfortunately, the topic of recent immigration is not often part of the curriculum (Graff, 2010). In many instances, units in classrooms at all levels treat immigration as a historical concept rather than a recent occurrence. Consequently, it is the two waves of historic immigration—from the early- to the late-nineteenth century and from the early- to the mid-twentieth century—that are studied (Graff, 2010). For many teachers, historical immigration is considered a safer subject than recent immigration and the anticipated issues and conflicts associated with it (Bersch, 2013).

A unit on recent immigration is grounded in social justice pedagogy. It gives students a sense that they have a place and meaning in their world. This pedagogy helps students develop positive social and cultural identities and encourages thinking that does not discriminate because someone is different. Therefore, recent immigration needs to be part of the curriculum if we wish to build a civic society based on social justice and the inclusion of all people in the fabric of the nation through our public education system.

INQUIRY UNIT ON IMMIGRATION TODAY

This instructional unit for the primary grades is divided into three phases: (1) identifying immigrants in our own community; (2) connecting today's immigration to our own families and communities; and (3) identifying the geographic and economic nature of recent immigration and its historical antecedents. The unit was guided by the following essential questions:

Who immigrated to my community from other countries?
Why did they come and where did they come from?
How has immigration changed over time and how has it stayed the same?

The two authors observed two second-grade classes who were using elements of this inquiry unit to study immigration in their community. The immigration unit was developed by the two second-grade teachers in conjunction with the school principal and the authors, who are teacher educators. The authors were invited to participate in creating and observing the unit because the principal was interested in integrating social studies and technology into the curriculum more than it had been in the past.

The school is located in Queens, New York, and all the students in each class were largely the children of immigrants. Only a few were immigrants themselves. In New York City, which is a city of immigrants, Queens County has the largest immigrant population, with nearly one-half of its residents foreign born in 2011 (The City of New York, 2013). The two second-grade classes drew students from across the county. Consequently they represented many of the countries of the world, including China, Guyana, Pakistan, Bangladesh, Columbia, and the United Arab Emirates, among others.

DATA AND ASSESSMENT

The focus of the authors' classroom observations was to determine the students' understanding of the content as guided by the unit's essential questions and to assess how well the students were able to demonstrate these understandings through digital storytelling. Evidence was gathered through classroom observations, written work contained in the students' social studies folders, students' written interviews with family members, and their presentation of the interviews using Pixie, a digital storytelling program. The observations occurred for a forty-five minute class period once or twice per week for two months. The researchers' primary interest was in the students' level of understanding of recent immigration through the lens of their own communities and families, as well as how local immigration fits into the broader picture of United States immigration. The researchers were also interested in the students' ability to produce and demonstrate their knowledge with Pixie, a digital movie making platform. The videos produced by the students were evaluated by the authors using a criterion-referenced assessment (Christie et al., 2015). The assessment contained the following criteria: (1) content & theme: were they clear and relevant? (2) images: did they match the content and give atmosphere and tone to the presentation? (3) organization: was it logical and coherent? (4) narration: was it clear and paced well? and (5) creator: did the student include self-identifiers? Each video was scored on a scale of 1 to 3, from lowest to the highest.

IMPLEMENTATION OF THE UNIT

Below are descriptions of the data collected from the authors' classroom observations and assessments. These descriptions are followed by suggestions for teachers who wish to implement a similar unit.

Phase 1: Identifying Immigrants in Our Community

In the second-grade classrooms in this study, the students engaged in centers to complete inquiry activities. In the first center, the teachers, the authors, and the students supplied pictures of businesses and people in order to look at their own community: Queens, New York. Students were given a structured inquiry sheet to use as they looked at the different pictures in the center. The sheet, adapted from inquiry activities on the National Archives and Records Administration website (2016), asked them to list their observations according to people, objects, and activities. Next they were asked to interpret what was the same and what was different in each picture. Finally they were asked to infer from the pictures what they learned about the different neighborhoods in their community.

Using a sample of ten students with a range of abilities from one of the classes, the authors counted their observations from the photographs and grouped them under general categories. The greatest number of students identified people in the pictures by their ethnicity, either because of their ethnic dress (e.g. Indians and Pakistanis) or the establishments in which they shopped or worked. One picture was of a coffee shop with the sign in Arabic and another was of a Greek food shop with the Greek flag hanging in the background. Some students identified people simply by gender, while others identified occupations in the photographs. For objects, the greatest number of students focused on transportation, such as buses, or on businesses such as stores, shops and restaurants. For activities, the students focused on interactions between people, such as buying and selling, or movement, such as walking or driving a taxi. When comparing the set of photographs to each other for similarities and differences, they identified some of the same elements in both categories. Writing and language were identified as different among the immigrant groups by four students, but the same by one student. Clothes were identified as different among the groups, since some pictures showed individuals in ethnic dress.

When the students were asked to tell what the photographs told them about their community, four students inferred from the photographs some of the major characteristics of Queens. They said that a lot of different cultures and languages exist in Queens. Others did not show this depth of understanding in their observations. They simply said that Queens is full of different people, places, markets and stores.

In a second center the students were asked to rank order by size the ten largest immigrant groups in Queens from the latest census data (The City of New York, 2013). This activity familiarized the students with the different immigrant groups, but could have been enriched with a survey and graph of the classes themselves to see if their ethnicity corresponded with the census numbers. For example, was the largest number of students in the class Chinese? If so, this result would correspond to the largest immigrant group in Queens.

Implementation. To begin the unit and engage the students before collecting evidence for the first work center, teachers can use Peter Sis's *Madlenka* (2000). In the book, Madlenka—whose New York City neighbors include the French baker, the Indian news vendor, the Italian ice-cream man, the South American grocer, and the Chinese shopkeeper—goes around the block to show them her loose tooth and finds that it is like taking a trip around the world.

For the second center, teachers can use the U.S. Census Bureau's American Factfinder section (US Census Bureau, 2017) to identify foreign-born populations in their area and build graphs for the students. The students can create a class census to determine if the ethnicity of their class reflects the Census Bureau's facts about immigrants in their community.

Phase 2: The Immigrant Experience in Our Community and Beyond

In this phase of the unit, students watched and critiqued videos of young immigrants from around the world who came to the United States in recent years. Then they created interview questions, practiced interviewing, and interviewed someone from their own family or community who is an immigrant. Last, they produced a video presentation of their interview using Pixie.

For information on young immigrants today, students used videos from the website *Immigration: Stories of Yesterday and Today* by Scholastic (2015). The site has five videos of children from Ukraine, South Korea, Sierra Leon, India, and

Mexico. Students completed an inquiry sheet that asked them to list what surprised them about the young immigrants' stories, how they were similar to themselves, how they were different, and what they learned from listening to the young immigrants' voices.

Using a sample of ten students from the second class, the authors coded their observations from the videos. The greatest number of students focused on holidays when listing information that surprised them. In particular, they were surprised to learn that Ashya from Ukraine celebrated Christmas on January 7 because of the Orthodox Christian calendar. For similarities among immigrant groups, the focus was again on holidays with the celebration of Christmas receiving the most comments. Five students listed elements of the immigrant experience as different from their own experiences, such as living in old houses in their homeland, being homeless in the United States, and moving from place to place, both internationally and domestically. The students in the two second-grade classes were largely the children of immigrants, with only a few exceptions. Therefore, they had not experienced immigration as the young people in the videos had. At least one of the students understood from the videos that one of the reasons for immigration was war in the young immigrant's home country of Sierra Leone. Another observed the feelings of loneliness that many immigrants experience after arriving in a new country. Other inferences were less insightful, saying for example that the young immigrants came from other countries and that their life was different.

As a final step in connecting their own knowledge with knowledge about today's immigrant experience, students prepared to conduct an interview with a family member, relative, or friend, who was an immigrant. The interviews were produced as a video. Interview questions were developed during whole class discussion led by the teachers. The students were urged to identify the differences between "talk long" questions, which encourage more complex answers, and "talk short" questions, which encourage short, often one-word answers. After collecting a pool of questions, they developed a Talk Long Immigration Interview Question protocol. The four interview questions were: (1) Can you describe why you moved to America? (2) Can you describe what life as an immigrant is like? (3) Describe what you felt like when you came to America, and (4) Describe how your country is different from America.

As a whole class, students conducted a practice interview with a recent immigrant from Taiwan, who was an assistant teacher at their school. They asked questions such as her first impression of America, what she ate in Taiwan, and how she liked American food. From this exercise, students found additional questions to ask. They included this extended pool of questions in their own interviews.

After conducting their own interviews, students prepared a storyboard with four scenes depicting the answer to each of the interview questions. In the first scene, they were told to add their picture and information about themselves and their interviewee, including their relationship with the individual, when they came to America, and where they were from. The storyboard gave them the opportunity to edit and reorganize the stories they heard. Finally, they created their own digital story in the computer lab using the storyboard as a rough draft.

In a lab session on movie making, students had the opportunity to edit, highlight, add, and subtract stories they wanted to use for their video using Pixie, a children's multimedia authoring tool. Students were guided to focus on typing their story first to prevent them from being overwhelmed by the technology rather than the power of their story (Ohler, 2006). Images were inserted to emphasize certain elements of their story; however, many students indulged in using the decorating tool solely for aesthetic purposes or for their own entertainment.

Implementation. In addition to viewing videos of young immigrants and creating their own video from an interview, students can also read excellent trade books on the immigrant experience for this part of the unit. Of particular note are *Migrant: The Journey of a Mexican Worker* (Mateo, 2014) and *I Hate English* (Levine, 1989). Each one shows the experiences of children from the two largest immigrant groups in the United States, Mexicans and Chinese. *Migrant* tells the story of an undocumented Mexican immigrant's journey to the United States with his family, describing the dangers they face crossing the border and hiding their documentation status. In *I Hate English*, a young Chinese girl finds it difficult to adjust to school and learn the alien sounds of English when her family moves to New York from Hong Kong.

In areas of the country with a lower immigrant population, full-class rather than individual interviews may be conducted. Local organizations representing various ethnic groups or local historical societies may be helpful in identifying immigrants. Additionally, interviews both written and oral can be located online at sites such as the Library of Congress and the National Parks site for Ellis Island. These resources may result in altering the emphasis of the unit away from individual students telling their own story.

Phase 3: Immigration in the Past

In order to understand immigration in the past and compare it to immigration today, the second-grade teachers again used the Scholastic website, *Immigration: Stories of Yesterday and Today* (2015). The students viewed photographs and videos of immigrants' arrival at Ellis Island at the turn of the twentieth century. The site offers an interactive floorplan of the main terminal and interviews with individuals who came to the United States through Ellis Island.

The purpose of the activity was to develop the students' skills at gathering, using, and interpreting evidence; to increase their chronological reasoning and understanding of causation; and to enhance their ability to compare and contextualize information. In pursuit of these goals the teachers used circle thinking maps, which are a type of graphic organizer. The inner part of the circle is used to write information that the student learned from the material and the outside of the circle is used to write any questions that the student might have after the activity.

After listening to interviews with immigrants who came to America through Ellis Island, the students filled in their circle thinking maps. One student completed the inner part of the map by saying that immigrants came from Italy, Poland, and Russia; it took weeks to get to New York, 3000 people were on the boat, and they could only bring stuff that they needed. In the outer part of the map, the student asked why it took weeks to get there and where the diseases came from, in response to the information that all immigrants were checked for diseases.

The students were then asked to write down their impressions of the trip to Ellis Island and facts that they learned about the Ellis Island experience. Using a sample of ten students from both classes with a range of academic abilities from high to low, we found that many noticed and recorded the same impressions and facts. Describing the trip to Ellis Island, at least two students used the descriptive adjectives, "bad, horrible, dirty, scary" and said, "the ship was rusty." Other descriptors used by the students were "smelly" and "people were sick, tired, and starving."

For important facts, the largest number of students said that 3000 people were on the ship to Ellis Island and that no food was on the ship. A smaller number reported that the ship was dirty, that passengers were only allowed one bag, that the journey took three weeks, and that passengers could not wash or brush their teeth. Other students said that many different languages were spoken and that immigrants were from different countries, but did not connect the fact that being from different countries resulted in different spoken languages.

Several of the students pointed out that the immigrants were checked for sickness at Ellis Island, particularly for trachoma, where button hooks were used to examine eyes. One student interpreted this evidence and said that even with the checks for sickness, most immigrants were allowed into the country. Two students were able to contextualize the Ellis Island experience chronologically. One student said that Ellis Island operated a long time ago and another attempted to supply dates for the experience.

In a full-class discussion on big ideas that resulted from studying immigration now and in the past, the students concluded that being an immigrant can be difficult but it can also be exciting. They observed that it is hard if you cannot speak English, that both yesterday and today immigrants have been seeking a better life, and that many hardships exist at home and in their new country.

Implementation. There are a variety of classroom materials available to study immigration in the past. On the Scholastic website *Asian Pacific American Heritage* (2016) students can view the story of Li Keng Wong, who immigrated to the

United States from China in 1933 through Angel Island. The site has links to a virtual tour of Angel Island and a written interview with Li Keng Wong. Two trade books for studying past immigrant children's experiences from an east coast and west coast perspective are *Landed* (Lee, 2006) and *The Matchbox Diary* (Fleischman, 2013). In *Landed* Sun leaves China to start life anew in America in 1882. Once in detainment and away from his family, Sun worries that he won't pass the oral exam and will be turned away from the land of his dreams. In *The Matchbox Diary*, a girl peruses her great-grandfather's collection of matchboxes and small curios that document his journey from Italy to a new country. These books are only a few of the many excellent children's books on recent and historic immigrant experiences.

DISCUSSION

This unit on immigration demonstrates a means for young students to begin their historical understanding through an empathetic study of individuals who have immigrated to the United States, both at the turn of the twentieth century and recently. Riley (1998) and Stern (1998) argued that it is through the voices of ordinary people that students can develop an understanding of history and consequently develop an empathetic stance towards historical events. Because this unit is based on the diverse assets that the students bring to class, they are able to understand how immigration has affected their own families, communities, and neighborhoods. The unit was designed to acknowledge and respect their personal family histories and different ethnic backgrounds. The students were able to share their knowledge with their peers.

Because the unit was implemented in Queens, NY, it was very common to see Spanish-speaking students helping other group members read signs in Spanish. When students saw Asian characters, they asked one of the authors, who is from Korea, to read the signs for them. Suddenly, the classroom became one of the immigration boats at Ellis Island or lounges at John F. Kennedy airport where 30 different languages were spoken. They learned about the history of diversity with the diverse assets they and their classmates brought to class.

The highlight of this empathetic experience was the students' interview with their family members (mostly their parents). In most cases, it was the first time they heard about their parents' difficult journeys to America. They discovered the story of their parents' journey and the story of the homeland they left behind. For all, it was the first time they heard about their parents' feelings on leaving their homeland and starting a new life in America. One of the students wrote about how he almost cried when he learned that his mom cried for most of her first night in America out of loneliness. Watching, reading, and listening to stories of immigrants who were their parents or grandparents engaged students with compassion and deepened their empathy when they retold the story. At the end of the unit, one of the students' mothers sent a letter to one of the teachers, writing that the unit changed their conversation topics at the dinner table.

SIGNIFICANCE

Most cities, counties, and towns throughout the United States contain immigrants. Consequently, this unit may be implemented in locations other than a multiethnic urban community, like the site of this study. This unit allows students to develop the power of their own voice through the process of creating immigration narratives. Most significantly, a valuable outcome of this unit is to guide students in identifying themselves within the larger context of their community's and country's history. Through this inquiry, students learn that the current multicultural assets of America are the product of immigrants, like themselves and their ancestors. America's present and future cultural diversity is defined by their ethnic heritage and the ethnic heritage of others. The purpose of this unit of study is for young students to understand that history is made up of individual stories of people who are famous and not as famous, and that they and their families are a part of this country's history.

REFERENCES

Bersch, L. C. (2013). The curricular value of teaching about immigration through picture book thematic text sets. *The Social Studies, 104*(2), 47–56.

Camarota, S. A., & Zeigler, K. (2014). U.S. immigrant population record 41.3 million in 2013. *Center for Immigration Studies*. Retrieved from http://cis.org/immigrant-population-record-2013

Christie, M., Grainger, P., Dahlgren, R., Call, K., Heck, D., & Simon, S. (2015). Improving the quality of assessment grading tools in master of education courses: A comparative case study in the scholarship of teaching and learning. *Journal of the Scholarship of Teaching and Learning, 15*(5), 22–35.

The City of New York, Department of City Planning, Office of Immigrant Affairs. (2013). *The newest New Yorkers: Characteristics of the city's foreign-born population*. Retrieved from http://www.nyc.gov/html/dcp/html/census/popdiv.shtml

Finkelstein, B. (2013). Teaching outside the lines: Education history for a world in motion. *History of Education Quarterly, 53*(2), 126–138.

Fleischman, P. (2013). *The matchbox diary*. Sommerville, MA: Candlewick Press.

Gonchar, M., & Schulten, K. (2017, January 29). Analyzing Trump's immigration ban: A lesson plan. *The New York Times*. Retrieved from https://www.nytimes.com/2017/01/29/learning/lesson-plans/analyzing-trumps-immigration-ban-a-lesson-plan.html?_r=0

Graff, J. M. (2010). Countering narratives: Teachers' discourses about immigrants and their experiences within the realm of children's and young adult literature. *English Teaching: Practice and Critique, 9*(3), 106–131.

Lee, M. (2006). *Landed.* New York, NY: Farrar Strauss Giroux.

Levine, E. (1989). *I hate English.* New York, NY: Scholastic Inc.

Levstik, L. (1997). Any history is someone's history: Listening to multiple voices from the past. *Social Education, 61*(1), 48–51.

Mateo, J. M. (2014). *Migrant, the journey of a Mexican worker.* New York, NY: Harry N. Abrams.

National Archives and Records Administration. (2016). *Photo analysis worksheet.* Retrieved from www.archives.gov/education/lessons/worksheets/photo_analysis_worksheet.pdf

Ohler, J. (2006). The world of digital storytelling. *Educational Leadership, 63*(4), 44–47.

Rabrenovic, G. (2007). When hate comes to town: Community response to violence against immigrants. *American Behavioral Scientist, 51*(2), 349–360.

Riley, K. L. (1998). Historical empathy and the Holocaust: Theory into practice. *International Journal of Social Education, 13*(1), 32–42.

Scholastic. (2015). *Immigration: Stories of yesterday and today.* Retrieved from http://www.scholastic.com/teachers/activity/immigration-stories-yesterday-and-today

Scholastic. (2016). *Angel Island: Li Keng Wong's story.* Retrieved from http://teacher.scholastic.com/activities/asian-american/angel_island/

Sis, P. (2000). *Madlenka.* New York, NY: Farrar Straus Giroux.

Stern, B. S. (1998). Addressing the concept of historical empathy: With frauen: German women recall the Third Reich. *International Journal of Social Education, 13*(1), 43–48.

US Census Bureau. (2017). *American fact finder.* Retrieved from https://factfinder.census.gov

CHAPTER SIX

"Act Like a Girl!"

Preservice Elementary Teacher Perspectives of Gender Identity Development
4th–5th Grade

ELIZABETH E. SAYLOR

Feminism, like social studies, is a democratic ideal, a social justice perspective, a movement that promotes advocacy for citizenship and civic engagement; it is all encompassing in the pursuit of equality and justice for all (Saylor, 2017). The canons of feminism and social studies education reinforce and support each other. Nonetheless, few elementary instructors are open to engaging in feminist discourse.

Gender inequality and sexism exist through explicit and implicit thoughts and behaviors. Research reveals that sexism, including gender stereotyping and sexual harassment, can be reduced through raising awareness and through the espousal of feminist perspectives (Becker & Swim, 2011; Becker, Zawadzki, & Shields, 2014; Cundiff, Zawadzki, Danube, & Shields, 2014; Zawadzki, Danube, & Shields, 2012). However, to reduce sexism with feminism, individuals (specifically women) must first be aware that we exist in a misogynistic, patriarchal society and recognize all of these nuanced undertones. However, there is a lack of research on what perspectives elementary teachers have regarding feminism, including sexism and gender identity development. Additionally, there is a dearth of research concerning how preservice teachers come to their understandings of feminism and what messages they received in school concerning feminism and their own gender identities. Exploring the development of teachers' understandings, ideologies, and beliefs can uncover their purposes for becoming teachers and possibly for decisions they may make in their future classrooms regarding their teaching practice and the curricular choices that ultimately affect student learning. A deeper understanding of preservice teachers' beliefs and understandings of feminism are important if teacher education programs are to foster reflective teachers who are conscious of the systemic, institutionalized oppression of women and all marginalized individuals and groups. A more rich understanding of their perspectives on this topic and of their understanding of the power they possess as instructional gatekeepers (Thornton, 1989, 1991) may reveal that preservice teachers teach to transform society as opposed to merely transmit information and perpetuate the status-quo.

The need for this study is supported by the contextual literature on the rich research efforts to construct teacher education and more specifically, social studies teacher education programs that confront the preexisting beliefs of students and beget educators who are oriented in teaching for reform (Barton & Levstik, 2004; Biesta, 2009, 2010; Fenstermacher & Richardson, 2010; McDonald, 2007; Osguthorpe & Sanger, 2013). This research accentuates the need for a crucial shift towards fostering in teachers a more critical viewpoint, so that they will believe their purposes for teaching are to work towards goals such as social justice, equity, democracy and citizenship. The research data included in this chapter were collected as part of a larger study, which explored preservice teacher perspectives of feminism, sexism, and gender identity development. This chapter was acutely focused on findings regarding preservice elementary teacher perspectives' of gender identity development and how it affected their work in their student teaching classrooms.

CRITICAL FEMINIST THEORY

A critical feminist theoretical framework was deployed as an orienting lens to examine and analyze the data. Although it is difficult to give a precise definition of the intricately complex and ever-changing idea of feminism, it is possible to assert that feminism "comprises various social theories which explain relations between the sexes in society, and the differences between women's and men's experience" (Ramazanoglu, 1989, p. 99). Ramazanoglu (1989) continues:

> Most feminist theories share certain beliefs and characteristics including: that much of what has been considered natural, normal, and desirable about gender relations has been challenged by feminism; that existing gendered relations which privilege men and subordinate women are unacceptable and need to be changed; that the point of feminism is to change the world; that feminism is provocative because it is deliberately politicized; that feminism always encounters resistances to its goals; that feminism does not start form an objective and detached viewpoint; and, that feminism questions why some knowledges are seen as more valid than others. (p. 103)

A key and important advance in critical feminist theory is the problematizing of gender and gender relations with the consequent understanding that gender cannot be dismissed or explained merely as an extension of nature or of natural differences (Ramazanoglu, 1989). Feminism "initiated the cultural work of exposing and articulating the gendered nature of history, culture, and society" and challenged "male-normative terms of discussion about reality and experience" (Bordo, 1990, p. 136).

The existing epistemological constructs of knowledge and power should continually be questioned. Critical feminist theory promotes the reevaluation of the current justified beliefs of knowledge and attempts to illuminate the undeniable nexus of power in our society. Feminist theory can inform educational research by catalyzing this reexamination and by creating spaces of empowerment for all people.

RESEARCH DESIGN AND METHODS

The research design for this study was an instrumental case study (Stake, 2000). The unit of analysis, or the case, was senior elementary education students enrolled in a teacher preparation program at a large public university in the southeast United States. The topic under examination (the phenomenon) was preservice elementary teacher perspectives of feminism and the experiences that have influenced their understandings regarding this topic.

The data sources consisted of two in-depth, semi-structured interviews, one focus group session, and participant journaling. These data sources were collected over a series of several months. Data was analyzed using a narrative analysis and categorical analysis. All of the data collected was additionally analyzed through a critical feminist lens as I am a feminist researcher and, "feminist research methods are methods used in research projects by people who identify themselves as feminist or as part of the women's movement" (Reinharz, 1992, p. 6).

CONTEXT AND PARTICIPANTS

To recruit participants for this study a recruitment email was sent to all seniors enrolled in the elementary teacher preparation program at the large university in the Southeast where I worked as a teaching assistant and instructor. Out of 52 students, four contacted me immediately to volunteer as participants. After my initial interview with each of the four participants, I asked if they could recommend at least one more individual for the study, and three of the four noted the same individual. I contacted this woman and she agreed to participate, thus completing a snowball sampling method.

All of the participants were White females, and all identified as coming from middle to upper class families and backgrounds. This research study took place during the spring semester as the women were completing their full-time student teaching experience in elementary schools. Four of the women were natives of the southern state in which this study took place. Sam[1] and Sarah were from small rural towns and noted their conservative Christian upbringing. Sue and Sophie were from small cities. Sue noted conservative undertones in her community. Sunny was raised in a large, urban city in the Northeast until middle school when her family moved to a suburban area outside of a large city in the south. She commented, "the transition of moving from north to south was huge."

Four women attended public schools for their primary and secondary education. One of these women, Sam, was home-schooled during middle school. The fifth woman, Sophie, attended parochial schools for elementary and middle school, completing her secondary education in a public school. Four of the women noted the lack of diversity in their primary and secondary experiences, while one woman, Sue, noted "some diversity" in her urban schooling prior to college.

All of the women stated their love of children, their enjoyment of working with children, and their perceived ability for working with children as reasons for choosing teaching as a profession. Sam noted that her choice to enter teaching was influenced by multiple family members in the profession and a calling from God.

This study focused on the ways that experiences contribute to the process through which preservice teachers form their beliefs, which ultimately inform their practice and possibly their purpose for teaching. Therefore, the following research questions were explored: (1) What are preservice elementary teacher perspectives' about gender identity development? (2) How did they come to these understandings? (3) What messages did preservice teachers receive in school about their own gender identity development? and (4) How did these understandings affect their teaching?

PERSPECTIVES ABOUT GENDER IDENTITY DEVELOPMENT

The participants' perspectives about gender identity development (GID) were complex and had multiple layers. The women appeared to shift their understandings of GID during college. Prior to college, the majority were unaware that gender (meaning the social constructions of men, women, transgender people, and other genders) and sex (meaning biological sex as determined by chromosomes) are not synonymous. During this study, many of the women were still working through their understandings of GID.

How They Came to These Understandings

All of the participants revealed that they had never participated in any explicit discussion regarding GID until college. They did discuss the implicit attitudes and behaviors that they were exposed to before college, additionally noting that they perceived children's experiences today as similar to their own concerning GID.

Parents and Families. Parents were noted by the participants as the most salient factor of a child's GID. All of the women agreed with Sue that GID of children begins "on the day they are born" or even prior, when the sex of a baby is announced. They noted that many parents select the room color, clothing, and toys according to the sex of the child, as well as the activities when they get a little older. Sarah explained, "I think adults treat babies differently in the toys they give them, in the way they hold them and coddle them or [if] they let them cry." Sunny added, "I don't think it's intentional. Even if it is or not, but it's everybody that's around. You can't escape it." All of the women noted items such as "dresses, ribbons, and dolls" and traits such as "non-athletic and submissive" as gender stereotypes with which they had personal experiences, but also which they observed in their student teaching placements as well.

Sam specifically noted, "We were on the playground one day during recess and a boy said to me, 'you can't play soccer, you're a girl,'" which Sam, a collegiate soccer player, had "heard her whole life." She connected the messages that she had received from parents and family members regarding GID as she was growing up to what her students were currently receiving from their parents and family members with regards to appropriate gender norms.

"Act Like a Girl." All participants in this study were told to "act like a girl" at various points throughout their lives. Sophie remarked that "from a very young age, even if it's not explicitly told, you need to 'act like a girl', [girls are told] you need to do this" because you are a girl. Parents, peers, and teachers typically made this statement in a disapproving manner. All participants were called a tomboy many times during development, most remembering this as being one of the first times they received feedback for behaving "atypically" for a girl. All recalled being called a tomboy in context of them participating in a sport or outside activities.

When the participants were asked if they had ever been told to "act like a girl," their responses were illuminating. Sam responded:

> When I was little, I was a daddy's girl and I wanted to be with him all the time … I would love to go hunting with him and I remember one day we stopped all of the sudden … My sister is the typical stereotypical white girl: … She was on the homecoming court as a freshman in high school. My mom said, "See why couldn't you be a girl and make homecoming court and do all this stuff? I thought when I made your dad stop taking you out to do things that would change things."

Sarah said, "When I was young, I wanted to wear basketball clothes and they didn't have any for girls. My peers and the teachers were always like, 'Why are you dressing like that? That's not how you're *supposed* to dress.'" She continued, "There is a stereotype around 'act like a girl': fix your hair every day, wear make-up every day, you can't get a job that's hands on. You have to get a job where you sit and look pretty. But, I don't feel that way." When Sue was posed the question, she responded, "I definitely was a tomboy in elementary based on the amount of sports I did, and I hung out with all guys. I was definitely told to be a girl, go to cotillion." Sue explained that cotillion is "like manners school. It has dancing, table setting, manners, how to be at a formal dinner. Very debutantish, very southern too." Sophie commented that "act like a girl" means to be "calmer, more polite, prim and proper." She also recalled her mother telling her to "not act like a boy" and her Girl Scout leaders told the girls to "act like a lady" if they were ever "acting out" because ladies should be "prim and proper." Sam concluded, "My parents have always encouraged me to be more girly." All of the women noted parents, community members, peers and teachers as forming children's GID.

School Messages

Teachers. All of the women agreed that schools and teachers played a major role in their GID. Sunny explained, "They're viewed as a role model and they're who the kids are with almost the most. They play the majority of the role of either saying yes or saying no to it [GID], assigning those roles." Sam agreed, "Kids look up to teachers absolutely, and anything a teacher says is okay or not okay influences a child."

Sarah commented, "I know teachers that line up their kids by boys and girls. This is happening in my school right now and it's perpetuating a stereotype. If you're a boy, you have to do this, etc." She continued, "We should work as educators to revert that and make it okay to choose what you want to be." Sophie agreed with Sarah's perspectives on the roles of teachers regarding GID. She stated that teachers, "need to express acceptance, no matter what someone chooses to play with or wear" and "children should be deemed gender-neutral till older." When explaining the role she felt teachers should play in a child's GID she said, "Teachers need to encourage all students to do all things and focus more on them as a person."

Sue felt that teachers play less of a role in elementary school, as young students are "more with family" during this time. But, she noted:

> Teachers are key during middle and high school when people are really wrestling with their identity. When I was figuring out my own life in high school, I relied on teachers to be my rock. Even if I was having a hard time with my family, I feel like my teachers were the very next person in my community that I would rely on. They have a unique role. They see you every day, [and so are a] strong influence.

Sam perceived teachers as having "a large role" in GID, but stated that she didn't believe they were the only strong influence. She stated, "I think peers definitely have some influence, and [there is] a huge home influence."

Peers. Consistent with the research, peers were perceived to have a strong impact on GID. When speaking about her experiences and for children in general, Sarah claimed that gender identity was developed "a lot through their experiences in school because that's when they're really around a lot more boys and girls." Sophie's high school experience drastically changed her perspective regarding GID, as her best friend identified as a gay male. She expressed that this was a "huge transition" and it "opened her eyes" because she started learning about "how people saw you and tried to put you in a box."

HOW GID UNDERSTANDINGS INFLUENCED THEIR TEACHING

Throughout the semester, the women noted a spectrum of ways in which their teaching was influenced by their understandings of GID. On one end of the spectrum, Sophie stated that she was "more aware of gender role stereotyping," which granted her a greater ability to recognize issues when they arose in her classroom. She also stated that she "felt more confident" addressing instances of gender role stereotyping with confidence in her elementary classroom placement.

Sam's Economics Lesson

Sam, who was from a conservative, fundamentalist Christian background, implemented a lesson on the gender wage gap in the United States during her economics unit in a 4th grade classroom. For this lesson, Sam created index cards which each had specific demographics, including a particular job, gender, race/ethnicity, and various monthly living expenses. She randomly passed the index cards out in an effort to simulate specifically that our gender and race are not a decision that we make, they are who we are—or rather, who society has constructed us to be, as both gender and race are social constructs. This lesson sought to introduce this complex topic by illuminating how these two factors, gender and race, have major economic implications for people's lives. Some of the boys in class received cards stating that they were women, possibly of another race, and what their annual salary was for their respective job. Sam retrieved her statistical data from the American Association of University Women (AAUW) (2017) in order to have accurate information with regards to women's earning in comparison to White men (e.g., Latina (54%), African American (63%), White-Non-Hispanic (75%), Asian (85%)). Sam reported that this activity was very enlightening for her students.

Sam concluded the lesson with a suggestion that I offered to her when she was initially designing the lesson. She was concerned that this activity would encourage the White boys specifically in class to feel empowered to perpetuate the status quo of their obvious power in society, while simultaneously causing the girls to feel further oppression by this understanding. I suggested that they close the lesson by opening a discourse examining all of the ways in which women making less money affected each of them. The students, identifying as both male and female, came up with some profound responses, including their mothers making less money for their families, their sisters making less for the same work, and a few also commented on the impact their future female spouses would have on their future families.

Sunny's American Revolution Lesson

Sunny's understandings also heavily influenced her teaching. She demonstrated a strong feminist identity and a belief in the importance of incorporating concepts of GID by creating a 3-week social studies unit on Sybil Ludington, Paul Revere, and sexism. Sybil was an individual that Sunny was introduced to during the "Herstory" lesson in her *Social Studies and the Young Learner* methods course in the fall semester.

Sybil Ludington is typically referred to as "the female Paul Revere." However, inarguably it would be challenging to find any literature where Paul Revere is coined as "the male Sybil Ludington," and herein lies one of the myriad issues with this story. Including Sybil in the elementary social studies methods course granted preservice elementary teachers the opportunity to learn about women like Sybil Ludington and her midnight ride of a 40-mile circuit alerting the Connecticut militia of an impending British attack. Many Americans are more familiar with Paul Revere's midnight ride of 20 miles, which ended abruptly as he was apprehended outside of Lexington, MA. The examination of these two heroes and their bravery can be exceptionally meaningful, and with the comparison of Paul Revere's ride, a social studies objective is typically covered in most states. A comparison of Sybil Ludington's and Paul Revere's midnight rides is *not* an exercise to marginalize Revere's role in our history: it is an exercise to equally elucidate Sybil Ludington's contributions.

While in her 5th grade student teaching placement, Sunny reviewed the state-mandated social studies standards that she would be required to cover for their upcoming social studies unit. The standards included teaching the American Revolution and Paul Revere. Sunny immediately noticed that no women were even mentioned in the standards. Thus, in an attempt to mitigate this limitation, she decided to introduce the class to Sybil Ludington. "If I was unable to find one 'model' text to introduce a heroine, I dug deeper to find multiple resources to help compare information, and guide the students to establish a new perspective," she stated.

She began the unit with the historical fiction poem by Henry Wadsworth Longfellow, "Paul Revere's Ride." Her goal was to compare this poem to the children's book, "Sybil's Midnight Ride," by Karen B. Winnick (2000). Sunny created a graphic organizer that allowed students to compare the two very different texts and the two characters that accomplished a similar task. "Paul Revere's Ride" was purposefully presented first. The class discussed the historical fiction account of Revere's ride within this poem, and the students also examined a primary source document in the form of a letter that Paul Revere wrote detailing his experience to Jeremy Belknap, circa 1789.

Sunny noted that during the discussion of the graphic organizers the class found a variety of colorful language, multiple perspectives, and unanswered questions. For example, Paul Revere's characteristics were common: brave, clever, and helpful. However, during the class discussion of the characteristics that Sybil Ludington portrayed, the conversation "took on a life of its own." Words such as *witty, savvy, perseverance,* and *determined* were elaborated on with evidence from the text. One student quoted, "Intelligent, since she snapped off a branch from a tree to bang on the doors so she wouldn't have to get off her horse every time." *Witty* was used to describe Sybil as she hid from a loyalist in the text, and "wooed" like an owl to mislead him. One student interjected the characteristic, *foolish,* and confidently defended his claim. Sunny reported the students became wide-eyed and rushed to defend Sybil's competence.

She used this moment to guide a debate with a series of questions such as: Should we use foolish to describe Sybil? Did anyone use the word foolish to describe Paul Revere? Comparing Revere's and Sybil's similar actions, what makes it okay to call Sybil foolish? Students connected the word foolish as being linked to her age and sex. Sunny stated that during this discussion one student "took center stage and claimed that because of her age, sex, and accomplishments, that she should be known as a historic heroine." The student who initially stated the term *foolish* convincingly erased the word from the characteristics list on his graphic organizer and replaced it with *brave.*

During another unit activity, Sunny stated that the students unknowingly elaborated on gender roles, past and present. This discussion prompted a student to describe the reason that Sybil was relatively unknown was because of sexism. This claim floored Sunny, but it also excited her. She asked the class to help define sexism. Sunny said that the reason she asked her students to do this was because in her social studies methods course she learned that it was essential when using and/or introducing a term that may be misunderstood or stereotyped by students, such as sexism, that everyone in the class understood it and had the ability to use it appropriately. As a class they worked to define sexism, and one student defined it as oppression "based on being a boy or girl." Together they made it their mission to inform others about Sybil and her accomplishments.

This particular class had a specific interest in reading graphic novels, so they decided to share Sybil's story by creating comic books of her midnight ride. The students individually organized the events, dialogue, and captions that would be in each frame of the comic book before beginning their final copy. The students uniquely expressed their interpretation of Sybil's bravery and accomplishment through words and art. The students each drew in different styles, fashioned covers, and created colorful dialogue between multiple characters, making it a creative summative assessment.

Sunny revealed that her students thrived in this creative setting. Struggling readers excelled at writing the dialogue. Many students with an IEP or 504 plan needed additional scaffolding when ordering the events in the story to build a cohesive plot and excelled at writing captions and dialogue that displayed the event accurately. Students created a comic book of a hero in which they were proud. They were also incredibly eager to publish their work. By the end of the unit, the students had created a reliable interpretation of a heroic tale. In their own way, the students wanted to mitigate the lack of awareness and information available about Sybil's story by creating their own, which promoted equity of information and the recognition of a lesser-known American Revolutionary hero.

SUMMARY

The interpretation of the data analysis regarding the preservice elementary teacher perspectives of GID yielded several salient findings. Almost all of their early exposures to GID were experiences concerning their appearance and behaviors, experiences during which they were taught to follow gender-normative behaviors and expressions. Participants stated that parents and families, teachers, and peers had great influence on the development of their own gender identity. The women perceived parents and families to be the most influential in the early years of development prior to elementary school.

LIMITATIONS

All of the women perceived teachers as having a *huge* role in GID of children as they make critical decisions including creating their classroom environment, selecting curricula, leading classroom conversations, and modeling (or not modeling) respect and tolerance for all children and their families. All participants also noted their belief in wanting to create an accepting environment for all children in their classrooms and setting a tone that allows children to express themselves freely with regards to gender. A few noted some discomfort with teaching GID in their elementary classrooms, but understood that it was the right thing to do as a teacher and leader. The discomfort with GID that one teacher expressed was due to her feelings of lacking pedagogical strategies to implement in her classroom. Others noted that because of the region in which they planned to teach, they were concerned about parental, co-worker, and community backlash. They were apprehensive that members of one or all of these groups might accuse them of having a "liberal agenda" or of "being a lesbian" and almost all were concerned that this could affect their future employment.

IMPLICATIONS: EXPAND ACCESS BY IMPLEMENTING FEMINIST THEORIZING IN SOCIAL STUDIES

Feminists have, since the early 1970s, criticized a variety of academic disciplines for being gender-blind (Kelly, 1988). The term "feminist methodology" first appeared in sociology, but I argue that salient points are applicable across disciplinary boundaries regarding these methods. One criticism of sociology is that it ignores feminist research in other areas. Educational researchers like Margaret Crocco (2005, 2008) and Nel Noddings (2001a, 2001b), among others, have called for feminist theorizing and research in the area of social studies.

Feminist theorizing and methodologies specifically interrogate socially constructed categories used to propagate privilege and power of certain individuals and groups. This is essential for all social justice work. As Crocco (2008) contested:

> The ultimate goal of feminist theorizing is to provoke change in the way of thinking about women, men and the human conditions, and thereby, to stimulate social change. Adopting new theoretical frameworks and discourses will provide social studies with a powerful and provocative set of tools to help reconsider the meanings of gender and sexuality for citizenship education. (p. 187)

Education and the education system of our democratic society should not model an intricately-designed machine functioning to maintain or perpetuate divisions in our nation. The literature suggests that feminist research fits hand in glove with the fundamental purposes of public education and even more acutely with social studies education. However, as this study indicates, preservice elementary teachers may have limited access to feminist theory and methods in their teacher preparation programs. Additionally suggested by the findings is the profound importance of critical exposures to feminism.

This research accentuates the need to deconstruct the current paradigm of simply training teachers to teach. It emphasizes the need for a crucial shift, which guides teachers towards a more critical viewpoint, believing their purposes for teaching to be more focused on goals of social justice, equity, democracy and citizenship. Social studies courses would be an excellent forum for such critical explorations.

NOTE

1. All names are pseudonyms.

REFERENCES

American Association of University Women. (2017). *The simple truth about the gender pay gap (Spring 2017)*. Retrieved from http://www.aauw.org/research/the-simple-truth-about-the-gender-pay-gap/

Barton, K. C., & Levstik, L. S. (2004). *Teaching history for the common good*. Mahwah, NJ: Lawrence Erlbaum.

Becker, J. C., & Swim, J. K. (2011). Seeing the unseen: Attention to daily encounters with sexism as a way to reduce sexist beliefs. *Psychology of Women Quarterly, 35*(2), 227–242.

Becker, J. C., Zawadzki, M. J., & Shields, S. A. (2014). Confronting and reducing sexism: Creating interventions that work. *Journal of Social Issues, 70*(4), 603–791.

Biesta, G. (2009). Good education in an age of measurement: On the need to reconnect with the question of purpose in education. *Educational Assessment, Evaluation and Accountability, 21*(1), 33–46.

Biesta, G. (2010). *Good education in an age of measurement: Ethics, politics, democracy*. Boulder, CO: Paradigm.

Bordo, S. (1990). Feminism, postmodernism, and gender-skepticism. In L. J. Nicholson (Ed.), *Feminism/postmodernism* (pp. 133–156). New York, NY: Routledge.

Crocco, M. S. (2005). Teaching Shabanu: The challenges of using world literature in the U.S. social studies classroom. *Journal of Curriculum Studies, 37*(5), 561–582.

Crocco, M. S. (2008). Gender and sexuality in the social studies. In L. S. Levstik & C. A. Tyson (Eds.), *Handbook of research in social studies education* (pp. 172–196). New York, NY: Routledge.

Cundiff, J. L., Zawadzki, M. J., Danube, C. L., & Shields, S. A. (2014). Using experiential learning to increase the recognition of everyday sexism as harmful: The WAGES intervention. *Journal of Social Issues, 70*(4), 703–721.

Fenstermacher, G. D., & Richardson, V. (2010). What's wrong with accountability. *Teachers College Record, (26)*, 26–28.

Kelly, L. (1988). *Surviving sexual violence: A guide to recovery and empowerment*. Cambridge: Polity Press.

McDonald, M. (2007). The joint enterprise of social justice teacher education. *Teachers College Record, 109*(8), 2047–2081.

Noddings, N. (2001a). Social studies and feminism. In W. E. Ross (Ed.), *The social studies curriculum: Purposes, problems, and possibilities* (Rev. ed., pp. 163–175). Albany, NY: State University of New York Press.

Noddings, N. (2001b). The care tradition: Beyond "Add Women and Stir." *Theory into Practice, 40*(1), 29–34.

Osguthorpe, R., & Sanger, M. (2013). The moral nature of teacher candidate beliefs about the purposes of schooling and their reasons for choosing teaching as a career. *Peabody Journal of Education, 88*(2), 180–197.

Ramazanoglu, C. (1989). *Feminism and the contradictions of oppression.* London: Routledge.

Reinharz, S. (1992). The principles of feminist research: A matter of debate. In C. Kramarae & D. Spender (Eds.), *The knowledge explosion: Generations of feminist scholarship* (pp. 423–437). New York, NY: Teachers College.

Saylor, E. E. (2017). Feminist theory in elementary social studies education: Making women an equal part of history. In S. Shear, C. M. Tschida, E. Bellows, L. B. Buchanan, & E. E. Saylor (Eds.), *(Re)imagining social studies education: Making controversial issues relevant and possible in the elementary classroom.* Charlotte, NC: Information Age Publishing.

Stake, R. E. (2000). Case studies. In N. K. Denzin & Y. S. Lincoln (Eds.), *Handbook of qualitative research* (2nd ed., pp. 435–454). Thousand Oaks, CA: Sage Publications.

Thornton, S. J. (1989, March). *Aspiration and practice: Teacher as curricular-instructional gatekeepers in social studies.* Paper presented at the annual meeting of the American Educational Research Association, San Francisco, CA.

Thornton, S. J. (1991). Teacher as curricular-instructional gatekeeper in social studies. In J. P. Shaver (Ed.), *Handbook of research on social studies teaching and learning* (pp. 237–248). New York, NY: Macmillan.

Winnick, K. (2000). *Sybil's night ride.* Honesdale, PA: Boyds Mills Press.

Zawadzki, M. J., Danube, C. L., & Shields, S. A. (2012). How to talk about gender inequity in the workplace: Using WAGES as an experiential learning tool to reduce reactance and promote self-efficacy. *Sex Roles, 67*(11), 605–616.

CHAPTER SEVEN

One Social Justice Music Educator

Working Within and Beyond Disciplinary Expectations
Kindergarten–5th Grade

ALISON LAGARRY

Music education is a field that is often seen as open and inclusive. If you ask music educators about this openness, many will tell you that there is a place for everyone in the music classroom; students who do not seem to fit in other school spaces find belonging there. Further, they will state that multicultural repertoire selections allow for engagement with diverse cultures and languages, adding to the narrative that music education inherently addresses concerns of cultural responsiveness. This supposition, that music education is already doing enough, may serve to prevent music educators from engaging in the critical questioning that is vital to social justice education (SJE) (Jorgensen, 2002). Music, as a discipline, has explicit expectations for which actions, attitudes, and experiences are viable for members of the discipline (Gustafson, 2009). The same can be said for the field of education. Many of these expectations, by nature, are exclusionary and highlight what Popkewitz (2009) described as "double gestures"—whereby delineating a *good* and *acceptable* member of a discipline automatically evokes the *unacceptable* member. For example, in music classes, much time is spent asking students to maintain a specific type of unmoving posture that corresponds with White European musical practice. Students whose musical traditions involve physical movement or improvised response may be penalized for engaging in practices outside of this sanctioned type of bodily performance.

When considering music educators' pathways to SJE, it is important to note that music educators are often those who *did* find a sense of belonging within the music classroom that seemed elusive elsewhere in the school. Thus, their hope for and confidence in the field as a *saving* space becomes problematic when they realize that not everyone experiences school music in the same way. In this chapter, I discuss how disciplinary expectations from both music and education shape and limit one music educator's conceptions of her personal identity and her role in the classroom. Using a narrative case study of this music educator as an illustration, I consider how teachers must examine their own experiences, assumptions, and disciplinary training on a daily basis in order to take on SJE as an on-going practice. The study focuses on one public elementary music educator, Amy,[1] who describes how her personal experiences helped her to understand SJE as an on-going imperative for practice. I use narrative data from Amy's interviews to highlight how she works to push beyond the disciplinary boundaries of music education. She noted that she must engage in identity reflection to reconcile her prior uncritical engagement with a new and evolving consciousness. Overall, this chapter highlights what *personal* work must teachers do in order to pursue social justice aims within and beyond their given discipline.

CONSIDERING TEACHER IDENTITY AS NECESSARY FOR SOCIAL JUSTICE MUSIC EDUCATION

Much of the prior research regarding cultural responsiveness in music education has centered on the merits and practical elements of teaching multicultural perspectives of music, as well as the socialization of pre-service music teachers into the professional field. Only recently has there been a call to shift the way the field conceives of multiculturalism and culturally relevant or culturally sensitive pedagogy (Abril, 2013; Allsup & Shieh, 2012; Gustafson, 2009; Jorgensen, 2002, 2003). In November 2014, the Task Force for Undergraduate Music Majors (TFUMM) put forth a report entitled, "Transforming Music Study from its Foundations: A Manifesto for Progressive Change in the Undergraduate Preparation of Music Majors". The task force put forth the question, "What contributions can music study make to broader educational and societal issues, including cultural diversity, multidisciplinary and transdisciplinary understanding, ecological and cultural sustainability, and social justice?" (Task Force on the Undergraduate Music Major, 2014, p. 10). The TFUMM proposed that undergraduate music curricula should, necessarily, put greater emphasis on creativity, diversity, and integration within the music curriculum. The recommendations of TFUMM are reasonable, yet they are notably focused on curriculum and not on the individuals who make up the field—neither students nor instructors.

Historically, the field of music education has constructed "professional" music educator identity as fractured from historical, political, and moral commitments, pushing these off as components of "personal" identity (Woodford, 2005). Several scholars have insisted that personal identity is vital to music educators (Bernard, 2005; Campbell, Thompson, & Barrett, 2010; Dolloff, 1999, 2007). However, the prevailing disciplinary research centers professional music identity as separate, and bound to explicit socialization processes (Isbell, 2008). In divorcing the profession of music education from political and moral obligation, there is a clear and problematic opposition to the aims of SJE. A primary assumption of SJE is the implication of the educator in the very same hierarchical structure they wish to critique. Thus, the personal identity of the educator is always implicated in professional identity. Any effort to maintain personal identity as outside the realm of teaching, then, is an effort to preserve the myth of schooling and teaching as neutral and non-political (Hinchey, 2004).

Despite the disciplinary trends present in the literature and in the practice of training music educators, there are practitioners in the field who seek to challenge this strategic fracturing of identity in the music classroom, and construct the field as inseparable from moral, political, and ethical responsibility. These educators often find themselves stuck in the middle of personal identity debates, wanting to serve the discipline meaningfully, but also understanding that the discipline does not exist outside critique. Like Amy, these teachers must actively and constantly seek to reconcile their personal experiences, training, and day-to-day practice with increasing social consciousness. Effectively, social justice music educators seek to work *within and beyond* the boundaries of music education, centering critique and equity at the heart of musical practice.

METHODOLOGY

Data Collection

Data for this study comes from a larger study of eight music teachers who self-identified as maintaining moral, ethical, and political commitments to equity within their classrooms. Music education was defined broadly, in order to attract participants from non-traditional settings such as churches, folk music centers, and non-profit music education programs. From this sample, Amy held one of the most traditional positions as a general music teacher in a public K–5 elementary school. The study was approached through the methodological lens of narrative inquiry (Chase, 2011; Maynes, Pierce, & Laslett, 2008; Riessman, 2008). This lens was chosen because of the centrality of identity construction within personal narratives, evoked here as a way to examine each participant's reflective development as a social justice educator. Each participant completed a series of three successive narrative interviews (Seidman, 1998). In the first interview, participants were asked to share their musical life story, including any experiences with music both in and outside of formal schooling. In the second interview, participants reconstructed a typical day in their current practice, including topics such as personal tasks, interactions, and challenges. Prior to the third interview, each participant was sent a transcript of their first two interviews to review. This transcript was used as a reflective artifact to spur conversation in the third interview. Participants were given leeway to question, rebut, and extend their offerings from interviews one and two. This also served as a member check, allowing participants to clarify or highlight what they believed to be the most salient points.

Data Analysis

All interviews were audio-recorded and transcribed in full. Data were analyzed using a dual level approach, using two of the four potential pathways for narrative analysis offered by Riessman (2008). First, all individual interviews were coded using the *dialogic/performance analysis* pathway, where the researcher takes special care to maintain context and temporality of the narrative. Rather than the miniscule codes of grounded theory (Charmaz, 2014), chunks of data are coded in order to prioritize the story—a type of performance—as told by the participant. This resulted in codes that were individual to each participant and did not translate across cases; a second round of coding was necessary to break the narrative data down into codes that worked across cases. In the second round of coding, interviews were coded using the *thematic/structural analysis* pathway (Riessman, 2008), an approach that is more similar to grounded theory, but still aims not to fracture data into its smallest component parts. Both levels of coding are included in this chapter because each pathway of analysis informed my interpretation of individual cases, including Amy's.

Researcher Positionality

As a former music educator, my own identity and positionality are implicated in the analysis of this data. I identify as a White, straight, cisgender woman from a rural area of the Northeastern United States. I entered the field of traditional music education with non-critical visions of helping students to find spaces of belonging in schools. Much like Amy, this was largely based on my own feelings of acceptance and success in the chorus room at my own high school. Over six years, I taught choral and general music at elementary, middle, and high schools. Through these experiences, I developed questions about equity and how it related to my own training within the discipline of music education. These questions led to further study of critical pedagogy and social justice education that have informed my practice ever since. My interpretations of Amy's narrative are inextricably tied to my own experiences.

NAVIGATING WITHIN AND BEYOND THE BOUNDARIES OF MUSIC EDUCATION

Context

Amy Harris is an elementary music educator at Lakeview Elementary School in an urban/suburban school district in the Southeast. She identifies as a Caucasian female,[2] and was in her early thirties at the time of the study. She taught general music to students in grades K–5. A colleague recommended Amy to me as a potential participant, and when I first had the chance to speak with her, she hesitated to claim herself as a social justice educator. She told me that she tried to maintain her commitments toward equity in the classroom, but did not feel like she was always successful. She also noted that at that her school, which boasted a population of 900 elementary students, intense scheduling constraints often prevented her from engaging in much social justice work. Despite these challenges, Amy told me that she was always reflecting on her relationship with her students, and how power might play a role. Based on this awareness of the presence of power in her relationship with students, we both eventually decided that she would be a good fit for the study.

In our first interview, we talked about Amy's history with music and ended up spending a significant amount of time speaking about her prior experience teaching in another state. Amy proselytized the wonders and benefits of her first teaching experience, highlighting the opportunity for significant professional development and interaction with like-minded music colleagues. Having attended the music conference in this state, I understand that music education there is highly structured, with a strong emphasis on vertical curriculum, abundant resources, and more efficient processes for curricular implementation. I also know, however, that the rigid structure of the music curriculum leaves little room for teacher or student agency. In our second interview, Amy compared the music education climate in her prior job to her current everyday practice in the Southeast. She stated that she wished she could do more in her present job: that she could see her students more often, and that there were more opportunities for her professional growth. In our third interview, several months later, Amy stated that she had reflected deeply on our earlier conversations. She had begun a new school year, and her schedule was just as hectic. Despite the challenges, she described dreaming of a music education utopia where students are engaged, and where she has the time to teach all of the musical skills and experiences that she believes are vital. We shared a number of our music teaching experiences during this interview, and at one point Amy interjected, recalling a moment in class during the past week when everything seemed to work perfectly. She described her feeling of "letting go" in that moment, and we ended the interview considering what letting go might mean for her practice moving forward.

The Desire To Do Well by the Discipline

Amy described feeling pressure to be hailed to as a "good" and high-quality music education practitioner. Throughout the interviews she explained her extensive training and professional development and how she used that training to plan meaningful curricular activities. She made clear that there are both written and unwritten disciplinary expectations guiding her thoughts on what she should be able to teach and how she teaches it. In our first conversation, she leaned heavily on the idea that the *what* (content) and *how* (pedagogy) of music education precede concerns of *who* is teaching and *whom* is taught. Her position at the time of the interview presented a number of logistical challenges that limited her ability to live up to her ingrained conceptions of what music educators should do, based on her school setting.

> [T]he school has just ballooned in size and gets bigger every year. It's been a real challenge being the only music teacher, and there's only one art teacher. So the arts here, I feel like, [are really undervalued]. I mean, it's a beautiful classroom; it's a beautiful school. But, it is really challenging for me to do my job as effectively as I want to and as I've been trained to do—with all of the things I experienced in my job in another state, and I saw the kids twice a week in there! I see the kids [here] once every eight days for 45 to 50 minutes, and that roughly equals about 20–22 classes a year. It's really hard to fit in half of what I need to. It's hard to maintain continuity. This summer my goal was to really knock out a curriculum that fits this situation and it's been super challenging, because I'm like, "I really want to do this activity, but I can't! I don't have time!" I need to teach this in second grade, but in order to do that, there's a process we have to follow. So when you're talking about trying to fit in the necessary concepts for music literacy, it knocks out some of the more whimsical activities that I would love to do that kind of just promote more of a love of music. It's really hard to balance those.

For Amy, the size of the school and inequitable distribution of resources limited the number of times she can see each student, and thus limited the amount of content she could teach each year. It was clear that she was not living up to her own perceptions of personal professional adequacy as a music educator, especially since she initially expressed that content was her primary teaching concern. This began to shift as she became increasingly conscious of the inequitable social systems that are at work both within and outside of her school.

Seeing Systems Within Music Education

A major shift in Amy's thinking came through her spiritual journey. As a child and young adult, she attended an Evangelical Christian church, but eventually transitioned to an emergent Christian church that focused on social justice, advocacy, and activism. She discussed how this new social justice lens helped her to see her earlier experiences in a new light, and how this started to expand her consciousness of the inequities around her:

> I would say I started to think about issues of equity moving here … and it kind of goes along with where my husband and I have landed spiritually. There was not a lot of emphasis growing up on social justice. In fact, we shied away from that. All the emphasis was on getting people saved. It wasn't about practical ways to promote social justice or equity. In fact, I went to school in a school district that had busing and I was part of, obviously, the White kids in the hometown, and we had African American kids getting bused in. [My thinking on that has shifted][3], and I think focusing my beliefs and just even growing up and just realizing that I was in a sheltered world growing up. Having moved several times in the United States, you see a lot and you realize what the real world is. I started paying attention more to society. This is what we talk about all the time at [our new] church; it's the least among us. Everything that you thought—but flipped.

This "flipped" way of thinking—that those with the least power and privilege should be elevated—pushed Amy to see that societal issues do not go away when you enter the music classroom. She elaborated on the ways that she began to recognize systems of power in her classroom, and how she attempted to work to balance these inequities. She also recognized her young self in the actions of one of her more privileged students, highlighting the extra attention that White students often get in classrooms.

> It is in the little moments when you have an opportunity as a teacher to elevate a child. If there's an opportunity for me to make a kid feel like he's smart or she's smart, or she's got abilities; you have to take advantage. I feel like you have to err on the side of choosing some kids more often a little bit, because it's gonna work out O.K. for that little White girl. You know what I'm saying, like in the grand scheme of things, she's in a position of power already. And yes, of course I'm here for that child too. It's not that there aren't things that she needs and ways in which I can be of service to her. [The thing is, the girl raising her hand], *it's me!* And I don't feel so bad, because I know she's gonna be O.K., because I remember that. How do you get that across to five year olds? I don't know! I think you just get it across in like, you see the teacher not calling on the same five White kids every time, and you see that this teacher, Mrs. Harris, she's really pretty good about picking everybody. When I walk in here, I don't know that I'm going to be the most special kid anymore. When I was student teaching, I got called out for calling on some of the same students all the time, and I did not even notice! But it takes practice. Getting to know your curriculum really well, and then your mind doesn't have to stay focused as much on "What am I gonna teach?"—methodology or process. Then you can be a little more open to what's really going

on in here socially. It's all these levels, you know? I'm trying to be more conscious of that, and it was not in my consciousness even [before this job], because it was never—I wasn't raised to be conscious of that.

Here, Amy also acknowledged that she was attempting to move beyond the *what* of music teaching and more toward a focus on who is present in the classroom. She noted that this was still a negotiation, however, and she struggled to push past her ideas of what a good music teacher *should* do, especially since this new consciousness was decidedly outside of the discipline. Despite this continued dissonance, Amy described how her newfound consciousness and reflection pushed her to be vigilant about critical reflection:

I'm always thinking about, was I fair? Or my mind is always going back sometimes maybe too much in the past and just re-evaluating. Did I take the right approach with that student? How could I have reached them more? Or saying, "Yeah! I did a good job with that and I should do more of this." So I'm always evaluating and always trying to do the next thing better.

This self-reflection positions Amy as a critical actor in the hegemonic power systems of society, schooling, and more specifically, music education. The more she recognized her role in these systems, the more she found herself willing to challenge the boundaries of traditional music education.

Letting Go to Engage—From *How* to *Who*

My final interview with Amy occurred three months after the first. She had the opportunity to read through the transcript of our first interview and had the following response.

I was just thinking in the transcript—I really am dreaming of this utopian music ed experience. You can see how badly I want that in my descriptions of things and where my concerns lie, and what my hopes and dreams are. I was just thinking that there definitely is that shift from my teaching experience in [another state] to my teaching experience here, and how that [previous] experience really focused on *how* to teach music—and I feel like my experience here has been everything but that. In a lot of ways, it's been how do you relate to your community? How do you deal with children? How do you diversify your curriculum, or just the way that you teach and act around kids, and handle situations? So I feel like, and I think that goes along with my experience with my packed schedule, and this school being so large, and not seeing the kids enough—I can't teach what I'm supposed to in the music ed world terms. I can't do it. So I feel like I'm having to pay more attention to relationships with the kids, and between kids. I do pay more attention, I think, to equity and to fairness and to all of those things that *would be* extra to teaching music—but really are kind of at the center. I think more than anything, I'm having to deal with those things first and foremost. It can't be that perfect music ed world utopian, perfect little Orff[1] class or Kodály class.

Amy's reflection on the transcripts and her emerging critical consciousness seemed to take further shape. In this quote she no longer held up her prior job as the epitome of proper music education practice. Rather, she realized the professional learning in her current position was not just an important addition, but the center of what *she* believed music education should be.

She further related her realization to her own spiritual formation and what it means to be moral:

> My spiritual formation has led me to believe that that's what I should do as a moral human being is to treat people the way I want to be treated, and even beyond that—because that's a little too individualistic—it's just much more of a big picture. It's not about me; it's about the greater whole. If I'm going to live my life, not looking out for my own back, but seeing how we as human beings create systems that work against other people, music can—in this microcosm of my classroom—it can help to break down those systems, and break down those barriers.

As we wrapped up our final interview, we were sharing our own classroom teaching stories, and she suddenly remembered a moment where she felt that she and her students were able to momentarily break down the barriers that she described. Teachers often attribute classroom success to whether or not students are cooperative. In Amy's case, she realized that she was the one who needed to be flexible and "let go" of her own disciplinary hang-ups to join in the classroom community of music-making:

> I think the best times in my classroom come from when the kids are just—they're making music. I had an experience yesterday, it was a very tough class, and I let go of that utopia thing that I was talking about and we had a play party. We did a song that was rhythmic and fun, and I had fun, the kids had fun. They were getting along, I started seeing this group of girls putting their arms around each other, and it was out of love. And it was girls who a few minutes earlier might have been making sneers at each other. This class has a lot of issues that way, relationship issues, but we were all on board. The class started off just horribly. And it ended up being one of the best classes that I've had in a long, long time. It's been tough this year. You know, I spent all this time creating this wonderful curriculum that I'm not able to teach. Yesterday was like, I was at the piano playing—and they were just doing—they were all on board. They were all participating. I don't know if that's because I let go, or if it was the make-up of the class, *but I think it was because I let go.*

Amy came to realize that her most critical work as a social justice music educator involved navigating both within and beyond the constraints of disciplinary boundaries. She acknowledged that this was difficult and often felt risky and frustrating, but the payoff for her students was well worth it. For her, the results were also meaningful and calmed her anxieties and self-judgement in ways that allowed her to feel successful as a music educator—though not in the ways she initially expected.

IMPLICATIONS AND CONCLUSIONS

Amy's narrative reflects an evolving self-awareness and consciousness that led her to consider how she must work both within and beyond the traditional limits of music education as a discipline. In considering these findings for educators in both music education and across disciplines, there are a number of meaningful implications. First, educators must be willing to do reflexive examination of their own autobiographies in order to re-contextualize and critique those things they hold as common sense (Boyd, LaGarry, & Cain, 2016). Further, they must recognize systems of societal inequity, and strive to situate themselves within these systems. Social justice educators in any field must also be willing to critique aspects of their disciplines that have been taken as given. They must develop the capacity to decide which disciplinary practices are worth preserving, and which are worth further questioning or abandoning altogether. This refers not just to content, but also pedagogy, disciplinary practices, and attitudes. For arts educators, this is particularly important in regards to aesthetic valuing (and de-valuing) of particular artistic works and cultural practices.

Navigating within and beyond a discipline can be frustrating, and even risky when accountability measures demand explicit modes of pedagogy and associated content. Like Amy, social justice educators must develop capacity for this navigation. Letting go, as Amy described, means taking the risk of being judged poorly as a member of the discipline. It also means allowing oneself to move past any personal anxiety at being perceived as someone who does not follow "rules" and traditions. In our third interview, Amy highlighted her growing conviction that relationships and people should be at the center of her practice—which further convinced her that challenging the boundaries of traditional music education was worth the risk. When asked what she hoped her kids would take away from her class, she stated,

> I hope that they look back and say, "You know, Mrs. Harris was for me." I hope that that's what they say. "There were people in my life in elementary school that were *for* me. She was one of them."

NOTES

1. All names are pseudonyms.
2. Identifications provided in Amy's own words.
3. Bracketed text is a technique of narrative inquiry where the author adds small bits of text to help the flow of participant narrative.
4. Orff and Kodály are two pedagogical approaches specific to music education. Each require multiple levels of specialized training, and are hailed as important traditional approaches to general music education.

REFERENCES

Abril, C. R. (2013). Toward a more culturally responsive general music classroom. *General Music Today, 27*(1), 6–11.

Allsup, R. E., & Shieh, E. (2012). Social justice and music education: The call for a public pedagogy. *Music Educators Journal, 98*(4), 47–52.

Bernard, R. (2005). Making music, making selves: A call for reframing music teacher education. *Action, Criticism, and Theory for Music Education, 4*(3), 2–36.

Boyd, A. S., LaGarry, A. E., & Cain, J. M. (2016). Moving from self to system: A framework for social justice centered on issues and action. *International Journal of Critical Pedagogy, 7*(2), 171–198.

Campbell, M. R., Thompson, L. K., & Barrett, J. R. (2010). *Constructing a personal orientation to music teaching.* New York, NY: Routledge.

Charmaz, K. (2014). *Constructing grounded theory* (2nd ed.). Thousand Oaks, CA: Sage.

Chase, S. E. (2011). Narrative inquiry: Still a field in the making. In N. K. Denzin & Y. S. Lincoln (Eds.), *The SAGE handbook of qualitative research* (pp. 421–434). Thousand Oaks, CA: Sage.

College Music Association, Task Force on the Undergraduate Music Major. (2014). *Transforming music study from its foundations: A manifesto for progressive change in the undergraduate preparation of music majors.* Retrieved from http://www.music.org/pdf/tfumm_report.pdf

Dolloff, L. A. (1999). Imagining ourselves as teachers: The development of teacher identity in music teacher education. *Music Education Research, 1*(2), 191–207.

Dolloff, L. A. (2007). "All the things we are": Balancing our multiple identities in music teaching. *Action, Criticism, and Theory for Music Education, 6*(2), 1–21.

Gustafson, R. I. (2009). *Race and curriculum: Music in childhood education.* New York, NY: Palgrave.

Hinchey, P. (2004). *Becoming a critical educator: Defining a classroom identity, designing a critical pedagogy.* New York, NY: Peter Lang.

Isbell, D. S. (2008). Musicians and teachers, the socialization and occupational identity of preservice music teachers. *Journal of Research in Music Education, 56*(2), 162–178.

Jorgensen, E. R. (2002). The aims of music education: A preliminary excursion. *Journal of Aesthetic Education, 36*(1), 31–49.

Jorgensen, E. R. (2003). *Transforming music education.* Bloomington, IN: Indiana University Press.

Maynes, M. J., Pierce, J. L., & Laslett, B. (2008). *Telling stories: The use of personal narratives in the social sciences and history.* Ithaca, NY: Cornell University Press.

Popkewitz, T. S. (2009). Curriculum study, curriculum history, and curriculum theory: The reason of reason. *Journal of Curriculum Studies, 41*(3), 301–319.

Riessman, C. K. (2008). *Narrative methods for the human sciences.* Thousand Oaks, CA: Sage.

Seidman, I. (1998). *Interviewing as qualitative research: A guide for researchers in education and the social sciences.* New York, NY: Teachers College Press.

Woodford, P. G. (2005). *Democracy and music education: Liberalism, ethics, and the politics of practice.* Bloomington, IN: Indiana University Press.

PART THREE

Middle Grades

Investigating Equity with Middle Grades Youth: Personalizing Justice for Students and Teachers

Middle grades, typically categorized in the United States as sixth through eighth, are those in which classroom curriculum tends to become more local and personal. Social studies in these grades, for example, generally includes the history of the state of students' residence, and in English Language Arts students often read novels that reflect their own positions as well as those of our diverse culture (Seglem & Bonner, 2016). Characterized as a unique time of life when students' identities are burgeoning, they are developing relationships with varied individuals (Previts & Bauer, 2017), and their cultural and social knowledge is forming, the need for social justice education in these grades is urgent. As students distinguish who they are in relation to our society, we want them to be critically conscious and able to discern their place in a democratic society. The teacher's role in middle grades education cannot be understated, as their respect and support can have drastic effects on student learning (Ryan & Patrick, 2001).

In this section, authors describe the ways they have studied social justice with middle grades students and explored approaches to teaching that accomplish equity-related goals within such spaces. Pennell and Fede's work in Chapter 8 aids students in naming and analyzing social justice topics; their chapter examines marriage equality in particular, through the avenues of mathematics and critical literacy. In a phenomenological study in Chapter 9, Cook and Martinez-Nichols explore how using story circles with middle grades students can build community and create more humanistic learning experiences. Greiner's Chapter 10 depicts a method for teaching World History through a focus on global human rights and scaffolds instruction for students to embark on social action for justice. Minshew, Horner, and Anderson consider how current technology initiatives in low-resource schools not only lend themselves to distinct challenges but also contain possibilities for equity in providing access and resources for students, particularly in math and science classes in Chapter 11. Morrison, Patterson, and Schindel propose ways in Chapter 12 to dispel commonly gendered aspects of science to illustrate how social justice education can play an important role in students' conceptions of STEM fields. Spanning a variety of critical topics, therefore, these chapter authors provide methods for approaching social justice at potentially pivotal moments in the lives of pre-adolescent youth.

REFERENCES

Previts, J. L., & Bauer, D. (2017). Forming relationships, creating curriculum. *Middle School Journal, 48*(1), 1–2.

Ryan, A. M., & Patrick, H. (2001). The classroom social environment and changes in adolescents' motivation and engagement during middle school. *American Educational Research Journal, 38*(2), 437–460.

Seglem, R., & Bonner, S. (2016). Disrupting complacency: Helping students find their voices through inquiry, literature, and technology. *Middle School Journal, 47*(5), 21–29.

CHAPTER EIGHT

Reading THE Math ON Marriage Equality

Social Justice Lessons in Middle School
5th–7th Grade

SUMMER MELODY PENNELL AND BRYAN FEDE

Summer: If anyone had asked me a few years ago what school subject was least likely to be a factor in my research, math would have been my top answer. I am a former high school English teacher and previously claimed to be afraid of math. Luckily for me, my research path took an unexpected turn out of my comfort zone. As graduate students, Bryan and I started talking about our shared interest in social justice and how his interests in critical math could combine with mine on queer pedagogy. What started as jokes about gay math problems led to a much larger project that changed the way I saw not only math but English Language Arts.

Bryan: "What is *gay math"?* This is a question I have been asked several times since I embarked on this project with Summer. I have to admit that I asked that question of myself five years ago as Summer and I mused about what a collaboration between the two of us might look like. As Summer began to gather and share literature on queer pedagogy, I began to realize that, far from a fringe theory, queer pedagogy provided a powerful lens for me to think about and enact the sorts of rich mathematical tasks and investigations that I want as the cornerstone of a mathematics program. It was also a perspective that allowed me to think about ways in which accessible mathematics might be used in building a critical awareness in students.

 Together, we co-created a middle school course called *Math for a Cause* in the fall of 2014, working closely with a classroom teacher, Morgan,[1] at a private

Quaker school in a southern state. We wanted students to read articles about social justice issues, create math problems from these issues, and share their findings with a larger audience. While the class did not go as neatly as planned (as is typical of classroom teaching), students did finish the course with expanded notions of math and an increased capacity for abstract thought.

In this chapter we will share examples from student work around marriage equality. In 2014, same-sex marriage was not yet federally legal, but individual states and circuit courts were granting these rights in some regions. Our students, whose school avidly supported LGBTQ (lesbian, gay, bisexual, transgender, and queer) communities, were talking about this issue amongst themselves and were eager to discuss it in the classroom. Furthermore, during our course same-sex marriage became legal in our state and was the cause of school-wide celebration. We harnessed this enthusiasm into our curriculum.

SOCIAL JUSTICE PEDAGOGY IN CONTEXT

For this study, we chose Rendón's (2009) definition of social justice pedagogy because we felt it best fit our context. She outlined a social justice education that entails:

> (1) having a 'critical consciousness' (from Freire); (2) taking action to transform entrenched institutional structures to ensure that people from all social group memberships have equal access to resources and opportunities; (3) acting with love and compassion to work with people who have less privilege and resources; (4) working to heal and to provide hope for all people, especially those who are victims of social and economic inequities; and (5) a socially engaged spirituality (Carrette & King, 2005) where individuals seek to improve their being and that of the larger collective. (Rendón, 2009, p. 10)

Because we were working with students and wanted to examine how they enacted social justice, this definition worked well as it lists both mindsets and specific forms of action. Further, the students were financially privileged (as they attended a private school), and many had other forms of privilege as well (such as racial privilege, as the majority were white). Helping students see that some people who are less privileged may face discrimination simply by being themselves was something we talked about as a teaching team. Finally, because of the Quaker background of the school, students were affected by ideas of Quaker spirituality. Though not all students were Quaker, the school was founded on these values, as reflected in this portion of their mission statement:

> [The Anchor School] is a vibrant and inclusive learning community empowering students to think critically, creatively, and independently. We foster active exploration and quiet reflection, individual endeavor and collaborative engagement. Inspired by Quaker

values—pursuit of truth, respect for all, peaceful resolution of conflict, simplicity, the call to service—we teach our children that it is possible to change the world. (The Anchor school website)

We also thought of social justice through a lens of queer pedagogy. Essentially, this means we were also interested in how our students and the curriculum could push us to consider norms and binaries that create social inequities. Unintentionally, queer pedagogy also caused us to question the norms surrounding our home disciplines (English for Summer, mathematics for Bryan).

RESEARCH METHODS

Summer was the primary researcher on the project, and she used post-critical ethnographic research methods (Noblit, Flores, & Murillo, 2004). Hytten (2004) emphasized that post-critical ethnographies in education have a fluid process, with constant "reflection and critique" (p. 102) between researchers and their collaborating teachers, so that "research subjects are not 'acted on' but instead are seen as knowledge producers whose voices are pivotal" (p. 102). Post-critical ethnography's focus on reflection and collaboration thus allowed the teaching team to continuously reflect and rework our approaches to the curriculum and instruction as the course progressed. However, Morgan saw the project as "ours" (Summer and Bryan) and so, while she participated in many reflective conversations after class in which we revised our methods and upcoming curriculum, she did not care to examine data (such as student work or transcripts of class discussions) with the researchers. Thus, the two researchers frequently met to discuss what we were noticing among student work and discussions.

All small and large group discussions were audio recorded and transcribed by Summer. These were the richest data sources as student conversations were more complex than what they translated to paper assignments. All data were coded by Summer with both open and deductive coding using MAXQDA, a qualitative software program.

THEORETICAL FRAMEWORKS

We used four theoretical frameworks (social justice pedagogy, queer pedagogy, critical mathematics, and critical literacy) because of their emphases on critical consciousness, dialogue, reflection, and social action. Social justice pedagogy was the underlying motivation for the curriculum. Queer pedagogy was the lens through which we viewed both social justice pedagogy and our curriculum: meaning, we questioned the norms of our own teaching, the school setting, and social justice issues. Critical literacy and critical math were the processes we asked students to use in their work. Though each of these pedagogies and frameworks may approach these tenets from different points of view or with different priorities, their underlying motivations and structures are similar. Each framework is also a mindset—a way of thinking about pedagogy rather than a set of prescribed techniques—which makes it possible to use them in combination. Despite the commonalities, queer pedagogy is unique. Instead of merely asking critical questions to encourage multiple perspectives in the classroom, *queering* pedagogy involves an attempt to disrupt the structures on which those perspectives stand. As such, it can be the most difficult to practice in real classrooms that have physical, intellectual, and emotional norms.

Queer pedagogy has a lot in common with the ideas of social justice educators. Both perspectives value dialogue (both student-student and student-teacher), questioning structures of oppression, encouraging social action (though not all queer pedagogy texts identify this as a goal), and including voices that are typically excluded (Kumashiro, 2001, 2009). Queer pedagogy also overlaps with tenets of critical literacy. The focus on print and other media in critical literacy is one major distinction between the two, as queer pedagogy is broader, and might examine rule systems as evidenced by behaviors, not only texts. Critical literacy asks students to read texts critically and discern underlying power structures, a goal shared by queer pedagogy (Britzman, 1995). Additionally, queer pedagogy fundamentally seeks to disrupt norms, binaries and hierarchies, particularly those that create and reify heteronormativity. Heteronormativity can certainly be considered under a critical literacy framework (e.g. Jacobi & Becker, 2013), but it is not a primary consideration.

There are some critical mathematics scholars calling for practices that relate to queer pedagogy, such as when teachers "periodically de-stabilize predictable conceptual boundaries between 'mathematical' and 'non-mathematical' activity [and thus] extended the domain of mathematics beyond that prescribed by textbooks and tests" (Hand, 2012, p. 241). Our study continued in a tradition of critical mathematics literacy, which Terry (2010) defined as combining critical literacies with mathematics. While Whitin and Whitin (2011) offered ideas for combining critical literacy and mathematics, their examples were often more focused on critical thinking—a fundamental aspect of critical mathematics—rather than creating social action, a fundamental aspect of social justice pedagogy. In this study, we attempted to add a queer lens to our critical literacy and mathematics in order to allow for a deeper questioning of social issues, which led to a questioning of mathematics and learning as well.

To intentionally create a queered math class, we worked to remove as many boundaries as possible. This included: (a) giving students guidelines but not strict instructions, (b) making the course student-centered and student-driven, rather than teacher-driven, (c) combining mathematics, literacy, technology, and current events in a single class to show students the fluidity of school disciplines, and (d) incorporating queer pedagogy tenets (shared by critical mathematics and critical literacy) of questioning, reflection, and dialogue. The difference between being student-centered in our class and others is that typically, even when an activity is student-centered, a teacher has an end-goal in mind. That goal may be a product students will create but is also usually a student learning goal. While we had vague learning goals of increasing students' capacity and understanding for social action, we had no idea what concrete learning goals the students would achieve from their explorations. This was scary and frustrating most of the time. However, when we began interviewing students a month into the course, we realized that they were beginning to change their mindsets about math itself. This was an outcome we could have never imagined, and we attribute it to the queer approach we took to the curriculum.

COURSE CONTEXT

As previously stated, the school where we conducted the course was a private Quaker institution. The middle school housed students in 5th–8th grade, and the twelve students in our course were in 5th–7th grade. Ten participated in the study: two fifth-grade boys; one sixth-grade boy; three sixth-grade girls; two seventh-grade boys; and two seventh-grade girls. Eight students were white, and two were mixed race (Asian and white). Our elective class was called *Math for a Cause*, and most of the enrolled students were interested in math, with a few more interested in the social justice aspect. Despite the title, it was an interdisciplinary course, and students analyzed a variety of difficult readings.

The class was student-centered and student-driven. Students worked primarily in small groups completing scaffolded activities, including:

1. *Read an article about their social justice topic.* The teaching team chose these initially, and later in the course the students chose from online news sources. Students answered questions designed to develop their critical literacies, such as "Who has the power in this article?" to help them analyze the information. One group found an article from a conservative religious organization about their reasons for opposing same-sex marriage and critiqued these arguments while discussing the article together.

2. *Identify relevant mathematics.* Using the article as a starting point, students identified statements of "fact" that might challenge the narrative as constructed in the piece. If in agreement with the article, student-groups attempted to identify supporting facts that might bolster the validity of the statement in the article. Whether challenging the narrative of the piece or

supporting the cause, students were asked to supply evidence that could be supported with mathematics. While students found that supporting their arguments with mathematics was difficult, their conversations often lead to "productive wonderings." For example, during the unit focused on same-sex marriage, one group wanted to find out how the percentage of Americans in favor of same-sex marriage had changed over time.

3. *Find the data necessary to solve the math problem.* This was the most difficult step, much more difficult than we anticipated. This was the first time the students had tried to both find and mine through dense numerical data. Often they would get distracted by data that was not relevant to the question they were interested in. For example, students who were looking at polling data on opinions about same-sex marriage started looking at opinions on same-sex couples adopting. While that may be related, it was not primary to their investigation. Because of the difficulties of both finding valid information and sorting through it, groups rarely completed their math problems. However, they were usually able to gain an idea of the scope of their question and how it related to broader social events.

QUEERED MATHEMATICS INSTRUCTION FOR SOCIAL JUSTICE

Because our course was student-driven, the mathematical lessons had to be planned in reaction to the directions students took in their mathematical inquiry into social justice issues. The fact that the mathematics slowly emerged from the interests of the student was an interesting pedagogical challenge as the teaching team had to be ready to deal with a variety of mathematical topics at any one time. Given that this was a mixed ability group, Morgan (the cooperating teacher) also had to deal with different levels of mathematical understanding. In other words, a teacher needed a broad understanding of mathematics in order to deal with the variety of mathematical situations that might be encountered, as well as have a deep (vertical) understanding of how students build mathematical understandings (i.e. trajectories) in order to ameliorate the differences in the mathematical abilities of the students in the class.

One of the common mathematical skills used in the class was calculating percentages. Morgan initially thought that the older students knew how to calculate percentages and that they could assist the younger students. However, when Summer listened to the audio recordings, it was clear that this was not happening. The students needed help in a few areas: (a) remembering (or learning) how to calculate percentages; (b) understanding how to read a complex text, rather than a single math problem, and determine what numbers were necessary to calculate a percentage; and (c) determining how to interpret the results from their calculations. Bryan and Morgan conducted lessons on percentages, including a worksheet Morgan created in which students calculated percentages related to race and the U.S. prison system. This activity allowed students to practice calculating percentages without having to do research themselves, and showed them how percentages tell a story and point towards the need for systemic change. This practice enabled students to be more successful when they worked to calculate percentages from complex texts when they worked in groups the next class period.

MARRIAGE EQUALITY MATHEMATICS FROM *MATH FOR A CAUSE*

Much of the work in our course was self-directed and open-ended: there was not one correct answer for every math problem, and students had to figure out the answers on their own with help from the teaching team when necessary. However, we began our final unit on marriage equality with all student groups completing the same task. As this was later in the term, we had learned that asking students to both sort through numerical data and solve math problems could be frustrating for them, so Summer created a worksheet so they could feel accomplished about their work before diving into more complex investigations on their own. The worksheet was about marriage equality in the local area, using numbers from an article in a local newspaper. This sheet had elements of ambiguity, as it asked students to estimate numbers of same-sex couples seeking marriage licenses based on a range of numbers (e.g., "The Register of Deeds said that normally the office processes between 12 and 15 marriage license applications per day. But on October 13th, the office processed around 50. Estimate how many of these applications were from same-sex couples"). For some students, this was difficult, as they were used to mathematics worksheets having only one possible answer per problem, rather than a range of possibilities. There was also self-guided exploration into potential wedding costs and room for student reflection. This self-reflection is important in social justice pedagogy, as students need time to think about what their findings mean, both for themselves and the broader community.

We also looked at polling data together (from www.pollingreport.com), to investigate how Americans' opinions on same-sex couples had changed. This required students to apply critical thinking and analytic reading skills to a dataset. Students worked together to answer the following questions:

1. In general, how have opinions about gay marriage changed over time? Give specific data to support your answer.
2. Compare the percentages of people who think gay couples should be allowed to adopt and should be protected against job discrimination with

the percentages of people who think gay couples should not be allowed to adopt and should not be protected against job discrimination. What do you notice?

3. Find data that asks people's opinions about same-sex marriage in general vs. data that asks about same-sex marriage in their state. Are there any noticeable differences? Why or why not?

4. Create your own math problem based on something else you can find in this data. Be sure to explain what you are looking for and then answer your question.

For the last question, one group was interested in finding the percentage of the population (for the year the poll was conducted) who were registered as Democrat, Republican, or Independent. They assumed that the Democrats, and possibly the Independents, would be more in favor of marriage equality and wanted to see if the numbers aligned.

From this introductory lesson, students found their own articles and data on marriage equality to create their own math problems:

1. What do you want your math problem to focus on? Give a specific example from your article. Just writing "marriage equality" is too big. Find something specific and related to social justice.

2. What information do you need for your math problem? Statistics, opinion polls, etc.?

3. What *social justice* question is your math problem going to answer? Example: Are areas populated mostly by white people given more funding for schools than areas populated by people of color?

It should be noted, however, that students often ignored our logically-ordered procedure and would immediately start looking through news articles or online data before fully forming a mathematical question or even a clear topic. Sometimes they could not find what they were looking for, nor could the teaching team, and initial ideas had to be abandoned. This exploration often guided their eventual question, and though we found it frustrating at the time, this freedom led to greater investment in their work and to greater gains in their abstract understandings of both mathematics and social justice.

As a teaching team, we had to let go of a carefully ordered classroom with procedural activities in response to this phenomenon, which was sometimes hard to accept. We had to rethink our perceptions of school and lessons. Often, student discussions were rich and full of debate, but very little of this animated engagement translated to the paper they turned in. Luckily we were recording their conversations so we did have evidence of student learning and engagement with the material. We suggest that classroom teachers sit in on more student conversations and make notes of student learning, or record short snippets (such as five minutes of conversation per group per week) to capture this data that evades traditional means of assessment. Recording student discussions can capture conversations that may be more animated in the absence of teachers, when students may be more open to expressing themselves.

For their final project on marriage equality, Ally, Rosette, and Ashley (sixth grade girls) continued looking at the polling data on same-sex marriage and calculated the average increase in support of same-sex marriage per poll over time (often this meant per year, but sometimes there were multiple polls in one year). While in prior math problems students had calculated averages that did not help them answer a question (likely because calculating an average was something they understood how to do), here, their averaging had a clear purpose. They were able to illustrate that, for each year since 2000, the average percentage of people in favor of marriage equality increased by 1.583% per poll. This difference in how they created and solved their math problem indicated growth in student understanding, both of what averages and percentages actually are, and how they can be used to illustrate a point. They made a video highlighting their data and encouraging people to vote for same-sex marriage legislation in their state.

Sum Dood (sixth grade boy), Justin Case, and Sue Denim (seventh grade boys) chose a different approach. They found data on suicide rates for LGBTQ people, and were interested in how these rates might correspond to marriage equality laws. At first they were comparing suicide rates and laws equally by year—for example, relating marriage laws in 2014 to suicide rates from 2014. However, they realized that the laws did not go into effect immediately and so instead compared suicide rates per state in 2014 to the legal status of same-sex marriage per state in 2013. They combined their findings and created a graph comparing the suicide rates for states that did not have marriage-equality for those that did, finding that states without marriage equality had a slightly higher rate (12.94 vs. 11.05). They also had a discussion about what these findings meant and how they should present their data:

Justin Case: Now write, "so now we have determined that the suicide rates of states that allow gay marriage is lower than the suicide rates of states that don't. So … if you wanted to lower the suicide rate you could make all states with gay marriage."

Sue Denim: So what's our conclusion? States that do have gay marriage have lower suicide rates?

Justin Case: Yes. To lower the suicide rate in the US you could just make it so-

Sue Denim: [talking while he types] "We do not know if the higher suicide rates are related to gay marriage."

Justin Case: Don't say that Sue Denim.

Sue Denim: But we don't-

Justin Case:	This [their website] is to say you should allow gay marriage because it will lower the suicide rate. That does not help with that.
Sum Dood:	Is that [correlation] really true?
Sue Denim:	Well, what if it's a scam?
Justin Case:	Well we still don't want to say that. We want to say, "to lower the suicide rate we should allow more states to have gay marriage."
Sue Denim:	Oh-kay.
Sum Dood:	One thing is, I still think this could be completely wrong.
Sue Denim:	Yeah.
Justin Case:	[Imagine] you have a serum that might kill somebody or it might save them. What do you do, would you give them the serum?
Sue Denim:	Yeah.
Sum Dood:	Well are they dying? If they're dying I would give it to them.
Sue Denim:	They're dying, yeah.
Justin Case:	They're not dying.
Sum Dood:	Oh. It might kill them or it might what?
Justin Case:	It might do nothing to them.
Sue Denim:	I would not give it to them.
Sum Dood:	Then, no.
Sue Denim:	That was an awful analogy.
Sum Dood:	If they were dying—that *was* an awful analogy. If they were dying sure I'd give it to them, because they might live. [All keep talking about the imaginary scenario.]
Justin Case:	Guys, I'm sorry I brought this way off track. But guys, we want it to say "Hey, let gay marriage be legal and it should lower the suicide rates."
Sum Dood:	No. We *think* it will lower the suicide rates. [Justin Case and Sum Dood keep arguing about how they should write about their findings on the website.]

This conversation allowed the boys to reflect on their feelings about how information is displayed and what language is necessary to get a point across. Ultimately, Justin Case won the argument and they decided to take out any uncertainty in their corollary statement. What their larger conversation illustrates is the boys reflecting together on their feelings about not only their answers, but how they presented their information. Sum Dood and Sue Denim felt uncertain about making such a bold statement, and felt that it was dishonest, especially when Sue Denim uses words like "scam." Justin Case also knew that it was not completely honest but he felt that was less important than making a strong message. As he tried to articulate in his fumbled analogy about the serum, if a message may save lives then he felt it is more important to make a strong statement even if it might not be true. According to Justin Case, convincing all the states to vote for gay marriage was the "serum" needed to prevent LGBTQ suicides.

STUDENT OUTCOMES

As we hope is evident, investigating social justice issues with mathematics allowed students to think about what mathematics is and does. While they perhaps did not gain many new concrete math skills outside of calculating averages and percentages, they learned a lot about how to read mathematical data and apply this data to questions about social issues. They learned that there are more ways than one to solve a math problem, and that not everything has one right answer. This was a breakthrough, as many students (including Ally and Sum Dood from the previous examples) told us in the beginning of the course that they liked math because it has rules. In *Math for a Cause* students learned to embrace ambiguity, to see mathematics as a process rather than a finite product, and were developing a critical consciousness that is necessary for social justice work. We also feel that learning that there is not always one solution to a problem will help students in social justice work, as these issues are nuanced and rooted in historical systems of oppression, meaning advocates must approach problems from multiple angles.

IMPLICATIONS FOR TEACHERS

We want to encourage teachers to embrace uncertainty and messiness that can, and likely must, accompany social justice teaching. While it was difficult for us to step back and let our students take control, we learned that the seeming chaos was productive. We encourage teachers to talk directly to students when they feel this way. Ask students what they are learning about the topic, what is important to them, and how they feel about topics. Through this shared reflection, teachers may learn—as we did—that what seems like a mess is in fact a catalyst for sophisticated learning.

We also encourage teachers to work outside of their comfort zones. Summer found that she could create mathematical lessons on her own, and that working outside her home discipline highlighted the strengths and weaknesses of each. Summer reflected that in ELA, multiple answers are already celebrated and this allowed her to create mathematics lessons incorporating ambiguity. She also realized that mathematics could be incorporated into ELA lessons, especially those on informational texts, as an additional layer of critical analysis. She encourages ELA teachers at all levels to work with mathematics teachers on teaching students to interpret numerical data. While many of our students understood that charts could be manipulated to influence public opinion, they had never considered things like the tone of the author when relaying numbers, or the way a question on a poll is phrased and how that might affect audience responses. By combining strengths of each subject, students may become better equipped to be critical consumers of information. This will help them not only be advocates for social justice, but more informed citizens.

The lessons for mathematics teachers are equally important. Traditional models of mathematics teaching do not often emphasize the part that mathematics plays across disciplines. Almost every argument has an underlying mathematical justification. Statistics and probability are the most frequently used mathematical tools outside of math class, but there are a variety of ways that mathematics can be used to justify a statement or shed light on a problem. Mathematics is the underlying way that human beings interpret their world. For example, we are sensitive to spatial relationships. When teachers and students look into their community, mathematics is literally all around them. We tacitly evaluate spatial relationships every day but forgo critical questions regarding the arrangement of objects in our neighborhoods. Who has convenient access to high performing schools? Who can access high quality medical care? Where are emergency services located? What is the response time within subdivisions of the community? How much open space is available for recreation purposes? Are all recreational facilities comparably equipped? The answers to all of these questions lie in an analysis of mathematics. We simply need to ask the appropriate questions of our students, develop their ability to analyze the situation, and empower and motivate them to *want* to do something with the knowledge that they uncover.

Knowing that mathematics exists all around is merely the first step, however. The next step for the teacher is making mathematics accessible. In our investigation we made assumptions about what students knew and were able to do mathematically. It turned out that some of our students were not mathematically capable of answering their own questions. That is okay. Mathematics is not always about answering the question, but knowing that the question exists. This was truly our purpose in developing *Math for a Cause*.

We were lucky to be able to try this program at a small, liberal private school that put little pressure on teachers to "cover the curriculum." Readers may be wondering how these lessons will translate to public school settings that have become consumed with accountability and standards. Here are a couple of suggestions. First, if teachers adopt a sociopolitical or social justice perspective they might simply judge *themselves* differently. Instead of looking at test scores, teachers might consider the ways in which their students creatively approach problems as well as recognize the way that students come to see a more positive relationship between themselves, mathematics, and their future (Gutiérrez, 2013). Second, teachers can be assured that they are addressing rigorous, standards-based mathematics and learn to justify this. One thing that we can all agree on is that context matters. Mathematics makes more sense when it addresses a subject that we care about. Finally, teachers should remember that small steps in teaching practices will make a large impact. The entire curriculum need not be a continuous sequence of social justice exercises. Teachers can, and should, use their curriculum, pacing guides, and school and district benchmarks, and build a social consciousness around these elements.

CONCLUSION

Students in *Math for a Cause* grew in their capacity to question not only social justice issues and the circumstances surrounding them, but also the norms of mathematics as a discipline. Through creating the curriculum, Summer and Bryan learned to question the norms of teaching in general and the disciplines of mathematics and ELA in particular. This process caused students and researchers alike to grow in our quest for social justice teaching and activism as we learned to let go of expectations and expand our thinking. This flexibility, as previously stated, is crucial to social justice practices that deal with overlapping systems of oppression and do not operate in an orderly, linear fashion.

NOTE

1. To protect the anonymity of our participants, all names except for the authors' are pseudonyms. Students chose their own pseudonyms.

REFERENCES

Britzman, D. P. (1995). Is there a queer pedagogy? Or, stop reading straight. *Educational Theory, 45*(2), 151–165.

Carrette, J. R., & King, R. (2005). *Selling spirituality: The silent takeover of religion.* Hove: Psychology Press.

Gutiérrez, R. (2013). The sociopolitical turn in mathematics education. *Journal for Research in Mathematics Education, 44*(1), 37–68.

Hand, V. (2012). Seeing culture and power in mathematical learning: Toward a model of equitable instruction. *Educational Studies in Mathematics, 80*(1–2), 233–247.

Hytten, K. (2004). Postcritical ethnography: Research as a pedagogical encounter. In G. W. Noblit, S. Y. Flores, S. Y. & E. G. Murillo (Eds.), *Postcritical ethnography: Reinscribing critique* (pp. 95–105). Cresskill, NJ: Hampton Press.

Jacobi, T., & Becker, S. L. (2013). Rewriting confinement: Feminist and queer critical literacy in SpeakOut! Writing workshops. *Radical Teacher, 95*(1), 32–40.

Kumashiro, K. (2001). Queer students of color and antiracist, antiheterosexist education: Paradoxes of identity and activism. In K. Kumashiro (Ed.), *Troubling intersections of race and sexuality: Queer students of color and anti-oppressive education* (pp. 1–25). Lanham, MD: Rowman & Littlefield Publishers.

Kumashiro, K. (2009). Teaching teachers to teach queerly. In W. Ayers, T. Quinn, & D. Stovall (Eds.), *Handbook for social justice in education* (pp. 718–721). New York, NY: Routledge.

Noblit, G. W., Flores, S. Y., & Murillo, E. G. (Eds.). (2004). *Postcritical ethnography: Reinscribing critique.* Cresskill, NJ: Hampton Press.

Rendón, L. I. (2009). *Sentipensante (sensing/thinking) pedagogy: Educating for wholeness, social justice and liberation* (1st ed.). Sterling, VA: Stylus.

Terry, C. (2010). Prisons, pipelines, and the President: Developing critical math literacy through participatory action research. *Journal of African American Males in Education, 1*(2), 73–104.

Whitin, D. J., & Whitin, P. (2011). *Learning to read the numbers: Integrating critical literacy and critical numeracy in K-8 classrooms.* New York, NY: Routledge.

CHAPTER NINE

Cultivating Communities of Care

Story Circles as Social Justice Practice
6th–7th Grade

COURTNEY B. COOK AND CELINA MARTÍNEZ NICHOLS

Kenneth Paul Kramer opened his book *Learning Through Dialogue: The Relevance of Martin Buber's Classroom* by claiming that "there exists a pervasive human relational problem in our culture, one shared by everyone … which drives a seemingly impenetrable wedge between us all" (2013, p. xxi). Beyond the scope of our personal (in)capacities to relate to one another on a human level, our contemporary educational, political, and social structures lend themselves ideologically and practically towards a project of dehumanization (De Lissovoy, 2010) which valorizes difference, individual merit achieved through competition, and, therefore, *isolation* over common experience and community. Rather than teaching community in our schools, teachers and students must navigate sociocultural and political powers of exclusion that work to divide us. bell hooks (2003) reminded us that one of the dangers we face in education is the loss of *feeling* community, which endangers our ability to feel connected to others and the world. She also argued that we have within us the agency to move beyond passive hopefulness in order to actively work, through intentional practice, towards a deeper sense of humanity and connection. As teachers, we are separated from one another and are asked to become complicit in teaching lessons of division through insistence upon individual merit, testing and assessment, and a rhetoric of "no excuses." What if we were to insist that one responsibility of educators is to encourage students to build relationships founded on practices of listening and learning from one another? How might we, through this insistence, work towards cultivating compassion and empathy as essential characteristics of democratic communities—by insisting, as Freire (1998) did, that teaching is first and foremost a human act?

The work discussed in this chapter is connected to important projects of humanistic and democratic education that prioritize the cultivation of the human spirit, assume dignity, honor difference, and encourage agency and transformation through relation with others (Aloni, 2013). To center the humanity of our students means we must center, in our classrooms, that which makes us most human of all: stories from our lives. Sharing lived experiences as an approach to working towards visions of a world founded upon love, faith, and humility (Freire & Macedo, 1987/2005) means dedicating teaching practices towards cultivating communities of care through relationship building. Informed by the conceptual framework of dialogue developed by philosopher and educator Martin Buber (1970), we imagine how personal story sharing through the method of story circles can offer teachers and K–12 students in diverse disciplines tools for building authentic relationships. At a time when educational and political structures are continuing to assault the very possibility of human community and connection, this work has never been more important.

CRITICAL PEDAGOGY AS SOCIAL JUSTICE

Critical pedagogy and humanizing education are central to social justice teaching. Critical pedagogy requires educators to remain dedicated to possibilities for justice-centered futures, and to invite students to analyze hidden relationships between power and knowledge (Freire, 1998; Freire & Macedo, 1987/2005; Giroux, 2013). Within this practice, teachers are called to encourage students to examine their own relationships and lived social realities within broader systems. Social justice educators will be hard-pressed to find critiques of systemic power embedded within test preparation materials or exercises that demand only rote memorization. Additionally, our students will fail to learn important practices of critical questioning if our pedagogy is itself uncritically defined by testing strategies. Alternatively, critical pedagogy seeks to activate student agency and consciousness through dialogue that interrogates taken-for-granted conceptions of "freedom, reason, and equality" (Giroux, 2013, p. xiv). It encourages students to become conscious citizens who imagine a world that could be, but is not yet. This work is based in transformative visions of democracy that begin by examining the grounds upon which life is lived, yet insist on working toward something better. What can be more powerful than teaching students that people cannot be commodified or counted and that each person carries within her valuable wisdom? Centering these knowledges in the classroom through dialogue, in the tradition of critical pedagogy, is one approach towards honoring students as, first and foremost, human.

If we are to believe Freire's conviction that "reading the world always precedes reading the word" (Freire & Macedo, 1987/2005, p. 79), then we must remember to honor students' stories as texts written from their often unacknowledged lives. From this viewpoint, critical educators are called to become experts, not only in reading curricular texts, but also in reading students' experiences as texts. Buber's (1970) work on humanizing dialogue provides models for putting this literacy into practice by inviting students to engage in critical reflection, vulnerable storytelling and listening, and a dedicated presentness to one another in classroom spaces.

Buber's (1970) theory defines dialogue as a meeting between people that requires a willingness to find meaningful relation and stands to deepen relationships with others. Invoking this conception of dialogue into classroom practice requires considering the ways relationships can develop and deepen through shared experiences. This theory of dialogue invites us to create moments that make possible honest and direct communication, mutual acts of being fully present, and feeling-based connections. By using story circles to create these shared moments, students and teachers have an opportunity to imagine what another is thinking, feeling, and experiencing without being asked to surrender their own personal values, beliefs, or understandings of the world (Kramer, 2013). Buber's (1970) theory requires a full presence and empathetic attention to the presence of another. If upon encountering one another, all participants can be fully attentive in mind and spirit, then possibilities for humanizing relations will emerge. In order to create conditions for humanizing dialogue to emerge in a debate-oriented culture, we offer models for structuring classroom conversations through the method of story circles.

Story Circles and Cultivating Communities of Care

Story circles, which are structured dialogue situations,[1] have a long legacy of being connected to social justice work. They were first developed as a means of connecting community efforts, activism, and education through *The Free Southern Theater (FST)*, a cultural branch of the Civil Rights movement. Founder John O'Neal, along with student activists, facilitated story circles within their communities to foster dialogue and educate larger audiences about stories from the Civil Rights Movement (Yuen, O'Neal, & Holden, n.d.). In their first usage, story circles were a means of cultivating community bonds and archiving local histories of those impacted by racial injustice in America. In practice it becomes clear that story circles, when practiced with care, have potential to serve the spirit of Buber's (1970) humanizing dialogue.

An important dynamic of the story circle process is knowing that everyone has a story to share and allowing stories to emerge organically[2] through a structured speech situation so that listening and learning is maximized. When introducing story circles, it is important to remind participants that deep listening is crucial, and that each person will have an opportunity to share *before* engaging in dialogue, known as "cross-talk." Cross-talk invites participants to reflect on the story they were called to share and to make connections to others' stories. This is the point at which participants are able to find connections while acknowledging individual differences, and it often happens that the connections are experience-based and feelings-centered.

Cross-talk invites students to engage in an uncommon experience of feeling in public and being vulnerable with (sometimes unfamiliar) others along the terrain of experience and difference. Theories of care provide us with insight into how teachers might consider community and relationship development in their classrooms in order to create the space for vulnerability. Noddings's work on care in schools reminds us that, while caring relations are sometimes challenging to cultivate within institutions, they are never impossible. Arguably, within our contemporary political moment, caring and human-centered relations are more important than ever. Noddings (2005) defined a caring relation as "a connection or encounter between two human beings"—a carer and a recipient of care—and suggested that "both parties must contribute" in particular ways (p. 18). It is a teacher's responsibility to help students "develop the capacity to care" (Noddings, 2005, p. 18). While we recognize that practices governing schooling do not center care-based relationships or feelings-centered pedagogy as standards for achievement, we have faith that teachers care deeply about their students. This means that as teachers we must think consciously about how we can restore communities of care in our classrooms, lead with that care, and be unafraid to be, first and foremost, human.

Further support for our concern with establishing authentic caring relationships in schools, Valenzuela's (1999) research exposed the ways that "schools are structured around an aesthetic caring whose essence lies in an attention to things and ideas" (p. 22). Rather than centering students' learning around "a moral ethic of caring" schools pursue a narrow logic that emphasizes objectives determined by standardized curricula and pressures teachers away from focusing on students' subjective realities (Valenzuela, 1999, p. 22). Authentic care, on the other hand, starts from the belief that "all people share a basic need to be understood, appreciated, and respected" (Valenzuela, 1999, p. 108) and that truly caring for students requires honoring "the material, physical, psychological, and spiritual needs of youth" (Valenzuela, 1999, p. 110). These knowledges can then be centered as the guide for educational processes. Story circles as practice in the classroom help support pedagogies that insist on hearing, seeing, and/or feeling what it is that others try to convey. Our research has shown that without a practice of centering students' everydayness through stories and feelings, alienation and division remain the dominant mode of being in our communities. Sadly, empathy, compassion, and connection become endangered.

RESEARCH METHODS: STORY CIRCLES AT VISION ACADEMY[3]

Given our aim to better understand how story circles impact students' relationships and capacity to connect, we adopted the qualitative research approach of phenomenology. This approach aims to identify "the essential components of … experiences which make them unique or distinguishable from others" (Pietkiewicz & Smith, 2012, p. 362). The goal is not to make claims of generalizability, but to better understand the shared experience of story circles from participants' perspectives. Our aim was to seek essence; a sort of intersection of feeling at the heart of the shared experience. We approached this goal of understanding story circle's potential as humanizing practice by inviting students to share individual stories through structured dialogue.

We entered the community as two female researchers familiar with the school community and invited students from Vision Academy to participate in a story circle for a duration of two hours. Vision Academy is a charter middle school located within an urban Texas district. Managed by a charter management organization, Vision embraces a "no excuses" system of accountability, standardization, and competition. This system is often realized through a narrow focus on the knowledge and skills to be tested; efficient, tightly-controlled and highly-regulated activities; teacher-centric practices; and highly-disciplined classroom environments (Golann, 2015; Goodman, 2013; Lack, 2009; Sondel, 2015). Comprised of 250 students in grades 6–7, Vision Academy has a racial demographic of approximately 96% Latino, 3% African American, and a remaining 1% white. The majority of teachers and administrators are white and originally from communities outside of Texas. Over 90% of the students qualify for the federal free or reduced-price meals program. The school's curriculum focuses on grade-level academic mastery with a stated goal of "college for all."

Purposeful sampling was used to recruit a small set of students to participate in the story circle. We sought to include a representative sample of students in terms of gender and race and purposely recruited seventh-grade students because of their familiarity with the school and with one another. This is consistent with the interpretive phenomenological analysis (IPA) tenet of recruiting individuals who share a common experience, yet vary in other characteristics (Smith, Flowers, & Larkin, 2009). Participants included three females (Beatriz, Daniela, and Esme) and three males (Alberto, Carlton, and Francisco); five students were Latina/o and one student was white. While all students were classmates, and therefore familiar with one another, their degrees of closeness varied.

In the initial stage of the story circle, we introduced the theme (or prompt) and explained the procedure to students. In this case, we asked participants to *"tell a story about a time you felt a sense of belonging, or the opposite, in your school community."*[4] We then invited students to take turns sharing personal, three-minute stories inspired by the prompt as we sat together in a circle. After each story, we asked everyone to pause, acknowledge the story that was told, and thank the storyteller for sharing before inviting the next student to share. We did this until everyone (including researchers) had an opportunity to share. The second stage of story circle was cross-talk. At this point we invited students to explore their experiences of sharing and listening as a group. Students talked to one another about the ways they experienced connection, distance, or surprise in relation to one another's stories.

Immediately following story circle, we asked students to write a letter to someone they felt that they trusted (their best friend, family member, etc.) about feelings they experienced at various points throughout the process, such as before and after, while sharing, while listening to others' stories, and while participating in cross-talk. We played music and allowed students to compose letters with the hopes that they would have time and space to intimately and honestly reflect on how the experience made them feel. Additionally, during this time we conducted semi-structured interviews with a random sampling of participants. The story circle and interviews were audio recorded and transcribed, and letters were collected as artifacts.

Using IPA, because of its usefulness in exploring how people make sense of their personal and social worlds, and of lived experience (Pietkiewicz & Smith, 2012), we placed the story circle and interview transcripts alongside students' letters. Our first step was to bracket what we identified as significant statements made by students. These significant statements offered insight into *how* students experienced (1) the story circle itself and (2) the act of sharing, listening, or relating to others through story. In the next step, we created a table with significant statements in order to analyze those experiences for underlying structures. We then developed a list of themes that described participants' common experiences. Following this step, we engaged in the process of clustering the themes into synthesized units of meaning in an attempt to understand the essence of the experience. We then used the clustered themes to write a "textual description" and a "structural description" (Creswell, 2013). In the final stage of analysis, we synthesized the structural and textual descriptions into an essence. In other words, after our individual analyses, we put our findings in conversation with one another and engaged in critically reflective conversation in search of language that honored students' experiences.

ANALYSIS

Our findings support the need for humanizing educational practices and the reliability of story circles to provide this type of experience in schools. All participants confirmed our suspicion that these types of spaces are generally absent from schooling practices by reporting that opportunities to share personal stories in classroom spaces were incredibly rare, most stating that it "never" occurred. Despite the fact that their stories were excluded from the spaces they inhabit every day, all student participants had an overwhelmingly positive experience of sharing in story circle and expressed a desire to engage in personal storytelling more often. Generally, the essence of the students' experience was relief, increased trust and closeness, and a heightened sense of belonging, and all students were surprised by how the experience made them feel more connected with one another.

The Relief of Sharing

Sharing today was kind of like feeling like it was easier to breathe.
—DANIELA, LETTER TO A FRIEND (OCTOBER 26, 2016)

Overwhelmingly, students expressed a feeling of relief after engaging in story circle. Relief was described as release of weight "off your chest," pressure "off your shoulders," or "like it was easier to breathe." Because students rarely, if ever, are given the opportunity to share personal stories in school, the opportunity to do so was liberating. Alberto stated, "sharing made me feel relieved because I usually never do this with anyone." Francisco added, "I feel as if I can finally let loose my past." Perhaps Daniela explained it best when she wrote:

> There's a sense of feeling trapped when people recognize only one part of you, which I think is what led to me never sharing things with people and turning any emotion into some sarcastic joke … it feels great to not *have* to do that.

We realize that students carry with them a weight that, from their perspective, requires them to perform a standardized way of feeling or, most concerning, perform *an absence* of feeling. Still, students expressed desires to feel lighter, to share and connect, and to have space to engage in this type of relationship-building that left them feeling less burdened. Daniela wrote, "there are still things I may never share, but to start with easy things still offers some kind of relief, like getting closer to that one destination." What is that destination? Perhaps it is trust, caring, sharing, being heard, being received with care, and connecting with others on a more human level. Story circles stand to offer secure spaces for dialogue in this much-needed pursuit of humanizing education.

Listening, Trusting, and Discovering Relation

It feels different now that we know each other's stories, like we've known each other forever.
—ESME, LETTER TO A FRIEND (OCTOBER 26, 2016)

A willingness to listen to others is essential to story circles. By having space to listen and learn from one another's stories, we learned that students felt closer to their peers. They developed new bonds that they identified in their own words as "trust" and that we understood as empathy. Carlton said that, through listening and connecting, he "felt what [other students] were going through." Another student, Beatriz, reflected, "when I was listening to the stories, it made me connect with the others … I felt as if my trust had grown with them during this time." Students also described this feeling as a realization of possibility for what this trust and closeness might mean. Esme, for example, expressed feeling "sad but kind of happy that there are other people like me who are kind of the same and I know if I have problems, I can tell them if I want to." Students believed that this new feeling would impact their future relationships with one another. Because students rarely, if ever, engage in storytelling in classrooms, they felt that sharing personal stories was challenging. Daniela suggested, "It's hard to share things since it always feels like no one would ever understand, but I think that changed a bit right now." Story circle emerged as a space to risk misunderstanding for Daniela, and allowed her to consider her desire to hear and be heard.

Acceptance Across, and Because of, Differences

Everyone's stories made me feel accepted, like we can all feel the same things even if it's in different ways.
—ALBERTO, INTERVIEW (OCTOBER 26, 2016)

Several students reported feeling a greater sense of acceptance and belonging within their peer group after participating in story circle. Having the opportunity to hear others' stories, particularly outside of established friend groups, allowed students to connect with one another. This chance relation through sharing resulted in an unanticipated feeling of acceptance. As Alberto's opening quote suggested, the structured approach to finding commonality despite difference made him "feel accepted." Similarly, Carlton expressed feeling "a sense of belonging" as a result of dialogue. Being acknowledged by other students through their connections to his story was a new and heartening experience for him. Francisco shared a similar sentiment in his letter: "I really hope this feeling of belonging stays in this group and we have time to share even more." This evidences story circle's ability to generate feelings of closeness and illuminates students' need to engage in personal storytelling as they navigate the common desire to belong in community.

IMPLICATIONS: CULTIVATING A CULTURE OF FEELING

Students' stories confirmed that schooling is often experienced as a process of alienation, unfamiliarity, and distance, despite the reality that each day they are the ones who fill the halls, classrooms, and desks with their hunger to be heard, to belong together, and to connect as humans in the spaces they share. Carlton said it plainly when he told us that school is a place where "teachers are more strict and don't show as much emotion." He unpacked the ways he has come to know teachers in his eight years of schooling across six schools and three states when he said teachers are "more like robots" and "less like people you can talk to." Taking risks to authentically *feel with* students has become increasingly absent, yet as Carlton reminded us, educational experiences that insist on being blind to feelings "doesn't make [him] feel very welcome." Students learn best from people they trust, from people who authentically care for and seek to understand them, and from teachers who have allowed these students to become critically familiar with themselves as well. For teachers this means *choosing* to orient our work towards community-building founded on honest relation and sharing.

Engaging in story circles in the classroom, according to students, requires that the teacher exhibit specific qualities. Students agreed that the teacher should show kindness, understanding, and a willingness to comfort them through sustained actions and attitudes. Without these qualities, students doubted their ability to be open, honest, and vulnerable in front of a story circle community. Story circles give us strategies towards *rehumanizing* education in a larger project of cultivating a culture of feeling. These students reminded us that sharing depends on trust, trust depends on relationships, relationships depend on shared time and experience with one another, and all of this depends on how well students feel they know their teachers as people, as humans.

Within a culture of feeling, teachers and students, must:

- Recognize that we are humans *first*
- Understand one another as complex emotional beings
- Understand that we all have complex self-knowledge of our own feeling selves
- Remember we all carry stories, and therefore wisdom, within us
- Believe we all have a desire to share stories and seek human connection through relation
- Believe in possibilities of living more authentic emotional lives
- Remain dedicated to holding spaces which honor openness, vulnerability, and feelings
- Remain dedicated to safety, community-building, and care-based pedagogy
- Work to expose the systems, structures, and barriers that discourage us from sharing, feeling, and honoring others' humanity

- Deepen emotional literacy: discourage shame that is often aligned with feeling
- Encourage one another to find relation to one another
- Encourage students to cultivate relationships with the content of the curricula (see Appendix)

The important project of working to develop a culture of feeling is *a choice*, a personal and professional orientation to human-centered and human-first pedagogy. The critical pedagogy that works to create opportunities for building relationships through humanizing dialogue is ultimately a project towards empathy and radical love. The compassion that is developed within these spaces helps us to imagine human solidarity on localized terms, and stands to inform possibilities for more expansive and global human connections. When asked about his education practices, Buber (1967) said:

> I have no teaching. I only point to something … I point to something in reality that had not or had too little been seen. I take him who listens to me by the hand and lead him to the window. I open the window and point to what is outside. (p. 693)

Might we imagine one of our roles as teachers to lead students by the hand towards the window? A window which exposes the unseen open hands of others willingly outstretched, ready to receive us? In Buber's charge, we must lead students to that open window.

Story circles are an effective strategy for multiple settings that help create safe spaces for dialogue to be experimented with. Storytelling and deep listening are primary vehicles for beginning the work of relationship-building and exchanges between students and teachers who are rarely offered the opportunity to share with one another beyond the limits of mandated curricula. We believe that re-centering our humanity must be counted as the most important standard of achievement in contemporary schooling. Grasping the hands of one another through story, deep listening, and being *with* promises that the road we make by walking will be guided by a deeper understanding of our common humanity, and move in a direction towards a world that is not yet, but *could be* founded firstly on love, compassion, and care.

APPENDIX

Teacher Toolkit: Story Circles in Your Classroom

You can adapt this process to fit the needs of your students across disciplines and grade level. Below we offer ideas and inspiration for future use.

Possible Topics:
Tell a story about a time ...

- your civil rights were/were not honored.
- you felt defined by an aspect of your identity that you cannot control.
- you felt supported or cared for, or the opposite, in a school setting.
- you felt a sense of safety, or the opposite, in a school setting.
- whiteness impacted your life.
- you felt unheard or unseen by someone in your community.
- someone's *idea* of who you are impacted your ability to be your fullest self.

Language Arts

Example: Anne Frank, *The Diary of a Young Girl*
Prompt: "Tell a story about a time when you were forced to follow a rule that you felt was wrong."
You might connect themes of civil disobedience, dignity, morality, sanctuary and safety during times of violence, and democracy-in-the-making from a connection between historic and personal examples, and with an emphasis on the human experiences shared in Anne Frank's diary and your students' stories.

Science/Technology

You may choose to create a topic related to bioethics, morality, or notions of "truth" as described within scientific research. Some possible examples could be: animal testing, genetic testing, the environment, or the Eugenics movement.

Civics/Social Studies/Art

One great way to engage students in thinking about politics and democratic engagement is to participate in the *United States Department of Arts and Culture*'s annual civic ritual called "People's State of the Union Address" which takes place in January. You can find story circle examples on USDAC's website (http://usdac.us/psotu) and engage in critical conversations about democracy, the importance of students' voices, and participation.

Physical Education

You might engage in lessons about gender, masculinity, femininity, sexuality, and ableism. You can hold a story circle where students can respond to a prompt like "tell a story about a time that you were expected to behave a certain way based on your gender" or "tell a story where you were made to feel less-able than you are because of another person's assumptions about what you are capable of achieving."

NOTES

1. A story circle is when anywhere from 5 to 8 people, plus 1–2 facilitators, and one scribe (optional) sit together in a circle with the goal of sharing stories from personal experience.
2. Participants are often nervous about sharing stories, or not being able to "come up with a story," but it is okay to remind them that there is a good chance they will be surprised by the stories they are inspired to tell. The element of surprise, of the story emerging suddenly, is important for the story circle. Encourage students to trust that a story will emerge when it is their turn to share and to trust whatever story comes to them in that moment. We have found it fruitful to discuss this element of surprise during the story circle with students.
3. "Vision Academy," like all names of place and participants included in this study, is a pseudonym we have used in order to protect the students' and community's confidentiality.
4. Prompt inspired by USDAC's 2015 People's State of the Union prompt (see Appendix).

REFERENCES

Aloni, N. (2013). Empowering dialogues in humanistic education. *Educational Philosophy and Theory, 45*(10), 1067–1081.

Buber, M. (1967). Replies to my critics. In P. Schilpp & M. Freidman (Eds.), *The Philosophy of Martin Buber*. LaSalle, IL: Open Court Publishing. 693.

Buber, M. (1970). *I and Thou*. New York, NY: Touchstone.

Creswell, J. W. (2013). *Qualitative inquiry and research design* (3rd ed.). Los Angeles, CA: Sage.

De Lissovoy, N. (2010). Rethinking education and emancipation: Being, teaching, and power. *Harvard Educational Review, 80*(2), 203–220.

Freire, P. (1998). *Pedagogy of freedom: Ethics, democracy, and civic courage*. Lanham, MD: Rowman & Littlefield Publishers.

Freire, P., & Macedo, D. (1987/2005). *Literacy: Reading the word and the world*. London: Routledge. (Original work published 1987).

Giroux, H. (2013). Prologue: The fruit of Freire's roots. In T. Kress & R. Lade (Eds.), *Paulo Freire's intellectual roots: Toward historicity in praxis* (p. xiv). New York, NY: Bloomsbury.

Golann, J. W. (2015). The paradox of success at a no-excuses school. *Sociology of Education, 88*(2), 103–119.

Goodman, J. F. (2013). Charter management organizations and the regulated environment: Is it worth the price? *Educational Researcher, 42*(2), 89–96.

hooks, b. (2003). *Teaching community: A pedagogy of hope*. New York, NY: Routledge.

Kramer, K. P. (2013). *Learning through dialogue: The relevance of Martin Buber's classroom*. Lanham, MD: Rowman & Littlefield Education.

Lack, B. (2009). No excuses: A critique of the Knowledge is Power Program (KIPP) within charter schools in the USA. *Journal for Critical Education Policy Studies, 7*(2), 126–153.

Noddings, N. (2005). *The challenge to care in schools* (2nd ed.). New York, NY: Teachers College Press.

Pietkiewicz, I., & Smith, J. A. (2012). A practical guide to using interpretive phenomenological analysis in qualitative research psychology. *Psychological Journal, 18*(2), 361–369.

Smith, J. A., Flowers, P., & Larkin, M. (2009). *Interpretative phenomenological analysis: Theory, method and research*. London: Sage.

Sondel, B. (2015). Raising citizens or raising test scores? Teach for America, "no excuses" charters, and the development of the neoliberal citizen. *Theory & Research in Social Education, 43*(3), 289–313.

Valenzuela, A. (1999). *Subtractive schooling: U.S.-Mexican youth and the politics of caring.* Albany, NY: State University of New York Press.

Yuen, C., O'Neal, J., & Holden, T. (n.d.). Junebug Productions: Color Line Project. *Animating Democracy & Americans for the Arts.* Retrieved from http://animatingdemocracy.org/sites/default/files/documents/labs/color_line_project_case_study.pdfhttp://animatingdemocracy.org/sites/default/files/documents/labs/color_line_project_case_study.pdf

CHAPTER TEN

Fixing THE World

Social Justice in World History
7th Grade

JEFF A. GREINER

Teaching for social justice in a social studies classroom seems to be a natural fit, and implementing an inquiry-based form of instruction seems to live alongside the goals of social justice easily. The natural inclination is to use social studies as a means of highlighting the historical injustices in society that continue to impact the lives of the disaffected in the modern world. When the prescribed content of the social studies class is world history, however, the equation changes. While it is easy to highlight inequity that has its roots in things like colonialism, slave trade, reactions to global wars, and more, those roots are so far removed from many students' experiences that it is often difficult to help them see that history as relevant to their lives. What is less difficult to accomplish, especially in the latter part of world history, is to help teach students about the power that they possess to impact the world, and for them to practice having such an impact.

Armed with these thoughts, I sought to create such a unit for the 4th quarter of my 7th grade modern World History course. I had worked to incorporate critical and social justice teaching methods all year, such as honoring student narratives, examining multiple perspectives, and examining concepts with a critical lens. All of that, however, felt as though it lacked the empowerment of actually taking an action and seeing how it impacts the world. On top of these goals, this was the first year where I tried to implement an inquiry-based organization of instruction, based on the C3 Framework for Social Studies State Standards (C3), published by the National Council for the Social Studies (2013). While I posit that inquiry-based instruction can generally facilitate a critical approach to teaching, in this case it also informed the format and design of my curriculum as being primarily organized around *compelling* and *supporting questions*. In the C3 framework, instruction is framed around these two types of questions. The Compelling Question is a large, overarching question. I like to use this question to engage students in thinking about relevant connections between history and their lives, by making the question as relevant to life today as it is for the study of the history being examined. Under the *compelling question* are a set of two to four *supporting questions* that focus more on the content and guide students to examine evidence that will ultimately help them answer the Compelling Question.

The unit I created—Globalization and Human Rights—is focused on world history in the post-Cold War era. I taught i to 7th graders in an urban middle school in the southeastern region of the United States. The students were demographically diverse because of the school system's policy of bussing and the school's magnet program that focuses on providing a wide variety of elective offerings so students can explore their many interests. Through this unit, students had the opportunity to examine such themes as the impact of global capitalism and their roles as members of a global capitalist system. The general outline was that students would examine why global human rights issues should be important to them, examine one example of a global human rights issue that was impacted by global capitalism (specifically South African Apartheid and the movement that ended it), and finally engage in a project culminating in the students working to make the world a better place.

FRAMEWORK FOR CRITICAL CONCEPTS

There are multitudes of approaches to social justice education that can be drawn upon for critical teaching. For the purposes of this unit, I kept in mind the following elements of critical teaching: (1) questioning the status quo—including the role of capitalism in the modern world (Giroux, 2004; Grande, 2015); (2) examining relationships of power and how people can change them (Giroux, 2004; Grande, 2004; Jennings & Lynn, 2005); (3) engaging students in dialogue as valued participants in creating knowledge (Freire, 1970/2000); (4) valuing the lived experiences and personal stories/perspectives of students (Freire, 1970/2000; O'Loughlin, 1995); (5) presenting information from multiple perspectives (Jennings & Lynn, 2005; O'Loughlin, 1995); (6) and giving students the opportunity to practice active citizenship (as C3 intends) (Giroux, 2004).

Questioning both the status quo and capitalism (the first element of critical pedagogy I considered) requires an examination of power, who has it, and what they are doing with it. Only through an examination of power can we understand what the status quo is, who benefits from it, and how capitalism impacts the lives of people. Scholars or critical theories state strongly that students should be taught to be critical to the point of questioning and challenging concepts that have become normalized in modern American society. Apple and Buras (2006) asked us to examine power when discussing the idea that knowledge is not neutral; they stated that asking "*whose* knowledge is most valued" (p. 18) exposes what counts, or does not count, as knowledge in the education system and society as a whole. Jennings and Lynn (2005) explained that critical theory is built on the idea of questioning and challenging the role of class and capitalism and that critical pedagogy must negotiate the issue of power. Swalwell (2013), when discussing social reproduction, explained that critical pedagogy must attempt to disrupt existing concepts of power and who has it and, as such, it only seems logical that students must be taught to identify power in the world, who has it, and how it is being used, as well as how it can be changed. Luke (2012) even suggested that being able to identify power can help students better understand the perspective of authors when examining text.

Valuing the stories and lives of students is the second element of critical pedagogy I kept in mind, and this element is found throughout social justice literature. O'Loughlin (1995) said "learning ought to be grounded in students' autobiographical stories of their lived experiences" (p. 111). Giroux (2004) stated "teaching in classrooms ... should not only simply honor the experiences students bring to such sites, but should also connect their experiences to specific problems that emanate from the material context of their everyday lives" (p. 500). These quotes emphasize the importance of respecting students' experiences as meaningful ways of understanding and interpreting curriculum. Similar concepts about the role of student experiences and how they should be honored to inform instruction can be found in many forms of critical pedagogy such as critical race pedagogy (Jennings & Lynn, 2005), LatCrit (Solorzano & Delgado Bernal, 2001), and Red Pedagogy (Grande, 2004).

The third element of critical pedagogy is engaging students in a process of dialogue where the students and teacher construct knowledge together, rather than knowledge being given to the students from the teacher (Freire, 1970/2000). Similarly, Giroux (2004) talked about the need to teach argumentation as it helps students better engage in democracy.

The literature on critical pedagogy also suggests that students should construct knowledge by examining multiple perspectives rather than relying on a singular authority. This is the fourth element of critical pedagogy. To some degree, engaging in dialogue suits that need, as students are examining the perspectives and lived experiences of the other people in the discussion, if not hearing the results of those experiences. In social studies we often examine various sources to understand a topic, so providing varied perspectives about a similar theme or topic highlights for students that knowledge is not without variability, based on perception. Avila and Moore (2012) explained that examining multiple perspectives in text is crucial to critical literacy so that students can understand that knowledge is not final or singular, but rather constructed from an individual's interpretations. Jennings and Lynn (2005) explained that counter-narratives (which I would argue are most possible when examining multiple perspectives) are supported by critical race pedagogy. McLaren (2009) put it well when he wrote, "the critical educator doesn't believe that there are two sides to every question ... For the critical educator, there are many sides to a problem" (p. 62).

Lastly, I intentionally laced a fifth element of critical pedagogy into the unit: the idea of citizenship and activism. According to Freire (1970/2000) "thought has meaning only when generated by action upon the world." North (2006) explained that education ought to ensure that students know how to act upon the world in such a way that it brings about their conception of the good. She cited Parker (2003) to illustrate the point, with Parker listing the "political behaviors" that students need to be taught, including, "voting or contacting public officials ... campaigning, engaging in civil disobedience, boycotts, strikes, rebellion, and other forms of direct action" (p. 34).

GLOBALIZATION AND HUMAN RIGHTS: LEARNING TO MAKE THE WORLD A BETTER PLACE

When designing this unit, I first designed a set of *compelling* and *supporting questions*. For a *compelling question* I like questions that are broad to be relevant to my students' contemporary lives, high-interest to promote engagement, and focused which will require them to examine the course content. To those ends I chose "What can we do to address global human rights issues?" The question isn't "what can be done"; it's "what can *we* do." I wanted students to consider the element of activism at all points throughout the unit as they see and consider the *compelling question*.

The *supporting questions*, focusing more on the content of the unit, were: "In what ways has the world become more globally connected?" and, "What do global human rights issues look like in the modern world?" The idea behind these questions is for students to build a narrative that addresses why they should care about global human rights abuses and what they can do about them. The first question addressed both of those things, since examining our connection to the world gives, if nothing else, selfish reasons to care about others in the world and their conditions. It also highlights our role in the system that leads to the abuse of others, so that students might discover that if they are part of the problem, they can also be part of the solution. These questions were addressed daily at the start of each class, previewing for students what they will be doing that day and how it should help them address the questions.

The second question focused on an example of a global human rights abuse, namely Apartheid in South Africa. It is of high interest, it is strongly connected to previous time periods of world history (i.e. colonization, decolonization), and it is an example of not only a human rights issue in the modern world, but also how the international community, and individuals, can act towards the liberation of others. Further, it presented an opportunity to examine how people can change power dynamics. South Africans went from a situation where the government used its power to implement racist Apartheid laws, to a point where the anti-Apartheid movement gained power and forced the government to change, effectively replacing it.

Finally, students stepped out of the inquiry questions provided for them, in order to engage in their own inquiry into modern human rights abuses. They wrote their own questions, examined resources from various perspectives, drew conclusions from their investigation, and then came up with ways they could leverage their power to try and have a positive impact. Lastly, they picked one of their ideas about how to use their power to make a positive impact, and they actually did it, making the entire academic process authentic and meaningful in a pragmatic way.

Supporting Question One: In What Ways Has the World Become More Globally Connected?

Three lessons addressed the first supporting question. The first introduced the unit as a whole. Students were introduced to the *compelling* and *supporting questions* of the unit as well as the general concept of human rights. I used a video from ultralized (2009) to introduce the topic, recognizing that the history presented is a bit simplistic. Students then engaged in an examination of rights, giving them an opportunity to express their own perspectives and narratives as they examined the Universal Declaration of Human Rights (UN General Assembly, 1948). I provided students with a copy of the Declaration (available through the United Nations website), had them identify the three rights they felt are the most important, and engaged them in a class discussion about those rights. The following questions guided that discussion: *What are human rights? Have your human rights ever been violated? How can the violation of human rights around the world impact us? What can we do about it? Is it possible for someone to violate someone else's human rights if they don't have power over them?* The discussion created an opportunity for dialogue in which the students were defining terms and expressing what they meant from their perspectives. They explicitly examined the role of power and practiced the skills of identifying it. They also practiced through a worksheet where they examined examples of power, how it is used, and where it comes from. These skills aided them later in the unit and outside of the classroom, since learning to identify power and its sources is crucial to being able to change power dynamics.

The second lesson involved giving some background information through direct instruction. In these moments I was continually framing the content through a critical lens and around the inquiry questions. Instead of simply writing down information about globalization they were asked to share their perspectives about it prior to the lecture. Even lecture notes can be framed as uncertain (i.e. what historians posit as positives and negatives) rather than presenting information as absolute fact. By alluding to vague authorship like "some historians," the information is less authoritative, easier for students to question, and encourages the teacher to present the content as one of many perspectives. The lectures were also constructed to ask students to question the value of globalization, which is the status quo, and is part and parcel with capitalism. More importantly, to conclude the lesson, students were asked to connect the concept of globalization to their personal experiences, by examining the impact of globalization in their lives and constructing meaning from those experiences (i.e. how would your life be different without globalization?). This lesson concluded by asking students to create a list of 20 things they own that came from other countries. This experience helped students create a personal narrative for globalization. The next day, they discussed the lists as we engaged in the examination of multiple perspectives.

On the final day of addressing *supporting question one*, students were asked to share their experiences investigating globalization in their own lives from the list of made in other countries. All students' experiences were equally valued by having students share what they discovered and marking it on a map of the world. Afterwards reviewed the concept and effects of globalization through a CrashCourse video (2012).

Students then examined multiple perspectives about globalization by analyzing a series of quotes. Not only did this utilize multiple perspectives, but it also led to a dialogue with students as they worked together to construct the meaning of the quotes and how they applied to our understanding of globalization. Some quotes were selected for their explicit critique of the impact of global capitalism. Sources of the quotes included Jimmy Carter and Nelson Mandela to Chinese Premier of State, Li Keqiang, and American economist/politician Phil Gramm. After students examined the quotes, they engaged in a class discussion about the role of globalization in their lives and others, as well as their general impression of whether globalization has been a net positive or negative for the world, their community, personally, or any other group they deemed appropriate.

Finally, I gave a formative assessment. Students created their own set of *compelling* and *supporting questions* about the topic of globalization. This provided a sense of both their basic understanding of the concept of globalization and their historical thinking about the subject, as well as provided them with practice thinking about creating their own inquiries, which they would do later in the unit. Moreover, it turned the teacher-student roles on their heads—as Freire (1970/2000) advocated—since students are accustomed to the teacher providing the inquiry questions.

Supporting Question Two: What Do Global Human Rights Issues Look Like in the Modern World?

The second supporting question introduced students to an example of a contemporary human rights issue in preparation for their later project. It also it gave them an opportunity to examine how power changed in South Africa as a possible template for how to change power dynamics elsewhere. The unit began by asking students to describe what discrimination looks like in the world today. I considered, alternatively, asking them to identify times when they had faced discrimination in their lives. However, as I shared the unit with other teachers, they expressed concern about making the subject that personal for 7th graders. Making it personal was appealing given that critical pedagogy encourages the examination of personal narratives—especially those that are from historically oppressed groups (Kohli, 2009; O'Loughlin, 1995), but it was determined to be too problematic. While making it personal may have provided a more meaningful and critical connection to the concepts, it could have alienated and singled out students who had negative experiences. Further, it could have reinforced stereotypes. Perhaps in the future it could be implemented with abundant pre-teaching and efforts made to create a safe classroom culture.

After briefly connecting to their ideas of discrimination, I introduced students to the concept of Apartheid. I tried to do so without injecting my own opinion into the description, allowing students to make their own judgments and create their own understandings. Students then examined a series of quotes about the government of South Africa at the time from people with varying opinions. This lesson concluded with a dialogue about Apartheid, its purpose, and resistance to it, framed by discussion questions like: *Why did these laws exist? Why did people think they were justified?* and, *How did people resist these laws?* For their homework the students examined excerpts from actual Apartheid laws and constructed their own interpretations of its impact and purpose, using excerpts from The Weinstein Company (n.d.)

Next, students learned background information on Apartheid and the resistance movement against it. I framed the lecture to examine Apartheid in terms of power and discuss how power was changed. The class looked at images and heard a narrative on how the resistance movement began eroding the power of the Apartheid government. Students considered if/what made the actions of resistance successful. I briefly described the events that led to the colonization of South

Africa, the creation of the Apartheid laws, and the resistance movement, highlighting international involvement. Guiding questions helped students focus on the dynamics of power and the process by which these changed in order to undo Apartheid, rather than being simply fact- or timeline-driven. For example, students considered broad questions like: *What was South Africa's role in globalization? How did Apartheid divide people? How did people start to take power to fight against Apartheid?* Students examined the structures of power and how to change them to make the world more just, and they also had the opportunity to construct knowledge based on their own perspectives. This also included primary source analysis in the form of contemporaneous photographs from South Africa.

The last lesson of this part of the unit focused on analyzing multiple perspectives about Apartheid towards the end of that government. Students examined a pro-Apartheid speech (*The Case for Apartheid*, 1953, by A. L. Geyer), an anti-Apartheid speech (*The Question of South Africa*, 1984, by Desmond Tutu), and a New York Times article from an outsider (Wren, 1991). The sources were excerpted to accommodate students' reading levels class time constraints. Wren's piece was selected because it present the idea that people can help address human rights issues even if they do not live in the place where the issues are happening. The lesson concluded with a silent discussion protocol in which students examined three critical questions on their own and then engaged in written dialogue about it with three partners. Questions were: (1) *How did the people of South Africa begin to make change so they could change things?* (2) *What role did the rest of the world have in changing who had power in South Africa?* and (3) *Could South Africa have ended Apartheid without the help of the rest of the world?*. While class discussions can result in meaningful dialogue, as a process it leaves out the voices of students who do not engage in verbal dialogues. The examination of this *supporting question* concluded with a formative assessment, similar to the previous one, which asked students to practice writing their own inquiry-style questions as if the entire unit was about Apartheid.

Project

In the last part of the unit students implemented their learning. The C3 inquiry arc includes a component called "taking informed action" wherein students use what they have learned from history to do something in the world today. Taking informed action can be time-consuming and often does not directly relate to content standards, and so it is likely to receive less attention. In this unit, however, there was an opportunity to make taking action relevant to the content standards: having students taking action in their own lives fits well with learning about that time period.

I started by doing a smaller version of the project together as a class. The model project was about mining conflict minerals in the Congo. These are often mined with forced labor and child soldiers and who destroy the local environment, killing local wildlife like endangered gorillas. Students examined how these minerals are often used in electronics purchased by American consumers, and how our economic choices impact things like child slavery/soldiers in Africa. Students completed a summary sheet, much like the one that they would use for their project, that asked them to describe the issue, create *compelling* and *supporting questions*, do research to answer those questions, and brainstorm ways that they could impact the issue positively. First students viewed a series of images that were seemingly unrelated: a gorilla, child miners, a cell phone, child soldiers, a map of Africa, etc. Then they identified the common theme represented by these pictures. They also viewed activist videos (e.g., Socialists and Democrats, 2015; ENOUGHProject, 2009). At this point students were able to create the inquiry questions and, with a sample article provided to them (Cellular News, n.d.) they practiced answering their own questions. Finally, they brainstormed possible solutions and discussed them with the class.

Lastly, students completed their own informed action project regarding global human rights issues. The first step of the project was for students to identify a global human rights issue. They were provided a list (with topics like the treatment of women in Saudi Arabia, or workers' rights in China), but I encouraged them to identify their own (for example, some examined issues like abusive treatment of women in India and drug trafficking in Latin America). They then engaged in independent, but supervised, research and constructed their own knowledge about their selected subjects. Students then created their own inquiry-based questions about the issue and answered those questions, after having examined multiple perspectives.

Finally, they brainstormed possible ways that they could act to make a positive impact based on their inquiry and then chose one to implement. They were provided examples of actions, but they were also encouraged to come up with their own. The most common form of action that students opted to take was to try to raise awareness. Many started social media campaigns, created posters to display around the school and community, or presented to local organizations. Others conducted a school-wide collection of supplies for a local organization that helps refugees, and others volunteered their time locally. A few also contacted government officials, asking them to take action on the issue that they had researched. I hope that, while they learned that they have power to impact the world, they also learned that when a large group of middle school students engages in activism at the same time, even if the projects are disparate and about different topics, the impact can be greater.

REFLECTIONS

Having researched, planned, and implemented this unit, I cannot help but reflect on the process. The students worked with inquiry-structured units from the beginning of the year, and so this unit represented a next step for them I was able to observe much about what students learned by seeing them engage in the final project. It was an activity that revealed what students understood about power structures and how they can be changed, while it also demonstrated how well students were able to take lessons from history and apply them to their lives. Moreover, it gave them an opportunity to practice being active citizens.

When students asked if they could run a school-wide drive to collect supplies for refugees, or if they could volunteer their time to help displaced people from around the world who were living locally, it was clear that these students were preparing to make the world a better place. When students created social media campaigns that were more attention-grabbing than your average social media post, and when those campaigns asked people not just to be aware, but to do something to help the situation, it was obvious that these students knew the role of awareness campaigns and how they can lead to further action. When students asked to examine topics like abuse of women in India they demonstrated an interest in the world's problems and a desire to have a positive impact on others' lives.

Regardless, the next time I teach this unit I will continue to evolve the way I guide the students through the process. Having different awareness campaigns working separately on the same issue can have an impact. If, however, a dozen awareness campaigns coordinated their efforts, they might have been able to examine how their efforts can make a bigger splash. I would also like to explore ways to encourage students to sustain their efforts to impact the world. While I consider it a success that some students engaged in a long-term effort to make a difference, it was clear that some students appeared less sincere in their efforts. While I do not expect that every student is going to embrace the lessons this unit can teach, making a deeper impact on more students is a worthy goal.

IMPLICATIONS

Using dialogue and having students construct knowledge is something teachers have been doing for a long time without considering its critical nature. Teachers have been using multiple perspectives for a long time as well. While I would argue that inquiry, as described in the C3 Framework, can be an ally to social justice instruction, it is not social justice instruction on its own. However, when these teaching methods are taken together with a framework like the C3 they start to encourage a more critical approach.

To be truly focused on social justice, however, the goal must be explicit and intentional. Simply following the instructions in a lesson plan, even a lesson plan designed for social justice, does not make a teacher social justice focused. To be social-justice focused, a teacher must explicitly and intentionally frame and implement lessons in a way that questions capitalism and power; that honors students' perspectives, narratives, and experiences; engages students in dialogue to co-construct knowledge; provides multiple perspectives; has students practicing active citizenship; and does so with a mindset focused on empowering students to make the world more just. Social justice pedagogy has the potential to give students a meaningful experience that can lead them to be more mindful of the state of justice in the world and their role in that state of justice. Teaching World History to 7th graders provides an opportunity for students to examine how the world is connected and recognize that, if there are injustices in the world, they can take part in making a difference to change those situations. They can impact the world, and if they would like to, they can use their power to make the world a better place.

REFERENCES

Apple, M. W., & Buras, K. L. (2006). *The subaltern speak: Curriculum, power, and educational struggles.* New York, NY: Routledge.

Avila, J., & Moore, M. (2012). Critical literacy, digital literacies, and common core state standards: A workable union? *Theory into Practice, 51*(1), 27–33.

Cellular News. (n.d.) *Coltan, gorillas and cellphones.* Retrieved February 22, 2017 from http://www.cellular-news.com/coltan/

CrashCourse. (2012, November 12). Globalization I – the upside: Crash course world history #41 [Video file]. Retrieved from https://www.youtube.com/watch?v=5SnR-e0S6Ic

ENOUGHProject. (2009, November 18). Conflict minerals 101 [Video file]. Retrieved from https://www.youtube.com/watch?v=aF-sJgcoY20

Freire, P. (1970/2000). *Pedagogy of the oppressed: The 30th anniversary edition.* New York, NY: Bloomsbury. (Original work published 1970).

Giroux, H. A. (2004). Public pedagogy and the politics of neo-liberalism: Making the political more pedagogical. *Policy Futures in Education, 2*(3–4), 494–503.

Grande, S. (2015). *Red pedagogy: Native American social and political thought.* New York, NY: Rowman & Littlefield.

Jennings, M. E., & Lynn, M. (2005). The house that race built: Critical pedagogy, African-American education, and the re-conceptualization of a critical race theory. *The Journal of Educational Foundations, 19*(3/4), 15–32.

Kohli, R. (2009). Critical race reflections: Valuing the experiences of teachers of color in teacher education. *Race Ethnicity and Education, 12*(2), 235–251.

Luke, A. (2012). Critical literacy: Foundational notes. *Theory into Practice, 51*(1), 4–11.

McLaren, P. (2009). Critical pedagogy: A look at the major concepts. In A. Darder, M. P. Baltodano, & R. D. Torres (Eds.), *The critical pedagogy reader* (pp. 61–83). New York, NY: Routledge.

National Council for the Social Studies (NCSS). (2013). *The College, Career, and Civic Life (C3) framework for social studies state standards: Guidance for enhancing the rigor of K–12 civics, economics, geography, and history*. Silver Spring, MD: NCSS.

North, C. E. (2006). More than words? Delving into the substantive meaning (s) of "social justice" in education. *Review of Educational Research, 76*(4), 507–535.

O'Loughlin, M. (1995). Daring the imagination: Unlocking voices of dissent and possibility in teaching. *Theory into Practice, 34*(2), 107–116.

Parker, W. C. (2003). *Teaching democracy: Unity and diversity in public life*. New York, NY: Teachers College Press.

Socialists and Democrats. (2015, December 18). Conflict minerals [Video file]. Retrieved from https://www.youtube.com/watch?v=CSe8LTqMZzk

Solorzano, D. G., & Bernal, D. D. (2001). Examining transformational resistance through a critical race and LatCrit theory framework Chicana and Chicano students in an urban context. *Urban Education, 36*(3), 308–342.

Swalwell, K. (2013). "With great power comes great responsibility": Privileged students' conceptions of justice-oriented citizenship. *Democracy and Education, 21*(1), 1–11.

ultralized. (2009, September 26). The story of human rights [Video file]. Retrieved from https://www.youtube.com/watch?v=oh3BbLk5UIQ

UN General Assembly. (1948). *Universal declaration of human rights* (217 [III] A). Paris.

The Weinstein Company. (n.d.). *Mandela: Long walk to freedom: The impact of apartheid*. Retrieved February 23, 2017 from http://weinsteinco.com/wp-content/uploads/2013/pdf/The_Impact_of_Apartheid.pdf

Wren, C. S. (1991, February 2). *South Africa moves to scrap apartheid* [Electronic version]. The New York Times.

CHAPTER ELEVEN

Technology Integration IN Urban Middle School Classrooms

How Does Culturally Relevant Pedagogy Support 1:1 Technology Implementation?
6th–8th Grade

LANA M. MINSHEW, MARTINETTE HORNER, AND
JANICE L. ANDERSON

Many schools are beginning to adopt one-to-one (1:1) technology initiatives as part of educational reform efforts with the goal of transforming teaching and learning. One-to-one (1:1) technology refers to classrooms and schools where every student has access to an individual device for instructional purposes. Laptops, iPads, and Chromebooks, for example, proliferate school technology initiatives and will continue to do so in the foreseeable future (Morgan, 2014). A portion of the technology initiatives that have brought 1:1 computing into schools have been funded by federal education reform efforts. These reform efforts, specifically the Race to the Top grant program, have provided millions of dollars to states for school transformation. In order to receive Race to the Top funding, states and districts had to devise a disbursement plan that would target the lowest performing schools in an effort to reform instructional practices and transform student learning (Boser, 2012). With resources to support instructional technology plans school districts recognized the promise of Race to the Top to spur educational innovation for students in the lowest performing schools and potentially affect the educational trajectory for historically marginalized students attending these schools. However, targeted low-performing schools of the Race to the Top program disproportionally serve students who come from lower socio-economic status and students who receive free or reduced-price lunches. The intent of educational reform plans was for low-performing schools to receive educational innovations in order to increase technology access and promote digital equity (Warschauer, Zheng, Niiya, Cotton, & Farkas, 2014). However, because of challenges teachers face when they initially implement technology, many of these schools have not had the learning outcomes that were anticipated.

The infusion of 1:1 technology into K–12 classrooms has necessitated a shift in teachers' thinking concerning both pedagogical practice and student learning. By placing a technological device in the hands of students, the intent is for teachers to be compelled to transition towards a student-centered pedagogy, thus allowing students to become more active in their learning. One-to-one technology also provides students opportunities to acquire critical skills (e.g. creativity, collaboration, and digital literacy) needed for future careers (Pellegrino & Hilton, 2012; Spires, Oliver, & Corn, 2011; Voogt, 2008). However, teachers often struggle to transition from a traditional teacher-directed pedagogy to a technology-infused, student-centered pedagogy.

Integrating technology for instructional purposes presents several challenges for teachers. Specifically, finding time to engage with and explore how to use technology for student-centered instructional purposes is often daunting (Minshew & Anderson, 2015). The current emphasis on student achievement on standardized tests, which leads many teachers to teach to the test, leaves little time for exploring new instructional practices. Teachers often need external support through professional development when initially becoming familiar with and implementing new technology and associated software for instruction. These challenges impact how effective teachers are in integrating student-centered lessons (Penuel, 2006). This is particularly true in the many 1:1 initiatives that have evolved out of school reform measures where teachers are expected to play a key role in the effectiveness of the implementation. These reform efforts have led many teachers to utilize technology as a means of drill-and-practice remediation, in particular with students of color (Staples, Pugach, & Himes, 2005). The technology is new and advanced, but teaching practices remain the same as they were 50 years ago (Vu, McIntyre, & Cepero, 2014), thus negating the innovation.

This study is a part of a larger design-based research project that examined teacher use of iPads at a school that adopted a 1:1 iPad initiative supported by Race to the Top funds. While the purpose of the larger study was to investigate ways in which teachers utilized iPads in instruction across content areas, a need for culturally relevant pedagogy for technology integration emerged as a theme. Culturally relevant pedagogy as defined by Gloria Ladson-Billings (1995) states that teachers must "develop students academically, [have] a willingness to nurture and support students' cultural competence, and ... their critical consciousness" (p. 483).

Culturally relevant pedagogy emerged regarding (1) teacher beliefs about student populations and how these beliefs impact teacher decisions when implementing the 1:1 initiative; and (2) the role of school culture in successful implementation of 1:1 initiatives. Specifically, we focused on the following research questions:

1. How do teachers' perceptions of their students affect integration, or lack of, the iPad in their classroom practice?
2. How do teachers and administrators situate their students within the larger school community?

BACKGROUND

Existing research on 1:1 technology initiatives shows that the initiatives are failing to meet expectations for transformative learning (Murray & Olcese, 2012). Teachers are key components for the success of 1:1 technology initiatives. According to Ifenthaler and Schweinbenz (2013), a majority of teachers are open to integrating 1:1 devices because they recognize that technology would enhance their practice. However, teachers who are not open to integrating technology are generally not confident with their technology skills or their ability to integrate 1:1 devices into their instructional practice (Ifenthaler & Schweinbenz, 2013). Further, how teachers actually integrate technology in the classroom is often dictated by school culture and administrative support (Fleisher, 2012; Greaves, Hayes, Wilson, Gielniak, & Peterson, 2012). These studies found that the more teachers collaborated and supported one another, the more successful those teachers were at implementing technology in their instruction. A logical conclusion could be drawn that the more support teachers receive for technology integration the more likely it is that they will be successful in utilizing the technology in their instructional design.

School culture influences how teachers negotiate technology initiatives in school reform contexts. Reform initiatives with heavy technology components require that the institutions (the schools and their administrations) commit, not only to providing technological resources that are necessary for integration, but also to support and provide structures that will allow teachers to begin to actualize technology use in their instruction. Staples et al. (2005) found that when principals empowered teachers to become technology leaders within their school, the level of curriculum—technology integration increased and technology became a part of the school culture. Conversely, in other studies where principals viewed the technology as an add-on, technology was used less and in more traditional forms (Staples et al., 2005). These outcomes often correlate to the socio-economic status (SES) of the school—the higher the SES, the better and more effective the integration. Warschauer et al. (2014) noted that the discrepancy between schools can be related to the effectiveness of the teacher and the PD support the teachers are provided. They also suggested that the financial burden of not only deploying the technology but also supporting teachers are two reasons that lower SES schools are less effective in regards to technology integration (Warschauer et al., 2014).

When considering teachers as change agents who use technology innovation as a key practice in education reform, the following dimensions must be considered: beliefs, attitudes, or pedagogical ideologies; content knowledge; pedagogical knowledge of instructional practices, strategies, methods, or approaches; and novel or altered instructional resources (Ertmer & Ottenbreit-Leftwich, 2010). Ertmer and Ottenbreit-Leftwich (2010) argued that pedagogical beliefs are the key variable. Hermans, Tondeur, van Braak, and Valcke (2008) found that teachers with constructivist, inquiry-oriented beliefs were more positive towards regular computer integration into their classroom instruction whereas teachers with more didactic or traditional lecture approaches were challenged by technology integration. Belief systems are defined as systems that "consist of an eclectic mix of rules of thumb, generalizations, opinions, values, and expectations grouped in a more or less structured way" (Hermans et al., 2008, p. 1500). Teacher beliefs are found to predict subsequent action (Haney, Lumpe, Czerniak, & Egan, 2002). Furthermore, teacher beliefs are heavily influenced by the subject and school culture in which they participate (Ertmer & Ottenbreit-Leftwich, 2010). Using the framework of teacher beliefs and how these impact pedagogical decisions and implementation, we will illuminate the challenges faced by teachers and how culturally relevant pedagogy could support teachers in implementing 1:1 technology in the classroom.

SCHOOL, STUDENT AND TEACHER CONTEXT

Caldwell Middle School,[1] the participating school in this study, received Race to the Top funds in order to utilize technology to improve student academic performance. The influx of technology at the school changed its distinction from a neighborhood school to a 1:1 Technology Magnet middle school. Caldwell Middle School is similar to most other schools receiving Race to the Top funding—it is an urban, Title I school, serving a population that consists mainly of students from low SES households. Caldwell also serves mainly students of color; the demographic profile at the time of this study consisted of the following: White, 8%; African American, 66%; Asian, 3%; Hispanic, 21%; Native American, 2%; and Multiracial, 2%. Eighty-percent of the students received free or reduced-price lunch, with 11% designated as having limited English proficiency, and 19% with disabilities.

Teachers and students at Caldwell Middle School had access to the 1:1 iPads for two years prior to our research team creating a partnership with the school. Teachers had experienced countless "one-shot" professional development (PD) workshops that introduced them to general apps such as Google docs, Quizlet, iMovie, and Wordle. These single-exposure PD sessions occurred during teacher planning periods, faculty meetings, and teacher workdays. With the help of the principal, four teachers were selected for initial phase of our partnership. The four participating teachers were members of a sixth-grade team of teachers and represented the four main subject areas taught in middle school: English-language arts, social studies, science, and math. We will focus the bulk of this chapter on the math and science teachers. Isabell, the math teacher, was a white female in her late 20s who had five years of teaching experience. Isabell was in her second year at Caldwell at the time of the study; she had previously taught for three years in the New York City public school system. Jake, the science teacher, was a white male in his mid-50s who had over 10 years of teaching experience, with 5 of those years being at Caldwell middle school.

Data points for the initial phase of our study included an interview with each teacher and multiple classroom observations that occurred periodically throughout the academic year. The beginning phase of the study was designed for researchers and participating teachers to become comfortable with one another and to observe how technology was being used during instruction. As time progressed, teachers and researchers began to design technology-integrated lessons together in attempt to model with teachers how technology could be used for a variety of instructional purposes.

FINDINGS

The main goal of our study was to examine how teachers utilized 1:1 technology for instructional practices and to provide teachers with various forms of support as they attempted to use the iPad for student-centered instruction. Upon entering the school and observing our participating teachers, we became aware of other challenges that the teachers faced beyond the introduction of 1:1 technology. The school culture, with a focus on improving student test scores, encouraged many teachers to have a deficit view of their students. Several administrative mandates, such as using Quizlet for test prep, had been placed upon teachers and students in an effort to improve student-testing outcomes. There was a prevailing notion throughout the school that the iPads were the key to student behavior and engagement. Since the iPads were a new addition to the school, several teachers felt that the technology could engage students in learning, whereas, prior to the introduction of the iPads, students seemed disengaged with course content.

Yet, two of our participating sixth grade teachers took a different approach with their students, and this impacted how they used the iPad in their classroom as well as how they viewed their students. Isabell, the math teacher, had mixed feelings about the use of technology to control student behavior and increase student engagement. She stated in her interview:

> It engages them more so than you would … but we are going to have behavior issues in our class regardless. Because most of our kids are great and even the kids that misbehave are great, but they're gonna do it whether they have the iPad or not. Just one day they might not be feeling it. But do I see how it has the potential to limit some behavior issues? Yes, because if they are engaged by the technology then they're not gonna feel the need to act out as much. But do I think it will eliminate everything? *No.*

Isabell was skeptical of the iPad as the key to her issues in the classroom. This may be due to how Isabell worked to develop relationships with her students. We noted that she took time to get to know her students on a more personal level, listening to them when they needed someone to talk to. During classroom observations throughout the school year, students seemed to act differently in Isabell's classroom compared to other classes. Students were more attentive and engaged. Students took directives and followed through with their actions in Isabell's class whereas this was not always the case with the other sixth grade teachers on Isabell's team. Student cooperativeness was not because Isabell had engaging technology enhanced lessons—most were teacher centered and used direct instruction—but because of the way she interacted with the students in and out of the classroom, taking a personal interest in their well-being. Isabell engaged in what Ladson-Billings would call *humanizing interactions* (1994). Isabell had a genuine interest in her students' lives and demonstrated on multiple occasions that she cared for their well-being. She was invested in student success both academically and socially, which proved to impact classroom behavior and engagement more so than did the presence of 1:1 technology.

Our research team met several times with Isabell and attempted to develop student-centered math lessons that engaged students with the iPads in a more exploratory way. An example activity was to use the camera feature of the iPad to have students capture angles they saw in everyday life. Students would then use a protractor app to measure the angles, and identify the type of angle they had captured. During our planning sessions, Isabell noted that she liked the idea of students being able to use the 1:1 aspects of the technology more in her math class. She indicated in her interview that she struggled with using the iPads for teaching math. She stated in her interview:

> I see how the other content teachers can use the iPad to teach, but math is different. Technology is difficult to use in math class because the students need to work out the problems and I really do not see a reason why the iPad needs to be used every day.

Isabell struggled to move past a traditional view of math education and did not use the 1:1 iPads in her class. The school administration, however, had established a policy that the iPad had to be used every day in every class. Isabell indicated that this policy felt restricting and did not fit with her beliefs about math instruction.

Isabell's apathy toward the integration of the iPad into her math instruction could be attributed, in part, to her struggle with the school culture, administrative pressures to use the iPad, lack of professional development, and the administration's perception of the iPad as the solution to student behavior. Isabell's own personal beliefs about teaching were what drove her to direct instruction. This was reinforced because the school culture affirmed her insecurities with technology through mandated use without content-focused PD or connection to innovative teacher practices with the technology. Spires et al. (2011) noted that teachers need PD that not only introduces them to the new technology but also identifies relevant ways the technology can be incorporated into specific content. Without adequate content-driven support, teachers are not likely to utilize the technology in their instructional practice. It could be inferred that Isabell felt that her current teacher-directed pedagogy, combined with elements of culturally relevant teaching, was more effective than the iPads.

Another way in which Isabell implemented culturally relevant teaching was through creating a classroom that personified a community of learners; she often put students in small groups to work through math problems and had students lead class discussions. Isabell also encouraged students to help one another understand how to work through the problem as opposed to just telling each other the correct answer. Isabell's classroom culture empowered students to be in charge of their own learning and understanding of mathematical concepts, which is another aspect of creating a community of learners. These actions reflect Ladson-Billings (1995) observations of culturally relevant teaching that emphasize the social relations among students and between students and teachers.

The science teacher, Jake, initially did not display aspects of culturally relevant teaching and reserved the majority of his technology use for direct instruction. In our initial interview Jake made comments such as "this particular population is not so interested in learning content as much as they are in learning drama." Jake perpetuated a deficit view of his students initially and subsequently had low academic and behavioral expectations for them. This is in contrast to Ladson-Billings' (1995) observations of teachers who utilized culturally relevant teaching when working in classrooms predominately filled with African American students. Ladson-Billings (1995) identified these teachers as believing that all students were capable of academic success.

When our research team suggested a student-centered iPad lesson that had students collecting information from around the school, Jake was hesitant and indicated that he was not sure it would work. Despite his hesitations Jake allowed the research team to co-teach a science lesson in his classroom on the topic of sound. Students, Jake, and research team members used the iPads to collect sound data from all over the school. Upon returning the classroom, students compiled their collected data, analyzed it, and engaged in lively discussions about conclusions they could draw based on their evidence. After nearly every class period during our observations of the lesson, Jake made comments about how engaged students were, how there were few behavior problems, and that the students were coming up with great ideas concerning the data they collected. Jake's comments about students indicated a slight shift in his perception of what the students were capable of accomplishing. He saw that all students in his class were capable and eager learners, and that, when given the opportunity, could engage collaboratively to discuss science. Upon subsequent visits to Jake's classroom to observe, it was noted that students were taking a more active role in their learning. Jake was using the 1:1 technology more frequently in student-centered ways such as having students create interactive concept-maps that displayed their individual understanding of a science topic.

Believing that students are capable learners is important for integrating 1:1 technology. The 1:1 technology allows students to be more autonomous and responsible for their own learning. This requires teachers to believe that students can be academically successful, which is a small, yet essential part of culturally relevant teaching. Ladson-Billings (1995) also emphasized social relations that teachers create among students that aid teachers in engaging in culturally relevant teaching. Ladson-Billings (1995) observed teachers creating communities of learners by encouraging students to work collaboratively and for students to share their individual knowledge with the group. In Jake's case, once he realized that students could work collaboratively and engage in discussion, his view of how he could utilize the iPads in his classroom began to change.

Both Isabell and Jake displayed different aspects of culturally relevant teaching in their classrooms. Isabell was already exhibiting elements of caring and perceived her students as being successful in math. This was demonstrated by her actions towards students and in the way she approached conversations with her students. Yet, Isabell struggled to use the iPad for math instruction with her students and maintained a teacher-centered pedagogy. Isabell's perceptions of students were counter to the dominant culture of the school, therefore potentially negatively impacting her ability to view technology as something positive for instruction. Jake, on the other hand, initially did not see his students' potential as science learners. His experience engaging with students during a student-centered, technology-enhanced lesson broadened his perception of his students. It encouraged him to view his students as capable of being successful in science and as learners in general.

IMPLICATIONS AND CONSIDERATIONS FOR FUTURE PRACTICE

A number of factors created substantial roadblocks for teachers as they tried to integrate technology for transformative learning experiences. While the lack of relevant and sustained PD was a determining factor, the school culture proved just as detrimental to the success of the 1:1 initiative. The preliminary findings suggest that school culture and teacher beliefs have tremendous impact on whether a school transformation effort has a chance to succeed.

While Ertmer and Ottenbreit-Leftwich (2010) suggested that pedagogical beliefs are the most important dimension on the continuum of change in educational reform, the discoveries made while conducting this larger study suggest that other dimensions are at play and warrant consideration, particularly since schools with high minority enrollment and high poverty schools are often at the center of such school reform efforts. Teacher content, pedagogical, and technological knowledge may have little impact on student learning when teacher attitude and beliefs contribute to a school culture that does not believe its population of students actually deserves rigorous curriculum that is innovative and uses 21st century tools and technology. The real reform must take place along these dimensions.

Simply providing the resources for the technology and cursory professional development do not address latent attitudes and beliefs teachers harbor about the population they teach. In such marginalized communities, no amount of technology or resources will change teaching and learning if the teachers do not believe that the students can actually learn with the technology and if the school culture does not recognize its population as learners who can "handle" a rigorous curriculum. Our findings about teacher expectations and beliefs are supported by other research findings that suggest teachers generally do hold different expectations for minority students, thus affecting student achievement and the types of activities students are presented during instruction (Van den Bergh, Denessen, Hornstra, Voeten, & Holland, 2010). Additionally, Staples et al. (2005) supported this finding by noting that teachers in poorer schools utilize technology to reinforce basic skills instead of supporting higher-order thinking skills.

Finally, Mouza (2011) considered technology initiatives in urban schools examining teacher efficacy and dilemmas related to implementation of technology initiatives, noting "cultural and organizational context impacted ways in which teachers applied learning from professional development in their teaching practice" (p. 25). The preliminary findings of this study support this assertion and warrant a closer look at such initiatives, particularly in school settings in which iPads and technology innovations are used to change teaching and learning for students in high poverty schools with predominantly minority populations. As school reform efforts are designed to close the ubiquitous achievement gap between racial majority and minority students, ill-designed reform efforts that do not address broader issues about teacher attitudes and beliefs about students will only widen the gulf and push marginalized student populations further behind their peers in a society that demands the skills and dispositions that can be gained from student-centered pedagogy.

CONCLUSION

Closer to the heart of the matter, teachers must first believe in their abilities to plan dynamic and engaging learning experiences that transform schooling for vulnerable students. Teachers must believe in the abilities of their students and value the knowledge that students bring to the classroom. In the case of Jake, students were able to share a multitude of experiences concerning sound and therefore could connect the science of sound to their everyday lives, making the learning experience more meaningful. Second, teachers must think of the technologies as tools that aid student understanding of complex phenomena and concepts, and assist students in communicating their learning and collaboration with other learners as generators of knowledge and not just as consumers of information. Isabell had already created a community of learners in her classroom; she merely needed to see the benefits of including the iPad into her existing practice. Perhaps most importantly, this orientation boosts the teaching and learning from a narrowed focus on tools to a focus on those 21st century skills and dispositions that education reform initiatives purportedly encourage and incentivize through grants like Race to the Top. While this boost in teaching and learning is good for all students, it is absolutely paramount if we are to change the trajectory of education for vulnerable populations of students disproportionately impacted by such reform initiatives that embed technology in the first place.

Our findings suggest that culturally relevant teaching is an important component in the implementation of 1:1 technology in the classroom. While our participating teachers did not appear to fully integrate culturally relevant teaching into their classroom practice, when it *was* observed by our team, it was effective in the creation of a classroom environment that supported student learning. These initial observations and our work with teachers prompted our team to add discussion of culturally relevant teaching to our technology PD sessions. In the PD and through the discussions that resulted, we used culturally relevant teaching to emphasize to our teachers that: (1) students in their classrooms were capable of engaging in student-centered learning; and (2) students content knowledge would improve given these opportunities. Additionally, we emphasized the role of students' prior knowledge in developing their conceptual understanding of disciplinary content. Acknowledging these lived experiences and connecting them to their classroom learning allows students to engage in learning that is both relevant and meaningful.

NOTE

1. School name and teacher names are pseudonyms.

REFERENCES

Boser, U. (2012). Race to the Top: What have we learned from the states so far? A state-by-state evaluation of Race to the Top performance. Center for American Progress. Retrieved from https://www.americanprogress.org/issues/education/reports/2012/03/26/11220/race-to-the-top-what-have-we-learned-from-the-states-so-far/

Ertmer, P. A., & Ottenbreit-Leftwich, A. T. (2010). Technology change: How knowledge, confidence, beliefs, and culture intersect. *Journal of Research on Technology in Education, 42*(3), 255–284, doi: 10.1080/15391523.2010.10782551

Fleischer, H. (2012). What is our current understanding of one-to-one computer projects: A systematic narrative research review. *Educational Research Review, 7*(2), 107–122.

Greaves, T., Hayes, J., Wilson, L., Gielniak, M., & Peterson, R. (2012). *Revolutionizing education through technology: The project RED roadmap for transformation.* Retrieved from http://www.iste.org/learn/publications/books/projectred

Haney, J. J., Lumpe, A. T., Czerniak, C. M., & Egan, V. (2002). From beliefs to actions: The beliefs and actions of teachers implementing change. *Journal of Science Teacher Education, 13*(3), 171–187.

Hermans, R., Tondeur, J., van Braak, J., & Valcke, M. (2008). The impact of primary school teachers' educational beliefs on the classroom use of computers. *Computers and Education, 51*(4), 1499–1509. doi:10.1016/j.compedu.2008.02.001

Ifenthaler, D., & Schweinbenz, V. (2013). The acceptance of Tablet-PCs in classroom instruction: The teachers' perspectives. *Computers in Human Behavior, 29*(3), 525–534.

Ladson-Billings, G. (1994). *The dreamkeepers: Successful teaching for African-American students.* San Francisco, CA: Jossey-Bass.

Ladson-Billings, G. (1995). Toward a theory of culturally relevant pedagogy. *American Educational Research Journal, 32*(3), 465–491.

Minshew, L. M., & Anderson, J. L. (2015). Teacher self-efficacy in 1:1 iPad integration in middle school science and math classrooms. *Contemporary Issues in Technology and Teacher Education, 15*(3), 334–367.

Morgan, H. (2014). iPad programs could lead to a bright future for schools. *New Horizons for Learning, 11*(1), 1–5.

Mouza, C. (2011). Promoting urban teachers' understanding of technology, content, and pedagogy in the context of case development. *Journal of Research on Technology Education, 44*(1), 1–29.

Murray, O. T., & Olcese, N. R. (2012). Teaching and learning with iPads, ready or not? *TechTrends, 55*(6), 42–48.

Pellegrino, J. W., & Hilton, M. L. (Eds.). (2012). *Education for life and work: Developing transferable knowledge and skills in the 21st century.* Washington, DC: National Academies Press. Retrieved from http://www.nap.edu/catalog.php?record_id=13398

Penuel, W. R. (2006). Implementation and effects of one-to-one computing initiatives: A research synthesis. *Journal of Research on Technology in Education, 38*(3), 329–348.

Spires, H. A., Oliver, K., & Corn, J. (2011). The new learning ecology of one-to-one computing environments: Preparing teachers for shifting dynamics and relationships. *Journal of Digital Learning in Teacher Education, 28*(2), 63–72.

Staples, A., Pugach, M. C., & Himes, D. J. (2005). Rethinking the technology integration challenge: Cases from three urban elementary schools. *Journal of Research on Technology in Education, 37*(3), 285–311.

Van den Bergh, L., Denessen, E., Hornstra, L., Voeten, M., & Holland, R. W. (2010). The implicit prejudiced attitudes of teachers: Relations to teacher expectations and the ethnic achievement gap. *American Educational Research Journal, 47*(2), 497–527.

Voogt, J. (2008). IT and the curriculum processes: Dilemmas and challenges. In J. Voogt & G. Knezek (Eds.), *International handbook of information technology in primary and secondary education* (pp. 117–132). New York, NY: Springer.

Vu, P., McIntyre, J., & Cepero, J. (2014). Teachers' use of the iPad in classrooms and their attitudes toward using it. *Journal of Global Literacies, Technologies, and Emerging Pedagogies, 2*(2), 58–76.

Warschauer, M., Zheng, B., Niiya, M., Cotton, S., & Farkas, G. (2014). Balancing the one-to-one equation. Equity and access in three laptop programs. *Equity & Excellence in Education, 47*(1), 46–62. doi:10.1080/10665684.2014.866871

What's Science Got To Do with It?

Possibilities for Social Justice in Science Classroom Teaching and Learning
8th–9th Grade

ALEXIS PATTERSON, DEB MORRISON, AND
ALEXANDRA SCHINDEL

As science teachers and teacher educators we have often experienced looks of confusion from other teachers and researchers when we talk about social justice teaching and learning in K–12 science classrooms. Typical of the queries we receive is: *What's science got to do with it?* Social studies or English seem to provide "natural" settings in schools for exploring social justice issues in the curriculum, but science is thought to be objective, free from the lens of political and ideological contexts and thus free from the need to consider how social justice intersects with science teaching and learning. However, science is anything but objective, instead being situated in participants' particular standpoints (Harding, 1986). Thus school science is certainly not objective or neutral in any way and is thus not free from the need to question curricular matters (Horton & Freire, 1990). In this chapter, we present narrative examples of social justice in science from our own practices as teachers and researchers to help educators envision transformative and justice-centered science teaching and learning. Specifically, we question: What does it mean to critically "read science" and "read the world with science" through teaching practices and learning experiences within science? We specifically include examples that support engaging students in scientific practices that are supported by the Next Generation Science Standards (NGSS)—notably, analyzing data, identifying patterns, and constructing evidence-based arguments—to demonstrate how social justice science can be grounded in deep engagement with scientific learning and relevant to current teaching contexts.

CONCEPTUAL FRAMING: SOCIAL JUSTICE SCIENCE EDUCATION

Theories of justice examine the conditions of quality of life and equality through the lens of the least advantaged, explore identity and positionality within historically situated and cultural contexts, and suggest ways to both confront and seek redress for injustices. Achieving social justice requires deliberate reflection on the social, cultural, historical, structural and political power relationships that cause oppression and diminish opportunities for students to flourish, particularly within colonized communities and land and among communities marginalized from full participation in science (e.g. youth, Indigenous peoples, communities of color, (dis) abled bodies, non-heteronormative sexualities) (Wheeler-Bell, 2014). Because injustice and oppression exist within schools—such as through exploitation, marginalization, powerlessness, cultural domination, and violence (e.g. through underrepresentation of cultural or ethnic communities represented in curriculum materials; see Young, 1990)—we consider how science education in schools may be differently and justly enacted to create socially transformative school science. We have found that, as science educators and researchers, these conceptions of justice help us to consider our own positions and interactions within the complexity of teaching and researching within K–12 schools.

In conceiving of ways to put social justice into practice within science education, we draw heavily from action-oriented goals of social transformation put forth by Paulo Freire (1970), who linked literacy and learning with critical understandings of the sociopolitical, cultural, and historical conditions of the world. Our goal is for students to use science learning for personally and/or publicly transformative actions, such as through questioning their views of science and scientists, as we describe below.

SCIENCE DISCIPLINARY CONTEXT

Drawing upon Freire, we explored multiple ways in which we "read the world" through our science learning activity. We have parsed Freire's (1970) lens of reading (i.e. comprehending the world and its injustices as they exist) in two ways: our explorations of how students and teachers "read science" and how they "read the world with science." In both instances we expand our thinking through detailed examples of science teaching and learning drawn from K–12 science contexts.

In thinking about what it means to "read science," we explore how students and teachers in science critically question who engages in science, what counts as science, and how science is done. If we accept that all activity is cultural (Rogoff, 2003) and thus science is a cultural activity (Tobin, 2006), then we must also understand that science—including all its participants, knowledge and practices—is always engaged in from a particular standpoint (Harding, 1986). Thus we need to ask the questions: Who is constructing this knowledge? And whose science are we learning? (Harding, 1991).

Additionally, we demonstrate how students and teachers "read the world with science," or leverage science understandings to examine power inequities in the world around them. Freire (1970) highlights how objects existed but were in the periphery or not yet "apprehended" by the individual. However, students' awareness is raised through problem posing education. Freire (1970) stated:

> That which had existed objectively but had not been perceived in its deeper implications (if indeed it was perceived at all) begins to "stand out," assuming the character of a problem and therefore of challenge. Thus, men and women begin to single out elements from their "background awareness" and to reflect upon them. These elements are now objects of their consideration, and, as such, objects of their action and cognition. (p. 83)

We argue that providing students with relevant and justice-oriented science instruction allows students to read information in the world that was always present, but not apprehended, using science as an analytic tool that inspires action. Examples from prior research suggest that justice-centered science roots learning about scientific concepts in youth's communities, concerns, and in relevant scientific issues. It further suggests that it is particularly powerful when the community's or the youth's concerns are the catalyst for their science learning (Morales-Doyle, 2015). This provides youth with opportunities to examine and critique power inequities in the world around them (Schindel Dimick, 2016) and to develop as "community science experts" who can engage their science "expertise and connections to engage community members and take action on local issues" (Calabrese Barton, Birmingham, Sato, Tan, & Calabrese Barton, 2013, p. 26).

Additional descriptive examples of reading the world through science can be found in *Rethinking Schools* publications (Dean, 2014; Lindahl, 2012; Zaccor, 2016). In one classroom-based example, Lindahl (2012) and her students drew on statistics from national and intercultural cancer databases to help students see how corporate and government policies, pollution, and racism play a role in the disparities of incidences of cancer and mortality rates across low-income communities and communities of color. She contended this would "arm [her] students with the tools and knowledge to face this disease and to consider the kind of social changes necessary to address both its causes and effects" (p. 16). As these examples begin to demonstrate, reading the world with science occurs when students utilize science learning to better understand inequities and how to counteract them.

RESEARCH CONTEXTS

In this work we used a multiple case study approach (Merriam, 1998) to examine examples of social justice science teaching and learning in varied contexts. This approach is in keeping with our theoretical framing which guides us to examine multiple perspectives on the construction of scientific knowledge and engagement in scientific activity (Harding, 1986, 1991). The two cases were chosen from our research to illustrate the conceptual ideas we explicate as aspects of social justice science teaching. The first case study was analyzed using a critical ethnographic approach (Carspecken, 1996). The second case study was a part of a larger qualitative study that used ethnographic methods including participant observations, audio and video recordings, and semi-structured interviews to collect the data (Bogdan & Bicklen, 2007). To ensure readability, each context is described in more detail when the cases are introduced.

SOCIAL JUSTICE SCIENCE TEACHING EXAMPLES

While research literature is somewhat thin in providing practitioners with examples of social justice science teaching, there is a rich history of such work in practice. Before going into examples drawn from our own practice, we want to acknowledge the constant efforts of some educators, not often documented, to improve the learning opportunities for youth who are historically marginalized in science learning contexts.

Reading Science

In thinking about how students and teachers can "read science," we consider three central concepts: who engages science, what counts as science, and how science is done. In classroom work, these three concepts can be thought of as work we do as educators around science identity development, science curriculum, and the practices of science. Each of these aspects of being able to "read science" are deeply subjective and situated in the power structures of our society; however, paradoxically they are thought to be power neutral by many educators, policymakers and community members (Eisenhart & Finkel, 1998; Hodson, 2003). We will examine several examples to highlight the non-neutral nature of coming to "read science."

Who Engages in Science. In working with students around the issue of who does science, they often feel that it is someone other than themselves. Thus in science learning settings, an important consideration is science identity development. Research has described science identity development in terms of discursive development with scientific literacy (Brown, Reveles, & Kelly, 2005) and through the social reinforcement of seeing oneself as a legitimate science community participant (Carlone & Johnson, 2007). To further examine this issue, we explore an example based in critical pedagogy, where students engaged in a critical analysis of "Who's a scientist?", examining what images influence our own identities and stereotypes of participation in science.

Many science teachers may be familiar with the "Who's a scientist?" activity. Here we asked middle school science students in a central U.S. context, which we refer to as Mountain Middle School's Science Community, to read more deeply into their initial work to examine and deconstruct stereotypes of who engages in science. The case study of Mountain Middle School's Science Community was constructed from ethnographic field notes, and teaching and learning artifacts collected over the course of two years by one of the authors who was a teacher-researcher in this location. The teacher was a white, middle class female who was multilingual and an immigrant. The students were diverse in terms of linguistic aptitudes, ability challenges, racial positioning, and economic lived experiences.

The "Who's a scientist?" activity was done near the beginning of the school year, after students had completed a number of activities to build a classroom culture for their science learning community.[1] All students were seated in table teams, to foster talk around their science thinking. The first part of the activity involved students drawing a science setting that addressed three questions: *What does a scientist look like? Where do scientists work?* and *What tools/resources do scientists use?* Students were encouraged to talk with their classmates as they drew. The teacher spent time talking with each group about their drawings to address the questions. This activity often ends here or with an all-class discussion that illustrates common visions or stereotypes present in the drawings; however, in the case of Mountain Middle School's Science Community, students were asked to push their thinking further, to actively engage in understanding implicit bias and to re-envision an alternative for their understanding of who can engage in science.

To this end, students participated in the science practices of data analysis and argumentation with evidence by posting their pictures on a wall and then, as a group, examining the "data" of the students' drawings for patterns and outliers. Students immediately saw common trends and started vocalizing them. To facilitate shared thinking, one of the students created a list of the observations. Things they noticed included that the scientists were mostly men, white, at lab benches, inside, using beakers, and finally that text, if there was any, was in English. Scientists in the images were almost always working alone. Outliers included scientists who were of color, working in outdoor locations, and using tools other than chemistry beakers. Also rare was youth engaged in scientific activity.

After finding these patterns and outliers, the students talked about why they had this shared vision of science activity. Did this reflect reality or was it a stereotype in our society? How did this shared vision of "scientist" and the "doing of science" limit our own participation and interest in science? What other data could they use to understand participation in science? What was their shared definition of science? Students became excited that maybe science could be something different than what they had envisioned and that maybe they had a place in it. This type of discussion has many paths that it could and should go down.

To foster a different way to "read science" in terms of who enacts science than the common stereotypes, students engaged in a *history of science* project. Each student found a scientist that they identified with in some way. Students wrote a one-page paper that included: biographical information on the scientist, how this person is a scientist (i.e. which definition of science or scientist is being referenced), and why the student cared about and/or identified with this person. The Mountain Middle School's Science Community shared their final versions of their science history narratives in a digital space (this could also be done on a science history wall) and referenced them throughout the year as they participated in learning that connected with these narratives. During initial sharing, students read at least five other papers, and searched for patterns and outliers in the pool of "data" (the stories as data). This allowed students to begin to see that there are different ways to imagine who can engage in science activity.

This activity has a number of important features that expand the way students "read science" in terms of science identity development. Students expand the normative image of who can do science to visions that can include them. This helps to foster science identity development in a culturally congruent way (Ladson-Billings, 1995); students do not need to be someone else to be a scientist. They also begin to understand how the messages they receive everyday construct normative stereotypes and are more aware of constructing counter-narratives to these images by critically questioning why such stereotypes exist (Barton & O'Neill, 2008; Solórzano & Yosso, 2002). Students begin to have an expanded understanding of the activity of science. Beyond their understandings of science, students also begin to see that they hold power in their learning and in the classroom space. They have generated resources for the classroom and for each other's learning. This reorganization of power, in who decides what is included in the curriculum, shifts students from passive participants to active agents in the classroom community (Hand & Taylor, 2008).

What Counts as Science. When we begin to plan learning around science, we start to think about science curriculum. In thinking about how to "read science" through what we bring to our science learning spaces, many educators draw heavily on existing curriculum resources or standards guidance documents that reproduce normative visions of science (Basile & Lopez, 2015; Hurd, 1994; Rodriguez, 2015). However, if we draw on an understanding of science as always from a particular standpoint, then when considering multiple perspectives on any form of knowledge we need to ask the questions: Who is constructing this knowledge? And thus, whose science are we learning? (Harding, 1991).

To explicate this idea of what counts as science, we highlight the work of Canipe and Tolbert (2016) who engaged 9th and 10th grade students in juxtaposing Western science with Indigenous science. In this case, students learned about changes in climate by examining evidence from both perspectives. Students were able to use this type of experience to question who creates knowledge and what knowledge is considered valuable for understanding climate change, how knowledge is legitimated and by whom, and how communities of people and scientists resolve scientific crises using tools and knowledge from multiple sources.

The work of Canipe and Tolbert (2016) illustrated the dynamic nature of what constitutes science. Windschitl (2004) documented several folk theories of science common among science teachers and illustrated that most of the teachers in his study used facts and concepts as objects of instruction. This objectification of knowledge can make the production of knowledge seem static. Yet, this inaccurately portrays how knowledge is (re)created. Freire (1970) described the dialectic of understanding as follows:

> For apart from inquiry, apart from the praxis, individuals cannot be truly human. Knowledge emerges only through invention and re-invention, through the restless, impatient, continuing, hopeful inquiry human beings pursue in the world, with the world, and with each other. (p. 72)

Thus, it is in our ability to learn to "read science" through the constant process of inquiry that we will better understand the world. Students in the Mountain Middle School's Science Community experienced this dynamic nature of knowledge in the examination of data of climate variation in the context of the variable phenomena they investigated. For example, students examining the impact of climate change on crop locations in the United States began to see patterns of crop shifts across locations over years. This data challenged their everyday understanding that particular locations always produced particular crops and showed how shifts in the environment are causing shifts in human activity due to new understandings about temperature and water availability.

Such reading is a human activity that is fundamentally dynamic in nature and should include thinking about how to expand science curriculum with ideas of what counts as science. This approach allows for the integration of history within science content learning while acknowledging the way in which scientific knowledge generation is a social activity engaged in by all people and transmitted through generations in multiple modes. Considering science in this way also allows students and teachers to engage in questions about why particular knowledge is prioritized in the curriculum more than other knowledge, and to interrogate the power dynamics behind curricular resource development. Emphasizing the history of science humanizes the production of science knowledge. This can highlight the way in which power intersects with scientific knowledge generation.

How Science Is Done. Science is done through shared practices that have been developed over time within the larger community of science. While there are many ways of knowing the world, to "read science" is to know the world through two related practices: critical thinking and evidence-based reasoning. Critical thinking, which can also be thought of as critical science literacy, lends itself to an analysis of power (Moje, Collazo, Carrillo, & Marx, 2001). Evidence-based reasoning also has a component of power ascribed to it as a practice, for example what counts as evidence is determined by who has status or power within the scientific community and past precedent on what has been seen as evidence (Aikenhead, 2006). To understand these two practices in the context of science learning, let us turn again to Mountain Middle School's Science Community.

In the spring semester, Mountain Middle School's Science Community members participated in learning around climate science. This topic is often considered to be a controversial topic to teach. Given this, the teacher organized student learning around the practices of critical thinking and evidence-based reasoning to encourage students to "read science" in terms of engaging in authentic science practices while learning about particular aspects of Earth system science. Students began by choosing a topic area within one of four broad constructs. In this way students were able to direct content learning towards their interests within a larger science community organization and around particular themes. For example, a student assigned the general area of ecosystems and may study orca whales because of a family connection to the West Coast. Students were then asked to determine if their topic area was impacted by climate change at all. They had to research climate variations in the particular region that influenced their topic. For example, they may limit the study of orcas to the west coast of British Columbia in Canada and, therefore, had to look up climate variation for that area. So in the case of the orca project, the student would research where orcas lived and identify historic and contemporary population and climate data.

In the process of research, students were asked to interrogate their data and sources by answering questions such as: Who authored the data? What methods of data collection were used? What kinds of errors were present in the data? What data was not included in your research that you thought should have been present and why? And when presenting research information that was not raw data they had to answer questions such as: What claims were made? What kinds of evidence were cited? Was this a primary data source? If not, what primary data sources did they reference to argue their claim? What possible motivations might the authors have had to argue their claim?

During this portion of the project, which included pre-work on climate change and post-work on mitigation and adaptations, students shifted from working in table team cross-theme groups to single-theme working groups. Each table team of four had one student studying each of the four major themes (e.g. ecosystems, agriculture, human health, and extreme weather). No two students in a class would be allowed to choose the same topic within a theme. Table teams were responsible for helping each other with critical thinking and evidence-based reasoning tasks throughout project work, and students were mentored on asking expansive questions to support each other's learning (Michaels & O'Connor, 2012; Michaels, O'Connor, Hall, & Resnick, 2010). Occasionally, students would reorganize for a class period into single-theme working groups to share common findings or support learning within specific themes.

Through participating in these practices of science, students came to understand and experience the collective nature of scientific activity. They learned that science is not a solitary activity but is an age-old form of inquiry in which humans make sense of issues important to them. Thus it is a cultural activity, full of meaning. Students in Mountain Middle School's Science Community found that science became something active and engaging to them when they could read themselves into the activity. Now let us explore how students can take their new understandings of science into the activity of *reading the world with science*.

Reading the World with Science

Science is deeply interwoven in our daily lives: its innovations and technology shape the experiences that we have in our communities. Thus, science knowledge and processes can provide a useful lens to better understand our individual and collective experiences. Indeed, science has been used to justify injustice historically (Brown & Mutegi, 2010) and can be a tool teachers use to highlight present injustice locally and globally (Upadhyay, 2006). For many students, the study of science can feel like the memorization of facts that are unrelated to their lived experiences (Calabrese Barton & Yang, 2000). We argue that by reading the world with science, teachers can increase student interest by making the topics relevant, as well as illustrate how science content knowledge can be applied to their everyday lives (Fusco, 2001).

A unit plan or curriculum that helps students read the world will include two major features: science content instruction and activities that require students to use science knowledge to understand and interpret current events. In addition, many teachers who help their students read the world with science also include an action component. Here, students take steps to address the injustices they have learned about and/or share their scientific knowledge and implications with community members.

We begin by providing illustrations of how students and teachers can read the world with science. This example comes from a recent study conducted in a high school physiology class within the California Bay Area. West Wood High School (WWHS)[2] is a charter school located in a suburban community in the California Bay Area. Although the surrounding community is quite affluent, WWHS serves one of the lowest-income communities in California. The school serves 281 students from predominantly Latinx backgrounds, with some students of African American and Pacific Islander ancestry. The physiology class was comprised of sophomores, with a few juniors and seniors retaking the course. Miss Lui, a second-year teacher at WWHS, taught the course and designed a nutrition unit that helped her students read the world through science.

One of Miss Lui's goals for this unit was to help her students understand the relevancy of nutrition and food options in their community. The unit was grounded in two guiding questions: How can I make sure that my family eats healthily? Why is that important? The students were provided with three lenses to understand the information they collected throughout the unit. The first was the physiological lens which encouraged students to consider how the body works. The second was the sociocultural lens and asked students to think about how their family and/or cultural traditions can influence what they eat. Finally, students were encouraged to consider how the amount of money they have might influence what they eat. This perspective represented the economic lens. These lenses provided students with multiple ways to see the world and helped them understand how science can be mired in politics, power, and injustice.

The first lesson in the nutrition unit asked students to consider how all three lenses worked to shape the experiences of people who live in communities similar to their own. Students were presented with graphs, excerpts from academic articles, and newspaper articles that helped them understand how diseases, poverty, the types of stores within the community, and other factors impact nutrition, as well as the impact of malnutrition on the body. After this initial lesson, students went on to learn about the types of vitamins, minerals, and nutrients within different types of foods through various lab activities. Students were given case studies of fictional diets consumed by WWHS students (these included breakfast, brunch, and lunch). They were asked to outline the nutrients in the food and make recommendations of what the fictional student should eat for dinner in order to have a balanced diet. Students ended the unit by (1) presenting information about important nutrients and minerals, healthy foods, and food-related diseases, and (2) writing a reflection in response to the guiding questions.

Through these activities, Miss Lui's students began to grasp that their bodies required certain nutrients, and they considered how much of those nutrients were in the foods they consumed. Finally, students began to understand that economic status and access to healthy food were correlated with each other. La'a, a sophomore in the physiology class, explained, "Our body is at high risk for disease if you have low income. So, like if people have high income they are able to buy expensive, healthy food ... so people who live in poor neighborhoods are more at risk." Jesus argued that "rich people can buy more healthy stuff, like organic stuff." As students learned about food through these three lenses, they began to utilize their science expertise to make sense of food and health inequities and place these concerns into an understanding of larger systems of oppression. This is a central focus of reading the world through science.

RECOMMENDATIONS FOR FUTURE PRACTICE

Conceptualizing social justice science education through *reading science* and *reading the world through science,* an adaptation of Freire's (1970) notion of *reading the world,* allows us to reframe the possibilities for science learning within formal K–12 contexts. Our examples stem primarily from our teaching and researching experiences in middle and high school settings; yet we believe these examples can be broadly applicable to multiple formal school science contexts, including elementary grades. Given our work, we make the following recommendations for justice-oriented science teaching and learning:

- Engage students in constructing identities of themselves as engaged members of science communities.
- Create counter-narratives against unproductive stereotypes of science and scientists.
- Disrupt power dynamics through student decision-making and by providing opportunities for students to enact their agency in curricular matters.
- Include multiple ways of knowing science within the curricula to alter whose knowledge counts as science.
- Provide students with opportunities to engage in the cultural and social activities of scientific meaning making.
- Engage students in scientific practices supported by NGSS—including analyzing data, identifying patterns, and constructing evidence-based arguments—alongside sociopolitical analysis to support critical consciousness around science issues.

Our hope in expressing our thoughts on social justice science teaching is not to prescribe a way in which such activity should be organized but instead to open and expand space for considering the ways in which such activity could be organized. We encourage teachers to explore the many variations that may come to be seen as social justice science teaching. Such teaching and learning centers students, values and builds upon their everyday experiences, and develops critical literacy practices so essential to effective democratic participation.

NOTES

1. The classroom community building work included relationship building based on respect for differences as resources to support our shared learning, as well as sharing our learning narratives that included both challenges and strengths. Students were beginning to understand that they were going to be asked to constantly examine power in their own histories, present experiences, and future visions within the context of science class.
2. This is a pseudonym used to maintain the anonymity of the high school and all names of participants are also pseudonyms.

REFERENCES

Aikenhead, G. S. (2006). *Science education for everyday life: Evidence-based practice.* New York, NY: Teachers College Press.

Barton, A. C., & O'Neill, T. (2008). Counter-storytelling in science: Authoring a place in the worlds of science and community. In R. Levinson, H. Nicholson, & S. Parry (Eds.), *Creative encounters: New conversations in science, education and the arts* (pp. 138–158). London: Wellcome Trust.

Basile, V., & Lopez, E. (2015). And still I see no changes: Enduring views of students of color in science and mathematics education policy reports. *Science Education, 99*(3), 519–548.

Bogdan, R. C., & Biklen, S. K. (2007). *Qualitative research for education: An introduction to theories and methods.* Boston, MA: Allyn & Bacon.

Brown, B. A., & Mutegi, J. W. (2010). A paradigm of contradictions: Racism and science education. In P. Peterson, E. Baker, & B. McGaw (Eds.), *International encyclopedia of education* (3rd ed., pp. 554–564). Oxford: Elsevier.

Brown, B. A., Reveles, J. M., & Kelly, G. J. (2005). Scientific literacy and discursive identity: A theoretical framework for understanding science learning. *Science Education, 89*(5), 779–802.

Calabrese Barton, A., Birmingham, D., Sato, T., Tan, E., & Calabrese Barton, S. (2013). Youth as community science experts in green energy technology. *Afterschool Matters, 18,* 25–32. Retrieved from http://ecommons.luc.edu/cgi/viewcontent.cgi?article=1082&context=education_facpubs

Calabrese Barton, A. C., & Yang, K. (2000). The culture of power and science education: Learning from Miguel. *Journal of Research in Science Teaching, 37*(8), 871–889.

Canipe, M., & Tolbert, S. (2016). Many ways of knowing: A multilogical science lesson on climate change. *The Science Teacher, 83*(4), 31–35.

Carlone, H. B., & Johnson, A. (2007). Understanding the science experiences of successful women of color: Science identity as an analytic lens. *Journal of Research in Science Teaching, 44*(8), 1187–1218.

Carspecken, P. F. (1996). *Critical ethnography in educational research: A theoretical and practical guide.* New York, NY: Routledge.

Dean, J. (2014). Carbon Matters: Middle school students get carbon cycle literate. *Rethinking Schools, 28*(4). Retrieved from http://www.rethinkingschools.org/archive/28_04/28_04_dean.shtml

Eisenhart, M. A., & Finkel, E. (1998). *Women's science: Learning and succeeding from the margins.* Chicago. IL: University of Chicago Press.

Freire, P. (1970). *Pedagogy of the oppressed.* New York, NY: Continuum.

Fusco, D. (2001). Creating relevant science through urban planning and gardening. *Journal of Research in Science Teaching, 38*(8), 860–877.

Hand, V., & Taylor, E. V. (2008). Culture and mathematics in school: Boundaries between "cultural" and "domain" knowledge in the mathematics classroom and beyond. *Review of Research in Education, 32*(1), 187–240.

Harding, S. G. (1986). *The science question in feminism.* Ithaca, NY: Cornell University Press.

Harding, S. G. (1991). *Whose science? Whose knowledge?: Thinking from women's lives.* Ithaca, NY: Cornell University Press.

Hodson, D. (2003). Time for action: Science education for an alternative future. *International Journal of Science Education, 25*(6), 645–670.

Horton, M., & Freire, P. (1990). *We make the road by walking: Conversations on education and social change.* Philadelphia, PA: Temple University Press.

Hurd, P. D. (1994). New minds for a new age: Prologue to modernizing the science curriculum. *Science Education, 78*(1), 103–116.

Ladson-Billings, G. (1995). Toward a theory of culturally relevant pedagogy. *American Educational Research Journal, 32*(3), 465–491.

Lindahl, A. (2012). Facing cancer: Social justice in biology class. *Rethinking Schools, 26*(4), 14–18.

Merriam, S. B. (1998). *Qualitative research and case study applications in education.* San Francisco, CA: Jossey-Bass Publishers.

Michaels, S., & O'Connor, C. (2012). *Talk science primer.* Cambridge, MA: TERC. Retrieved from https://inquiryproject.terc.edu/shared/pd/TalkScience_Primer.pdf

Michaels, S., O'Connor, M. C., Hall, M. W., & Resnick, L. B. (2010). *Accountable Talk® sourcebook: For classroom conversation that works.* Pittsburgh, PA: University of Pittsburgh Institute for Learning.

Moje, E. B., Collazo, T., Carrillo, R., & Marx, R. W. (2001). "Maestro, what is 'quality'?": Language, literacy, and discourse in project-based science. *Journal of Research in Science Teaching, 38*(4), 469–498.

Morales-Doyle, D. (2015). *Science education as a catalyst for social change? Justice-centered pedagogy in high school chemistry* (Unpublished doctoral dissertation). University of Illinois at Chicago, Chicago, IL.

Rodriguez, A. J. (2015). What about a dimension of engagement, equity, and diversity practices? A critique of the next generation science standards. *Journal of Research in Science Teaching, 52*(7), 1031–1051.

Rogoff, B. (2003). *The cultural nature of human development.* Oxford: Oxford University Press.

Schindel Dimick, A. (2016). Exploring the potential and complexity of critical pedagogy of place in formal science education settings. *Science Education, 100*(5), 814–836.

Solórzano, D. G., & Yosso, T. J. (2002). Critical race methodology: Counter-storytelling as an analytical framework for education research. *Qualitative Inquiry, 8*(1), 23–44.

Tobin, K. (2006). Editorial: Toward a cultural turn in science education. *Cultural Studies in Science Education, 1*(1), 7–10. doi:10.1007/s11422-005-9006-5

Upadhyay, B. R. (2006). Using students' lived experiences in an urban science classroom: An elementary school teacher's thinking. *Science Education, 90*(1), 94–110.

Wheeler-Bell, Q. (2014). A critical pedagogy against consumer capitalism: A normative approach. *Critical Education, 5*(9), 1–16.

Windschitl, M. (2004). Folk theories of "inquiry:" How preservice teachers reproduce the discourse and practices of an atheoretical scientific method. *Journal of Research in Science Teaching, 41*(5), 481–512.

Young, I. (1990). *Justice and the politics of difference.* Princeton, NJ: Princeton University Press.

Zaccor, K. (2016). Lead poisoning: Bringing social justice to chemistry. *Rethinking Schools. 31*(1). Retrieved from http://www.rethinkingschools.org/archive/31_01/31–1_zaccor.shtml

PART FOUR

High School Grades

Justice and Teens: Curricular Approaches to Equity in High School

Secondary students, many on the brink of active political participation, have already begun to interact with the world of social justice. Many engage in social media, at the very least witnessing the daily swarm of debates on topics ranging from immigration to equity for transgender individuals. Some are already active in marches for women's rights or standing up for a local cause at their high schools or in their communities. As future participants in our democracy, it is vital that we ensure our adolescent youth are involved in considering multiple perspectives, debating critical issues (Hess, 2009), and recognizing complicity in oppression (Applebaum, 2001). These students will be the ones who lead our country, lobby for political decisions, and teach the next generations. In these formative years we must impact students' capacity for and confidence in effecting social change.

Because social justice issues do not occur in content areas, it is imperative that we address equity and justice across contexts. Several authors in this section focus on teachers' pedagogies and, through qualitative study, describe the methods by which educators enhance their students' critical consciousness through their disciplinary connections. In Chapter 13, Boyd, Bauermeister, and Matteson analyze a reading project in an English classroom in which students were allowed to select the novels they would read and this helped them become more critical consumers of classroom material. Dyches examines an English Language Arts teacher's approach to fostering her students' sociopolitical consciousness through intertextual connections between poetry and current social movements in Chapter 15.

Parkhouse details the methods that one U.S. History teacher used to balance her students' recognition of oppression with their belief in the potential for change. These methods, detailed in Chapter 17, included noting historic examples of resistance and debunking common misconceptions and simplifications.

Other authors investigate educational opportunities constructed specifically to engage their students with justice, such as Pattison-Meek in Chapter 14, who explores one teacher's formation of a rural-urban intergroup encounter through which rural teenagers actively engaged with immigrant youth. Shuttleworth and Donnelly's Chapter 16 examines the creation of "official knowledge" with Newcomer English-Learners to illustrate a method for introducing such students to the notion of challenging the status quo and engaging in activism. Still others explore how secondary curriculum can be re-structured to reflect more inclusive and critical approaches. Through a Youth Participation Action Research framework in Chapter 18, Gibbs identifies the ways that U.S. history curriculum can center issues of social justice and thereby re-envision standard curriculum. DeMartino and Rusk explore in Chapter 19 a U.S. government classroom to posit methods for integrating students with disabilities into an ethnic studies class and to more deeply consider curricular content as well as co-teaching models. In these chapters, we see not only how teachers work within their classrooms to facilitate students' critical knowledge, but also how they inspire youth to become agents of change in their own worlds. If we are to truly achieve social justice in education, we must include opportunities for activism, especially with those poised to enter their adult lives, so that they can continue such work when they leave our classrooms and become members of our society.

REFERENCES

Applebaum, B. (2010). *Being white, being good: White complicity, white moral responsibility, and social justice pedagogy.* Lanham, MD: Rowan & Littlefield Publishers.

Hess, D. E. (2009). *Controversy in the classroom: The democratic power of discussion.* New York, NY: Routledge.

CHAPTER THIRTEEN

"Project Read Freely"

Using Young Adult Literature to Engender Student Choice in an English Language Arts Classroom
9th Grade

ASHLEY S. BOYD, ALYSSA BAUERMEISTER, AND
HOLLY MATTESON

Sometimes what you really want to do is just pick up a book and read it. Sometimes you don't want to think about 'oh my god why did he kill Lennie. Why would he do that?' You don't want to spend half an hour at 9 o'clock thinking about that. You just want to read.

—OLIVER, STUDENT PARTICIPANT

In his explanation of *aliteracy*, the notion that individuals are capable of reading but choose not to, Donald Gallo (2001) famously wrote, "We are a nation that teaches its children *how* to read in the early grades, then forces them during their teenage years to read literary works that most of them dislike so much that they have no desire whatsoever to continue those experiences into adulthood" (p. 36). His statement echoes research that has shown cumulative declines in students' attitudes towards reading over time, particularly in grades one through six (McKenna, Kear, & Ellsworth, 1995). What is it that is making our students no longer want to read? How can we empower them in a system where most decisions are made for them, where bells dominate their lives, and where curriculum is divided into disciplinary silos that, as a consequence, also separates their interests?

The research described here sought to answer those questions by offering a method for engaging students in reading in a way that attempted to embolden them. Our investigative team was composed of a university-based researcher who works in English Education (Ashley), an English teacher student intern in an initial certification master's program (Alyssa), and an undergraduate English

Education student who served as a research assistant (Holly). Our secondary English language arts teacher intern and her ninth grade students engaged in a reading venture, titled "Project Read Freely," specifically focused on student choice in curricular decisions around the use of young adult literature (YAL). We wanted to develop students' agency, cultivating their identities as *readers* and as individuals with a voice, and not merely performers in an academic milieu. We focused specifically on YAL due to its relevancy to students' lives (Gallo, 2001), documented impact on reading engagement (Ivey & Johnston, 2013; Moje, Overby, Tysvaer, & Morris, 2008), and reflection of content aligned with our social justice goals (Glasgow, 2001). Utilizing YAL as a medium then, we sought to expand traditional curricular and classroom structures to more fully incorporate secondary students as discerning and capable scholars.

Specifically, our guiding research questions were:

1. How can we empower students to make their own curricular choices in a secondary English Language Arts classroom?
2. How do students respond to the implementation of a reading project with an open structure?

We conceptualized this project's relationship to social justice in two ways: first, we sought a more just schooling environment where students were allowed to make content decisions. Scholars have documented the power differentials in schools and classrooms in which curriculum is an entity which the teacher, who is all-knowing, deposits into students' minds (Freire, 1970) and is thus external to the learner (McLaren, 2003). Those who have experimented with student-led curriculum projects noted benefits that relate to social justice, such as cultivating students' critical dispositions (Epstein, 2014) and helping to promote social action (e.g. Morrell & Duncan-Andrade, 2005/2006). Second, we structured (or, rather, un-structured) classroom activities in such a way that students engaged with one another in authentic, critical dialogue about the socially relevant topics raised in the novels they read. Dialogue is central in social justice pedagogies (Freire, 1970; Parsons, 2006). The project design then, as well as the outcomes, aligned with educational goals for social justice in that they empowered students as democratic participants in a social environment.

YOUNG ADULT LITERATURE IN CLASSROOM
CONTEXTS: USES AND ABUSES

To situate the scope of this study, we looked at how YAL has been utilized in classroom practice. Our exploration led us to three primary foci when using YAL in the classroom. First, we found YAL is integrated as a text studied by a whole class in order to supplement and support the requirements of the high school curriculum (Wilder & Teasley, 1998). For instance, Jackett (2007) used *Speak* by Laurie Halse Anderson (2014) to instruct students on literary theories and code-switching to demonstrate intertextual references, helping students gain different perspectives of the text. YAL in the classroom is also implemented as a bridge to canonical texts. This includes relying on common themes to make connections between the two types of texts, thereby making the canon less intimidating (Herz & Gallo, 1996). One example from Herz and Gallo's (1996) work illustrated a teacher's use of *Hamlet* by William Shakespeare (1892) as a complement to *The Chocolate War* by Robert Cormier (2014). Moreover, YAL has been used for independent reading assignments (Groenke & Youngquist, 2011). While these methods are noteworthy for bringing YAL into the classroom, we approached the use of YAL with the goal of disrupting the typical structures of classrooms and curriculum in the descriptions above. That is, in the spirit of Paulo Freire's (1970) work, we sought to liberate students from the traditional structure of school in order to engage their critical literacies.

THEORETICAL FRAMEWORK: LIBERATING THE CURRICULUM

Paulo Freire (1970) posited: "liberating education consists in acts of cognition, not transferals of information" (p. 60). In other words, liberation in education consists of students becoming aware of the world around them and taking a critical approach to learning instead of memorizing static facts and figures. According to Freire (1970), one consequence of the banking concept of education is that it eliminates students' ability to have a stake in their education by removing the opportunity to contribute in the curriculum decision-making process. Thus, students accept their situation as status quo, without a critical consciousness to discern their power. In contrast, a problem-posing approach looks to remove the hierarchy of the teacher-student dichotomy while simultaneously creating consciousness. The goal is to equalize both teacher and student to a place where they learn—and teach—about the world around them from each other.

We placed our study within this paradigm of equalizing education. We were looking to blur the teacher-student dichotomy in pursuit of a liberating education. We focused on breaking current classroom structures to engage students' critical literacies; to challenge and question students' perspectives of the curriculum; to disrupt the traditional (teacher) perspective of educational practice; and to explore the value of YAL in the English classroom. We hoped to teach students the practice of critical literacy by having them question axiomatic curriculum (Behrman, 2006; Campano, Ghiso, & Sanchez, 2013). However, we recognize that our study is not a full liberation—ultimately as teachers in a public school system we retain more power than students. We were not ignorant of the structures in which we resided, but instead hoped to distort the boundaries for students to see that power comes *from somewhere*. We hoped to facilitate their awareness that this power must not be taken for granted, but that it can be questioned and, as a result, students can have a stake in curriculum development.

THE PROCESS: IMPLEMENTING CHOICE AND AUTONOMY

The "Survey to Literature" class in which this study occurred was at a public high school in a university town and was composed of 29 ninth-grade students. There were 14 male students in the class and 15 female. Most of the students identified as White, with two identifying as African American and one as Asian. The course provided students with an overview of literature while building baseline skills of writing and grammar. The conventionally-used texts were primarily canonical and aligned with the content structure of the other ninth grade courses at the high school.

The first step of our process was using the online survey software program Qualtrics© to administer a survey to discover students' current profiles as readers and to solicit their interests in reading. To develop this, we modified both an existing reading attitudes survey tool (Wigfield & Guthrie, 1997) and an existing interest survey (Lesesne, 2005). Our initial survey was a thirty-item questionnaire using two personal identification questions. It included 25 Likert scale prompts including those such as "You read a lot," from which students selected options from the rankings of "strongly agree" to "strongly disagree," and open-ended prompts asking student to offer additional information on themselves and their desired genre for reading. Finally, we asked students a rank-order question with genres of YAL. The seven categories offered to students were based on our research on the most popular categories of YAL: relationships, dystopia, fantasy, sports, historical fiction, realistic fiction, and social justice.

Next, we compiled the survey results to examine students' rankings and to form reading groups of three to four members. Student groups were initially determined based on the genre interest students conveyed on their surveys and more definitively narrowed based on personality and the cooperative potential of each group member as determined by Alyssa (the student intern). We then developed a *short list* of texts for YAL novels in each genre, and each group chose one novel from a catalog (that we supplemented with book cover images and written descriptions). As a research team, we endeavored to choose contemporary, recently published novels written by established authors in the YAL community. In the end, each group was given the chance to choose from two novels and determined their book choice by popular vote. We utilized grant funds[1] to purchase the books.

For the remainder of the project, we fashioned loosely structured individual and group opportunities for responding to the reading. We wanted to include discussions that mirrored real-world scenarios for reflecting on reading with peers, such as book clubs. Therefore, students met to discuss their books once per week in class. We intentionally allowed students to individually determine how many pages they read in the time between book group meetings rather than assigning specific page goals for students. Unlike traditional *literature circles*, we did not assign rigid roles for students or require that they select page number goals as a group. The unit stretched over approximately five weeks, during which several students finished their initial books and read other novels.

Prior to discussion group meetings, students were provided with "Daily Starter" handouts that asked them to not only share how much of their novels they had read, but to disclose specific details about their feelings about the novels, the authors, and reading in general so that we could track their responses throughout. These were completed independently before group assemblies. Some of the questions varied from meeting to meeting, but all were designed to encourage students to think specifically about their reactions to their novels as a whole rather than solely to the content of what they had read, again to include the students as democratic, knowing participants and readers. One of our concluding questions asked students to analyze whether the books were successful in their pursuit to appeal to young adults in general and to each student as a young adult, personally.

Finally, students completed a post-reading survey at the end of the study that was similar to our first questionnaire but slightly modified. Through this second iteration, we wanted to note any changes in students' reading attitudes and to examine their qualitative responses to the project. Questions encouraged students to answer based on their personal connection with the project as well as the books they read. The post-reading survey contained the same 25 Likert-scale items as the initial survey but contained different open-response prompts including: "What have you learned about yourself as a reader through this project?" and "What feedback can you offer about the structure of the reading project?" We also devoted an entire class period to a reflective whole-class discussion on students' thoughts on both the project and reading in general. Students were asked to share things they liked about the project in addition to areas that could be refined and altered. This de-briefing time was also meant to further cultivate students' critical literacies by giving them a voice in curriculum and illustrating that they are allowed to have opinions about what they read and classroom activities.

METHODS: EXAMINING THE CLASSROOM CONTEXT

For our purposes here, we analyzed the data qualitatively using the software HyperResearch©. Data included the students' qualitative responses to the pre-and post-surveys, their "Daily Starter" sheets, fieldnotes from classroom observations by Ashley, students' responses to book-related activities in class, Alyssa's daily reflections, and the transcript of the debriefing session at the end of the reading project. We first engaged in open coding of each data point separately (Strauss & Corbin, 1998). We then used those codes to generate categories and concepts, and from these we developed larger themes (Charmaz, 2006) from across the data set.

We also examined the students' verbal and written responses through a discursive lens (Fairclough, 1995; Tannen, 1989), noting particularly how they responded to the texts and the project. We were interested particularly in the topics of students' conversations in class, how they framed discourse around specific issues, and where silences existed (Huckin, 2002). Since the conversations were largely left unstructured by the teacher, we felt these would be illustrative of students' genuine reactions to the texts. From this analysis, we identified emergent themes that primarily spoke to our second research question, noting how the students responded in nuanced ways to the reading project. In this chapter, we share two of the major findings we identified from the data set: slight shifts in students' identities as readers and the prevalence of organic conversations in classroom discussions that resulted from both structured and unstructured activities.

PATTERNS AND OUTCOMES: STUDENT RESPONSES TO READING FREELY

Effects on Reader Profiles: Opening Spaces for Reading for Pleasure

Through our analysis of the students' reader profiles in the Likert scale portion of the survey, we did not find radical changes in students' attitudes toward reading. For the most part, those students who identified as readers prior to the YAL unit continued to identify as such, and students who did not like reading maintained similar sentiments. While this at first seemed defeating, we were buoyed by slight shifts in student responses that indicated some effect and spoke to our larger purpose of blurring the lines in traditional academic spaces and, especially, to creating a more authentic, real world experience in which participants talk and share their reading.

For instance, Oliver,[2] a White male student, initially identified himself as a reader. In the pre-project survey, he disagreed with statements such as "You feel you have better things to do than read" and "You are willing to tell people that you do not like to read." He agreed with statements including, "You have a lot of books in your room at home" and "You love to read," In the open-response comment section, however, Oliver provided a more nuanced portrait of himself as a reader, avowing, "I like reading simply for fun. If there is a book that I really like, I will finish it quickly, and move on to the next book. However, if it's a book I don't really like, it might take me a while to get through it." Although he classified himself as a pleasure reader, he nonetheless affirmed his affinity for reading.

Based on his genre preferences, Oliver was assigned to the fantasy group, which chose *Throne of Glass* (Maas, 2012) as their focal text. Flying through this book the first weekend after it was assigned, Oliver read four total books during the time of the project. In one of his "Daily Starter" assignments, Oliver shared that he "literally couldn't stop reading" and was "up until 1:45 am on Sunday reading my book." Alyssa reported that he often came in before and after school to chat with her about the book he was currently reading in the project.

While his reader profile remained strong, then, there were some positive shifts in his reader identity markers that warrant attention. He changed, for instance, his feelings about the statement, "You like to read a book whenever you have free time" from "undecided" to "agree" as well as "You like to stay at home and read" from "disagree" to "undecided." Perhaps most noteworthy to our examination here, his feelings about the item, "You like to share books with your friends" altered from "undecided" to "agree." In the comment section at the end of the post-reading survey, Oliver shared, "I learned that I actually missed reading in big amounts and I am glad that I got the chance to read a lot again." Even if, perhaps, his notions of a reader identity did not shift drastically, by appealing to Oliver as a pleasure reader, we were able to blur the lines of in-school reading with reading that, to him, was engaging. Highlighting the import of student interest, he noted, "I liked that the genres were exactly the ones I like. It was very exciting reading them and I couldn't put the books down."

Another student, Harley, a White female, revealed similar minor shifts in her reading persona. Alyssa shared about Harley, "Originally I think she would have identified as not a reader, because she said it was always really difficult for her to find good books to read." Although part of this observation was confirmed in Harley's pre-project comments in which she stated, "I tend to take a little bit of a longer time reading a book but when I finish I am able to remember most small and important details throughout the book," the summation of Harley's selections in the pre-reading survey actually identified her as a reader. For instance, she agreed with statements like "You love to read," and disagreed with items such as "You seldom read except when you have to do a book report." From these responses, we were led to believe that Harley maintained an affinity for reading prior to our project.

Harley most desired to read books with relationships as their focus. Her indications were used to place her in the corresponding group, which chose to read Rainbow Rowell's (2013) *Eleanor & Park*. Like Oliver, Harley was captivated by her book and reported in a "Daily Starter" activity, "I didn't want to set it down and I liked that." Later she wrote that she "enjoyed it [the book] more because

I just wanted to finish it." Harley read a total of two books over the course of the project.

Also similar to Oliver, slight modifications in Harley's pre-and post-reading surveys indicated small shifts in her views. For instance, her response to, "You like to read a book whenever you have free time" changed from "undecided" initially to "agree" after the project, and "It takes you a long time to read a book" from "agreed" to "undecided." This is significant given her initial concerns about the time it took her to read a book. That she experienced a shift here, combined with her enthusiasm for the books, points to a relationship between interest and endurance; perhaps having an affinity for the topic of the book and finding it engaging led to her being able to finish faster. Harley confirmed this in the post-reading survey, disclosing, "I liked this reading project a lot more than normal because the books were geared towards our generation and they made me want to read instead of feeling like I have to."

Echoing Oliver's notion of reading for pleasure, here Harley concluded that the project afforded her a space for reading that did not feel like assigned work but rather provided her with options and allowed for her self-direction. Also resembling Oliver, Harley changed her stance on "You like to share books with your friends" from "agree" to "strongly agree," reverberating the social nature of the project and the more authentic sense of sharing related to books we hoped to facilitate. Although there may not have been statistically significant changes exhibited in the larger body of data with regard to reader profiles, Oliver's and Harley's cases demonstrate that there were some aspects of the project that affected individuals' reading-related outlooks in more nuanced ways. Through these traces, we were able to gain a snapshot of how students understood reading in the context of the school—what constituted traditional reading and what did not—and how those distinctions affected their reader identities.

Prevalence of Organic Critical Conversations

A second theme in student responses was the prevalence of organic critical conversations generated through not only reading the books, but the accompanying activities that Alyssa (the teacher intern) designed. This was evident across observations by Ashley as well through Alyssa's reflections on class time. Students' analytic discussions resulted from the unstructured and structured portions of the teacher's plans, but the fact that both solicited students' critical literacies emerged in our analysis.

First, students raised topics in their self-directed discussions that were political and dealt directly with sociocultural issues. For instance, one group's chosen book, *Carry On* (Rowell, 2015) led students to consider sexual orientation and homophobia in the United States. Although there was no clear consensus among the participants, the theme (as a point of discussion and sometimes contention) was ongoing throughout their book meetings. In addition, readers of *Between Shades of Grey* (Sepetys, 2011) considered the use of violence in government dealings. One student shared that this was an aspect of the book he would rather not encounter, while his peers felt it was a necessary component to communicate the author's message. Finally, students who read *The Impossible Knife of Memory* (Anderson, 2014) spent time exploring the notion of post-traumatic stress disorder and discussing how and why it might plague adults in our current social and historical context. These conversations, animated and lively, were mesmerizing to witness. While we realize they were broached because of the content of the books, students' focus on the issues, their agreements and disagreements on them, as well their articulations of related current events and concerns are not elements that could have been scripted by a teacher. Given the space to explore and time to simply discuss the texts, the students elected to engage with these topics and to delve into areas that might have led to discomfort. And, they did this all on their own.

The focus of students' conversations, however, was not only on the broad sociopolitical issues raised in the texts. They also argued, at no prompting from Alyssa, the merits of the books in terms of their literary, aesthetic, and emotional appeal, much like in typical book clubs. One student, Jocelyn, said that she was at a part in her book that was so well-written, she couldn't "not continue to read." Many discussed wanting to know how their novels ended, making predictions about the plights of the main characters. They also critiqued the authors, for example, for leaving events unresolved, and they noted questions they would like to ask the author.

What we found particularly interesting were conversations about why students did not like their books when those instances arose. In a few cases, students shared that they did not enjoy the content of their book because it was unrealistic or the plot because it felt predictable. In another example, even though the student selected sports as their favored genre, they did not like that the chosen book *All American Boys* (Reynolds & Kiely, 2015) centered specifically on basketball, a sport for which they had little affinity. Most prominent was the fact that even though these students attested to being dissatisfied with their novels, they actually read them in their entirety and engaged in debate to justify their claims. Because they were not being held to page number requirements or tested on the texts, they could have stopped reading, but they did not.

In addition, students also engaged in critical conversations about the protagonists, the relationships, and the everyday issues that connected specifically to adolescents. Such exchanges ranged from a debate on, as one student labeled it, the "two awkward love interests" in *Throne of Glass* (Maas, 2012) to, as another noted, "the emotions of the young adult characters" as serious entities, "which shows us how they are going through life," even in the fantasy genre world portrayed in

Throne of Glass (Maas, 2012). Others discussed how *Eleanor & Park* (Rowell, 2013) reflected "the way we are treated" and "what happens at home." Here was a book written about "heavy" subjects (including poverty and domestic abuse), and students were able to engage with the love story as an entryway into these issues, which are also present in some adolescents' lives. This novel allowed students to consider domestic violence and talk about it as it occurred in the novel while considering the events in a real world capacity. Even when a text did not seem to explicitly focus on an adolescent issue, such as in a dystopian work, students noted that the book nonetheless had "teenager-related issues," by the sheer parallels they saw in the obstacles faced by the protagonist and those in their own lives. In fact, they said of *Partials* (Wells, 2012), "it contains adventure, responsibility, and the stress of young adulthood." They thus read themselves into the texts, furthering their demonstration of critical literacies.

As mentioned previously, students' critical conversations arose by nature of both the unstructured activities and structured assignments in class. On some occasions, students were given free time to share a passage from the book that was memorable, and it was within these discussions that sociopolitical topics were raised. In other instances, minor structure was provided that solicited students' personal reflections on the book. In one class activity, Alyssa instructed students to write one word on the board that summarized their book thus far. As students shared their words, this led to an assessment of the book and in many cases, resulted in debate with their fellow group mates. The structure here, although somewhat loose, led to more complex dialogue.

Finally, in another exercise, Alyssa provided more guidance for an in-class group activity that (perhaps unintentionally) fostered students' critical responses: creating an online presentation using Prezi. Required elements included a summary of the book that did not contain spoilers, an artistic representation of the novel, a tagline to represent and advertise the novel, and a recommendation for "who should read this book." While this assignment was structured in many ways, it also afforded students the space to consider how the text would appeal to adolescents like themselves. Thus, students began to see the value in peer recommendations for books. Many students found this task highly engaging and eagerly worked during the class period to divide components and reach a consensus on how they wanted to deliver their information.

IMPLICATIONS AND CONCLUSIONS

Given these student responses to the project and related activities, we were left with several questions to ponder: What does it mean to liberate curriculum? How can we determine if our social justice purposes have been met in our work with students? And, how might we adjust the reading endeavor for future iterations to better judge its impact on students and meet their diverse needs?

We feel that we were able to meet our goal of illustrating for students curriculum as a dynamic entity. That students were able to select books according to their interests, read at will, and argue the merits and shortcomings of the readings they undertook demonstrated their recognition that curricular content exists by someone's choice. We realize, however, that we were not able to truly and wholly liberate curriculum. While we provided choice, those choices were within a limited scope. Perhaps in future iterations of the project we can be more open to students selecting literature from their personal, peers', school, and local libraries in order to provide even more options. Although teachers are often regulated in public schools in the extent to which they can blur the boundaries of curriculum, we do feel that offering choice as much as possible will motivate and engage students, and offering material that is relevant to their lives, such as YAL, is necessary.

The students' engagement in critical conversations is one demonstrable outcome of using relevant material, and it signaled one way our social justice aspirations were fulfilled. Throughout the unit, students' considerations of the ways their books reflected current sociopolitical issues and their debates on those issues, their relation of the texts to their own lives, and their question-ing of authors' purposes and viewpoints all indicated their developing critical literacies. This finding leads us to recommend that English educators continue to seek ways for students to critically engage in the classroom outside of tra-ditional norms—beyond discussion of theme, symbol, style, etc. and to listen for analysis that reflects profound consideration of current events or draws con-nections among topics with creative and critical acumen. We were encouraged by the presence of this dialogue and its organic appearance; yet, in future work we hope to delve further into the topics that students raise and push them to consider issues beyond conversation. We hope to move into research and action, extending students' reading beyond the text and into deeper exploration of the topics they raise.

As evidenced by the themes we noted in students' responses, we feel that providing youth with more authentic reading experiences is crucial. Allowing them to "just read" was valuable as it affected their reading identities and helped them discern curriculum as an entity in which they could participate, rather than a practice that is forced upon them. If we hope to create lifelong learners and readers, we must provide pleasurable, equity-oriented reading experiences for the students in our classrooms.

NOTES

1. This study was funded by the Edward R. Meyer Project Grant awarded by the College of Arts and Sciences at Washington State University.
2. All references to students are pseudonyms.

REFERENCES

Anderson, L. H. (2014). *The impossible knife of memory*. New York, NY: Penguin Group.

Behrman, E. H. (2006). Teaching about language, power, and text: A review of classroom practices that support critical literacy. *Journal of Adolescent and Adult Literacy, 49*(6), 490–498.

Campano, G., Ghiso, M. P., & Sanchez, L. (2013). "Nobody knows the … amount of a person": Elementary students critiquing dehumanization through organic critical literacies. *Research in the Teaching of English, 48*(1), 98–125.

Charmaz, K. (2006). *Constructing grounded theory. A practical guide through qualitative analysis*. London: Sage.

Cormier, R. (2014). *The chocolate war*. London: Penguin Books.

Epstein, S. E. (2014). *Teaching civic literacy projects: Student engagement with social problems*. New York, NY: Teachers College Press.

Fairclough, N. (1995). *Critical discourse analysis*. London: Longman.

Freire, P. (1970). *Pedagogy of the oppressed*. New York, NY: Continuum.

Gallo, D. (2001). How classics create an alliterate society. *The English Journal, 90*(3), 33–39.

Glasgow, J. N. (2001). Teaching social justice through young adult literature. *English Journal, 90*(6), 54–61.

Groenke, S. L., & Youngquist, M. (2011). Are we postmodern yet? Reading *Monster* with 21st-century ninth graders. *Journal of Adolescent & Adult Literacy, 54*(7), 505–513.

Herz, S. K., & Gallo, D. R. (1996). What is young adult literature anyway? Can it be any good if students like it? In S. K. Herz (Ed.), *Hinton to Hamlet: Building bridges between young adult literature and the classics* (pp. 9–11). Westport, CT: Greenwood Press.

Huckin, T. (2002). Textual silence and the discourse of homelessness. *Discourse and Society, 13*(3), 347–372.

Ivey, G., & Johnston, P. H. (2013). Engagement with young adult literature: Outcomes and processes. *Reading Research Quarterly, 48*(3), 255–275.

Jackett, M. (2007). Teaching English in the world: Something to speak about: Addressing sensitive issues through literature. *The English Journal, 96*(4), 102–105.

Lesesne, T. (2005). *Making the match: The right book for the right reader at the right time: Grades 4–12*. Portland, OR: Stenhouse.

Maas, S. J. (2012). *Throne of glass*. New York, NY: Bloomsbury.

McKenna, M. C., Kear, D. J., & Ellsworth, R. A. (1995). Children's attitudes toward reading: A national survey. *Reading Research Quarterly, 30*(4), 934–956.

McLaren, P. (2003). *Life in schools: An introduction to critical pedagogy in the foundations of education* (4th ed.). Boston, MA: Pearson Education.

Moje, E. B., Overby, M., Tysvaer, N., & Morris, K. (2008). The complex world of adolescent literacy: Myths, motivations, and mysteries. *Harvard Educational Review, 78*(1), 107–154.

Morrell, E., & Duncan-Andrade, J. (2005/2006). Popular culture and critical media pedagogy in secondary literacy classrooms. *International Journal of Learning, 12*, 1–11.

Parsons, E. C. (2006). From caring as a relation to culturally relevant caring: A white teacher's bridge to black students. *Equity and Excellence in Education, 38*(1), 25–34.

Reynolds, J., & Kiely, B. (2015). *All American boys.* New York, NY: Atheneum Books For Young Readers.

Rowell, R. (2013). *Eleanor & park.* New York, NY: St. Martin's Griffin.

Rowell, R. (2015). *Carry on.* New York, NY: St. Martin's Griffin.

Sepetys, R. (2011). *Between shades of gray.* New York, NY: Penguin.

Shakespeare, W. (1892). Hamlet. In B. Mowat & P. Werstine (Eds.), *Folger Shakespeare library: Hamlet by William Shakespeare* (Updated ed.). New York, NY: Simon & Schuster. (Original work published 1603.)

Strauss, A., & Corbin, J. (1998). *Basics of qualitative research: Grounded theory, procedures and techniques.* Newbury Park, CA: Sage.

Tannen, D. (1989). *Talking voices: Repetition, dialogue, and imagery in conversational discourse.* Cambridge: Cambridge University Press.

Wells, D. (2012). *Partials.* New York, NY: Balzer + Bray.

Wigfield, A., & Guthrie, J. T. (1997). Relations of children's motivation for reading to the amount and breadth of their reading. *Journal of Educational Psychology, 89*(3), 420–432.

Wilder, A., & Teasley, A. B. (1998). The high school connection: Young adult literature in the high school. *The ALAN Review, 26*(1). Retrieved from http://scholar.lib.vt.edu/ejournals/ALAN/fall98/wilder.html

CHAPTER FOURTEEN

Geography Matters

Face-to-Face Contact Pedagogies to Humanize Unfamiliar Ethnocultural Differences
9th Grade

JOANNE M. PATTISON-MEEK

Canada is a multicultural state that is home to Indigenous Peoples (First Nations, Metis, Inuit) and settler populations, and continues to receive thousands of new immigrants from around the world each year. The extent of diversity present within the country is distinctive, including wide-ranging ethnic, racial, religious, and language diversities. The political inclusion of Canada's diverse populations, known as multiculturalism in English Canada, emphasizes cultural retention: protecting the values and practices of different ethnocultural populations from being absorbed into mainstream cultures (Gérin-Lajoie, 2012). In other words, diverse groups are supported by law and encouraged to maintain their identity differences as opposed to assimilating.

Citizenship education policy requirements across Canada, determined at provincial and territorial levels, have been a means to nurture students' understandings and respect for social diversity, equity issues, and associated identity rights (Bickmore, 2014). As yet, there has been very little research to explore the ways in which social studies teachers in Canada's rural regions teach citizenship education, especially in relation to ethnocultural diversity, so their reasons for doing so and their students' responses to this remain unknown. In what ways do teachers implement subject matter and pedagogies probing and affirming perspectives in relation to Canada's vast ethnic, cultural, linguistic, racialized, and religious populations in rural classrooms, where such diversities are sometimes rare?

In this chapter, I present a classroom case study that examines pedagogical challenges and opportunities faced by one social justice-committed teacher to affirm ethnic identity diversities viewed as absent in her rural community. Working with a class of Grade 9 geography students in rural southern Ontario (Canada), Mrs. Thomas deemed as a priority face-to-face human contact pedagogies to provide opportunities for her students to humanize ethnoculturally different and racialized young people. Her facilitation of a rural-urban intergroup encounter with newcomer immigrant youth in a nearby urban area expands our pedagogical insights of multicultural citizenship education in under-studied, majority-white and rural high school classrooms.

MULTICULTURAL CITIZENSHIP EDUCATION

Citizenship education and multicultural education are related areas of study. As a bridge between the two, multicultural citizenship education aims to provide youth with knowledge and skills to learn, live, and participate in an increasingly diverse democratic society (Banks, 2009; Dilworth, 2008; Sleeter, 2014). Teaching for multicultural democratic competence includes nurturing students' "personal and intercultural communication skills; knowledge of cultural, social, and political systems; and [their] ability to critically think about civic and political life among and between diverse groups" (Dilworth, 2008, p. 425). Some theorists advocate for multicultural citizenship education as a way to mitigate discomfort and anxiety about social differences that can lead to prejudice and discrimination between divided social groups (Banks, 1994; Camicia, 2007).

Human relations (intergroup education), as a dialogic approach to multicultural citizenship education, emphasize affective dimensions of citizenship such as empathy and tolerance (Sleeter & Grant, 2009). A version of human relations pedagogy designed for high-conflict societies, called intergroup contact, aims to support students to communicate with, accept, and learn from people who are different from themselves, while dismantling negative feelings and stereotypes (e.g., Tal-Or, Boringer, & Gleicher, 2002). Face-to-face intergroup dialogue processes encourage people from diverse social identity groups to share different perspectives and insights into social conditions, to open opportunities to shift negative intergroup perceptions into positive, affective connections with Others (Nagda, Kim, & Truelove, 2004; Zuñiga, Nagda, & Sevig, 2002). Students' intergroup learning could potentially nurture inclusive understandings of citizenship in which students are less likely to marginalize and oppress those with whom they are unfamiliar or hold partial views.

LITERATURE REVIEW

Multicultural citizenship education is not always viewed as relevant in predominantly white and/or rural school contexts. For example, in a survey in one southeastern state in the United States, secondary school administrators in rurally-located schools tended to hold negative perceptions of multicultural education, compared to administrators in urban and suburban schools who expressed more value (McCray, Wright, & Beachum, 2004). In the study, administrators who shared support for multicultural education were more likely to work in school communities with racially and ethnoculturally diverse student populations, compared to administrators in schools populated primarily by white students. None mentioned their community's lack of visible diversity as a reason to support multicultural education. Thus, citizenship education for diversity is sometimes assumed to benefit non-white and urban or suburban students.

While scholarship in the fields of citizenship education and multicultural education is diverse and abundant, not surprisingly, it is focused almost entirely on racially and ethnoculturally diverse populations in urban contexts (Atkin, 2003; Ayalon, 2003; Reed, 2010), or on rural or suburban schools in the United States that had already experienced an influx of racial minority students (Heidlebaugh-Buskey, 2013; Rhodes, 2014). Applying implicitly urban multicultural citizenship education theory to all contexts (such as rural classrooms) does not consider local social, political, and population factors—and so may not represent a fair reflection of the broader factors that affect pedagogy (see Williams, 2013). Teachers practicing in rural classrooms, especially those also comprised of primarily white students, are left with the complex task of translating multicultural education curricula designed for racially and culturally diverse and/or diversifying (sub)urban contexts for the cultural milieu of rural schools and their communities (Yeo, 1999).

A multicultural citizenship education should not be limited to settling social anxiety in settings faced with changing ethnic demographics. Citizenship education for diversity can also affirm the democratic principles of social justice, through rejection of all forms of discrimination and oppression based on human differences in schools and society. If young people are to learn, assert, and maintain the values and principles of democracy, opportunities must be available to all students—urban, rural, and the spaces between—to learn what a pluralist, justice-oriented way of life entails and to experience how it might be led.

METHODOLOGY

The findings presented in this chapter are drawn from a larger multi-case study. The research involves constructivist analysis of social studies teachers' understandings and practices of democratic citizenship education in rural high school classrooms populated by majority white students. The study is intended to develop pedagogical insights from various classroom cases that might be useful to teacher educators and teachers in similar secondary school classrooms. My aim is not to generalize, but instead to illustrate and analyze issues and options in multicultural citizenship education.

Much research in citizenship education, particularly in rural areas (because of distance), relies on survey data (Burton, Brown, & Johnson, 2013). In contrast, this qualitative study presents what occurred inside classrooms through teacher and student voices—often missing in published research—to represent a comprehensive view of the tensions teachers may face when selecting subject matter and implementing pedagogical practices. The vivid descriptions provided by case study may permit readers to experience the issue(s) for themselves (Rossman & Rallis, 2012). This process of applying insight to the original data is "part of the [ongoing] knowledge produced by case studies" (Stake, 1981, p. 36).

Data from the classroom case presented in this chapter are derived from 16 classroom observations of one experienced teacher's *Geography of Canada* classroom (Grade 9; ages 13–14), two 30–40 minute teacher interviews, four 15–25 minute student group interviews, and analysis of classroom documents (including student written work). Using multicultural citizenship education as a guide, the analytic procedure involved locating, selecting, and synthesizing the raw data in typed transcripts of interviews, field notes, and quotes/passages from documents. Data analysis was inductive: the development of analytical categories and coding to represent distinguishing characteristics of the data was ongoing and intuitive (Altheide, 1987). Through this process I was better able to illustrate and explain the situational complexity of Mrs. Thomas's multicultural citizenship pedagogy shared below.

CONTEXT AND PARTICIPANTS

The official Ontario grade 9 *Geography of Canada* curriculum invites teachers to explore questions with their students such as, "In what ways can cultural diversity enrich the life of a community?" and "How can schools help newcomers?" (Ontario Ministry of Education, 2013, pp. 98–99). These questions can be challenging to explore in some white and rural classroom contexts where students' exposure to ethnocultural diversity and recent immigrants is limited. Teachers' and students' belief systems and experiences are, to some degree, shaped by the geographical relations and spaces in which they find themselves (Kenway & Youdell, 2011). How might such contextual factors contribute to what teachers bring to their citizenship education for diversity? Thus, I sought social studies classrooms located in high schools in predominantly white and rural settings as a key element in the research design.

I chose to name Mrs. Thomas's school and community *Hoffmann* to reflect the German-Dutch and Mennonite heritage prevalent in the local area. Mrs. Thomas, white and in her mid-40s, had 20 years of teaching experience. She had a reputation of being a renegade among the school staff for her classroom work promoting social justice and anti-discrimination education. She viewed growing up in rural northern Ontario to benefit her teaching because she understood Hoffmann's "very Anglo" setting and some of the mindsets of her students. There were 22 students in her *Geography of Canada* class: 18 boys and 4 girls, 21 of them were white. All community, school, teacher, and student names are pseudonyms to protect participants' identities and research locations.

TALKING TO STRANGERS: RURAL-URBAN INTERCULTURAL CONNECTIONS IN ACTION

The study found that teaching for inclusive citizenship in relation to ethnocultural diversity in Mrs. Thomas's primarily white, rural setting presented a pedagogical challenge. She acknowledged that her students in general, largely owing to their community settings located outside of racially and ethnoculturally diverse (sub) urban centers, had had limited opportunities to interact across race and ethnicity that differed from their own. Mrs. Thomas viewed this as both a deficit in her students' citizenship education—particularly in the context of Canada's pluralist democracy—and also as an incentive to democratize her geography teaching.

When introducing a 3-week unit of study on the topics of immigration policy and multiculturalism in Canada, Mrs. Thomas explained to her geography class that she thought the local Hoffmann community would, in time, become less monocultural (white and Christian). As Canada continues to increase its acceptance of new immigrants from around the world each year, she reasoned, urbanization would creep closer to Hoffman. Further, because of these changes, she stressed to students that they would inevitably encounter more people of different racial, ethnic, and religious backgrounds in the future. She felt that her students' infrequent interactions with different identity groups might impede their ability to respectfully interact with such diversity in Canada's changing demographic landscape.

In light of her demographic challenge, Mrs. Thomas deemed as a priority facilitating a rural-urban intergroup encounter with newcomer immigrant youth in a nearby urban area. She sought to create authentic learning interactions to expose her students to different narratives, specifically those of youth belonging to racialized and cultural groups different from their own. Through this experience, she endeavored to support perspective sharing between her students and newcomers, to learn about different social identities and citizenship experiences, and to interrupt some students' previously expressed anxieties about ethnocultural differences.

Mrs. Thomas had professional contacts in an urban public school located a 30-minute drive from Hoffmann. With their help, she coordinated two class trips. For the first trip, she transported her "country kids to the city" to spend a morning interacting socially with a class comprised of racialized, immigrant youth (ages 12–16). Most of the students in the urban class were newly-arrived (less than one year in Canada) from (sub)tropical, conflict-affected countries. The small class of 13 students was preparing for integration into mainstream classrooms through accelerated English and numeracy learning. To protect the anonymity of the students, I will refer to their program as AIC (for accelerated integration class).

Mrs. Thomas spent 8 class sessions leading up to the first excursion readying her students to engage respectfully with AIC students. For many, this was their first occasion to meet and converse with newcomer Canadians about their pre-immigration and refugee experiences. One way Mrs. Thomas prepared her students for the intergroup encounter was to present short videos documenting the challenges for children living in conflict-affected areas of the world.

In one instance, she showed a 6-minute video depicting life in an over-crowded refugee camp near Goma, in the Democratic Republic of Congo. "I want you to be sensitive to the fact that some (AIC students) did come from really heavy experiences. So to understand their stories, let's take a look at one situation," said Mrs. Thomas before the clip. One scene erupted in gunfire, showing groups of children fleeing from tarp-covered huts into nearby forests for refuge. The class sat in silence as Mrs. Thomas began her debrief:

Mrs. T:	What was going through your minds when you watched the video?
Logan:	How that boy lost his family. He didn't know where they were.
Mrs. T:	How did that make you feel?
Logan:	Sad. *(He takes a deep breath and sighs loudly)*
Jack:	I'm shocked that soldiers just come in and take everything. They don't think about the people.
Mrs. T:	How do you think it works then if those children, they spend maybe five years in that environment, and they come to Canada? How do you think they might feel in a Canadian community for the first little while when they've grown up with that?
Jack:	Free.
Mrs. T:	So can you understand why people living in these circumstances would want to flee to places like Canada?
Jack:	Makes me feel lucky to be here and not there. I'm happy to be Canadian.

This conversation implied that at least one student believed refugees would be grateful to come to Canada, regarded by both Mrs. Thomas and Jack as a safe haven and "free." Jack's last comment suggests that the viewing experience enhanced his appreciation for his citizenship privilege. Mrs. Thomas provided students, through graphic footage, with a vicarious experience to promote a feeling of empathy toward refugees by inviting students to contemplate what it might be like to grow up in war. Logan and Jack's responses, body language, and general silence in the room suggested that Mrs. Thomas's approach had evoked a degree of compassion among students.

In advance of the intergroup encounter, Mrs. Thomas assigned students into small groups to compose interview questions to ask AIC students (AIC students had also prepared questions). On the day of the trip, each group was placed with two-to-three AIC students to form learning buddies. Mrs. Thomas told her class that they had permission (communicated through the AIC teacher) to ask newcomer students about their pre-immigration experiences in their home countries. She expressed to me that she hoped the prepared interviews would ease students into more unstructured, engaged conversations.

On the morning of the trip, before students disembarked from the bus, Mrs. Thomas turned to her unusually quiet class, sitting still in their seats, and said sternly, "Be respectful. Be polite. Make me proud." Quietly, the students filed out of the bus—only the clicking sounds of some students' cowboy boots broke an anxious silence. Two AIC students, one boy and one girl, greeted the group at the front doors; both were non-white, and the girl wore a *hijab*. They led students to a classroom with chairs arranged in a large circle. A few desks were pushed together in the middle, covered in an assortment of food. A smell of fragrant spices filled the air. The AIC teacher, Ms. Clark, invited Hoffmann students to sit on one side of the circle, while AIC students, all non-white, sat opposite.

Ms. Clark broke the uneasy silence and extended a warm welcome to the guests. She explained that her students came from around the world and "have had life experiences that are probably very different from your own." She went around the circle and invited each student to say their name and where they were born. AIC students shared that they were from a variety of countries, such as Sudan, Iraq, Bangladesh, Rwanda, Yemen, Pakistan, Myanmar, and Somalia. As a lesson in citizenship, this circle process encouraged a climate of respect and offered all students an opportunity to participate through speaking and listening in the intergroup introductions.

Next, Ms. Clark and Mrs. Thomas led a series of human relations activities to draw students' attention to their similarities and differences. For instance, a teacher would read a statement, and students would step into the circle if the statement applied to them. Some questions demonstrated for students their cross-group commonalities, such as, "Step into the circle if you like to grow things," or, "if you have a cell phone." Establishing that similarities exist among students is key to help reduce tension and promote favorable intergroup relations (Parker et al., 2010). Some students laughed when differences between the two groups appeared stark, such as living in an apartment building (all Hoffmann students remained standing still while all AIC students stepped forward). However, the group grew quiet when the majority of AIC students signaled that they had experienced war.

After, teachers assigned students to small mixed groups. More than two-thirds of students easily transitioned into unstructured conversations after asking their prepared questions (e.g., favorite pastimes/food, reasons for coming to Canada). The room was abuzz with animated talking and laughter. A female AIC student asked her group why some of the Hoffmann boys wore camouflage, because in her home country, only soldiers wore such clothing. A conversation in an all-girl group emerged on the topic of various religious head coverings (Hoffmann students: *why do some Muslim girls cover their heads and others don't?* AIC students: *why do some girls here* [in Ontario] *cover their heads and wear long dresses?*—referring to some Mennonites). In another group, Alex, a Hoffmann student who had shown no previous visible interest in the trip, appeared deep in conversation with a male student from Myanmar over photos Alex displayed (on his phone) of his family's tractor. On this day, cell phones were used—not for texting or work avoidance—but as tools to promote student engagement, such as sharing with new acquaintances students' lived stories through photos. All Hoffmann students appeared engaged in talking and/or listening intently in the group conversations. The arranged interviews supported students to actively listen to unfamiliar social and cultural perspectives that differed from their own (Parker, 2010).

The food at the center of the room also served as a talking point for conversations to flourish among intergroup members during lunch. AIC students stepped up to the table one by one and shared details about the particular dish they had brought for the large group. Ms. Clark explained that it had been the students' idea, not her own, to each bring different foods to teach about their diverse cultures. Mrs. Thomas shared with me later that she had been worried her students would react negatively when invited to try the food because it was so different from what they were used to (e.g., curry, spicy). To her delight, all but two students sampled from the table, some filling their plates a second time. The sharing of traditional food, under these circumstances, did not appear to trivialize cultural expressions (e.g., Gorski, 2008), but served as an invitation to Hoffmann students to bridge differences and engaged students from both groups in cross-cultural dialogue using food as a frame of reference.

For the second class trip, AIC students travelled to Hoffmann High School a few days after the city visit to reconnect with the geography class, have lunch, and visit a local dairy farm "to experience rural life in Canada." Many of Mrs. Thomas's students appeared enthusiastic to host the visitors, many wanting to share foods that connected to their own family backgrounds and/or rural roots. Food appeared to inspire many Hoffmann students to recognize differences among their own European-Canadian traditions and thus ethnocultural diversity among themselves—assumed to be rather homogeneous prior to the trip. For example, Austen, of Mennonite heritage, arranged for his grandmother to bake a traditional dessert. Earlier, Austen had openly exhibited resistance to learning about Muslim identities, but he now appeared keen to share his family traditions with his AIC learning buddies (one of whom was Muslim). After the first visit, he told me how he thought AIC students were brave. "It's really difficult for them—some of what they've been through. I think them coming (to Hoffmann) is important too, so they can learn about us." Dairy farming was a significant piece of Austen's lived experience and social identity: the arrival of visitors provided him an opportunity to participate and share his farm roots with classmates and the guests. For Austen, multicultural citizenship seemed to be more meaningful when the pedagogy included and supported his own social expressions.

On the day of their second meeting, Mrs. Thomas asked students to work collaboratively in mixed Hoffmann/AIC pairs to complete a Venn diagram. For this, students chatted to first identify some ways they thought they were different (e.g., *Muslim, Christian*), and then to identify what they had in common (e.g., *we like sports*). Mrs. Thomas employed this strategy to scaffold dialogue—for students to engage with and compare their personal stories with newcomer students. Advocates of a human relations approach to multicultural citizenship suggest that educators must cultivate skills that promote acknowledgement and respect for individual differences as well as commonalities (Johnson & Johnson, 2002).

The expectation (or hope) that intergroup interchange may lead to affective dimensions of citizenship, such as empathy and understanding, centers on the presumption that learning about strangers can inspire students to feel commonality—that *they* are like *us*—and demystify differences (Sleeter & Grant, 2009). For instance, Jack shared in class his anxiety about meeting AIC students the day before the first trip:

Jack:	I can't explain it. I feel nervous about tomorrow!
Mrs. T:	You may find that the people you meet are very similar to you. You've been expecting them to be very different.
Jack:	Like, do you mean similar to us now? Or back then? *(in their home countries)*
Mrs. T:	I want to pitch the idea that your learning buddy may have had a dairy farm in their home country (similar to Jack). But maybe they don't now because they live in (name of city)—but some of you might have that rural connection in common.
Jack:	Really? I didn't think about that. Cool!

Here, Mrs. Thomas eased the social distance between the two different groups to encourage positive interactions to develop. She applied the same strategy when she asked students to show their differences and commonalities using the Venn diagrams: to see the self in the Other. Both the structured intergroup interviews in the first visit and the pair-produced Venn diagrams in the second visit supported inclusive, conversational spaces for all students to share their similar and different lived experiences.

A strength of this intergroup approach is that it may counter some students' misconceptions about the immigrant Other. For instance, during Mrs. Thomas's trip debrief with her students, Jimmy expressed his surprise to learn that both of his learning buddies had not wanted to immigrate to Canada. Two students also shared that their AIC buddies had had to leave family members behind to flee to Canada; one student had not seen his mother in two years. This seemed to conflict with some Hoffmann students' prior beliefs: they exhibited confusion about why a peaceful Canada, with its assumed rights and freedoms, might not be a desirable place to live for someone who had experienced war. This transformative realization, a result of intergroup dialogue, evidently challenged some students to rethink their assumptions about the circumstances under which some people arrive to Canada and the hardships they endure.

IMPLICATIONS AND IDEAS FOR FURTHER RESEARCH AND PRACTICE

Mrs. Thomas's facilitation of students' exposure to stranger narratives supported interruption (Haroutunian-Gordon, 2010) to dismantle assumptions and misunderstandings held by some students concerning immigrant and/or racialized identities. Through inviting students to engage with unfamiliar Others, as well as encouraging the building of bridges between differences, Mrs. Thomas hoped to nurture students' understanding, comfort, and respect for their different and similar lived citizenship experiences. Such in-person dialogic interaction, albeit within two intergroup visits, promoted respect from which justice transformation may grow (e.g., understanding the importance of religious accommodations) and supported students' capacity to view human difference as desirable for a more just democracy. A caution: teachers must be vigilant when facilitating intergroup dialogue so it is not taken up as uncritical tourist curriculum (Derman-Sparks, 1989).

Future qualitative studies that focus on various geographic and social rural landscapes are also needed, to broaden our emergent view of pedagogical possibilities for multicultural citizenship education. For instance, research in rural contexts that are not necessarily predominantly white, but that include racialized student populations (e.g., Indigenous). Also, how might some teachers already employ information and communications technologies (e.g., social media) to facilitate face-to-face, intergroup contact pedagogies that connect rural students to the broader world? Such research could further our understandings of how teachers may address different kinds of social differences, and guide their students to reflect on multiple understandings of citizenship and citizen issues in different contexts.

The case study presented in this chapter provides practical guidance to support teacher development and teachers' pedagogical learning. Through the wisdom of practice shared by Mrs. Thomas, this research illustrates one demonstrably feasible way of teaching multicultural citizenship education in similar majority-white, rural classroom contexts. Thus, this study may have implications for educational researchers, teacher educators, school administrators and teachers to make citizenship education for diversity relevant (and prioritized) in settings having low levels of racial and visible ethnocultural diversity. The findings also inform social justice-oriented educators grappling with how to approach diversity education in other apparently-homogenous environments, such as suburban student populations, and in school settings that are in the early stages of, or anticipate, racial and ethnocultural diversification.

REFERENCES

Altheide, D. (1987). Ethnographic content analysis. *Qualitative Sociology, 10*(1), 65–77.

Atkin, C. (2003). Rural communities: Human and symbolic capital development, fields apart. *Compare, 33*(4), 507–518.

Ayalon, A. (2003, Fall). Why is rural education missing from multicultural education textbooks? *The Education Forum, 68*(1), 24–32.

Banks, J. (1994). Transforming the mainstream curriculum. *Educational Leadership, 51*(8), 4–8.

Banks, J. (2009). Diversity and citizenship education in multicultural nations. *Multicultural Education Review, 1*(1), 1–28.

Bickmore, K. (2014). Citizenship education in Canada: 'Democratic' engagement with differences, conflicts and equity issues? *Citizenship Teaching and Learning, 9*(3), 257–278.

Burton, M., Brown, K., & Johnson, A. (2013). Storylines about rural teachers in the United States: A narrative analysis of the literature. *Journal of Research in Rural Education, 28*(12), 1–18.

Camicia, S. (2007). Prejudice reduction through multicultural education: Connecting multiple literatures. *Social Studies Research and Practice, 2*(2), 219–227.

Derman-Sparks, L. (1989). *Anti-bias curriculum: Tools for empowering young children*. Washington, DC: National Association for the Education of Young Children.

Dilworth, P. (2008). Multicultural citizenship education. In J. Arthur, I. Davies, & C. Hahn (Eds.), *The sage handbook of education for citizenship and democracy* (pp. 424–437). Los Angeles, CA: Sage.

Gérin-Lajoie, D. (2012). Racial and ethnic diversity in schools: The case of English Canada. *Prospects, 42*(2), 205–218.

Gorski, P. (2008). Good intentions are not enough: A decolonizing intercultural education. *Intercultural Education, 19*(6), 515–525.

Haroutunian-Gordon, S. (2010). Listening to a challenging perspective: The role of interruption. *Teachers College Record, 112*(11), 2893–2814.

Heidlebaugh-Buskey, P. (2013). *A multiple case study on the phenomenon of culturally responsive pedagogy in rural western North Carolina* (Doctoral dissertation). Western Carolina University, Cullowhee, NC.

Johnson, D., & Johnson, R. (2002). *Multicultural education and human relations: Valuing diversity.* Boston, MA: Allyn and Bacon.

Kenway, J., & Youdell, D. (2011). The emotional geographies of education: Beginning a conversation. *Emotion, Space and Society, 4*(3), 131–136.

McCray, C., Wright, J., & Beachum, F. (2004). An analysis of secondary school principals' perceptions of multicultural education. *Education, 125*(1), 111–120.

Nagda, B., & Kim, C., & Truelove, Y. (2004). Learning about difference: Learning with others, learning to transgress. *Journal of Social Issues, 60*(1), 195–214.

Ontario Ministry of Education. (2013, Rev.). *The Ontario curriculum, grades 9 and 10: Canadian and world studies.* Retrieved from http://www.edu.gov.on.ca/eng/curriculum/secondary/canworld910curr2013.pdf

Parker, W. C. (2010). Listening to strangers: Classroom discussion in democratic education. *Teachers College Record, 112*(11), 2815–2832.

Parker, W. C., Cookson, P., Gay, G., Hawley, W., Irvine, J. J., Nieto, S., … Stephan, J. W. (2010). Education and diversity. In W. C. Parker (Ed.), *Social studies today: Research and practice* (pp. 67–76). New York, NY: Routledge.

Reed, K. (2010). Multicultural education for rural schools: Creating relevancy in rural America. *The Rural Educator, 31*(2), 15–20.

Rhodes, M. (2014). Dynamics of diversity in a rural school. In C. Howley, A. Howley, & J. Johnson (Eds.), *Dynamics of social class, race, and place in rural education* (pp. 243–265). Charlotte, NC: Information Age Publishing.

Rossman, G., & Rallis, S. (2012). *Learning in the field: An introduction to qualitative research.* Thousand Oaks, CA: Sage.

Sleeter, C. (2014). Multiculturalism and education for citizenship in a context of neoliberalism. *Intercultural Education, 25*(2), 85–94.

Sleeter, C., & Grant, C. (2009). *Making choices for multicultural education: Five approaches to race, class and gender* (6th ed.). New York, NY: John Wiley.

Stake, R. (1981). Case study methodology: An epistemological advocacy. In W. Welsh (Ed.), *Case study methodology in educational evaluation.* Proceedings of the 1981 Minnesota Evaluation Conference, Minnesota Research and Evaluation Center, Minneapolis, MN.

Tal-Or, N., Boringer, D., & Gleicher, F. (2002). Understanding the conditions necessary for intergroup contact to reduce prejudice. In G. Salomon & B. Nevo (Eds.), *Peace education: The concept, principles, and practices around the world* (pp. 89–107). Mahwah, NJ: Lawrence Erlbaum Associates.

Williams, D. (2013). When 'minimalist' conceptions of citizenship reveal their complexity. *Citizenship Teaching and Learning, 8*(3), 357–369.

Yeo, F. (1999). The barriers of diversity: Multicultural education and rural schools. *Multicultural Education, 7*(1), 2–7.

Zuñiga, X., Nagda, B., & Sevig, T. (2002). Intergroup dialogues: An educational model for cultivating engagement across differences. *Equity & Excellence in Education, 35*(1), 7–17.

CHAPTER FIFTEEN

"I, Too, Sing America"

Operationalizing #WeAreNotThis and #BlackLivesMatter in an English Classroom
9th Grade

JEANNE DYCHES

The power and purpose of literature instruction in the secondary English class-room has long been a matter of contestation. Despite its dogmatic qualities that include suppressing the voices of teachers by limiting the culturally responsive practices they perform (Bissonnette, 2016) and dismissing marginalized students from canonical conversations (Bissonnette & Glazier, 2015; Carter, 2007), literature instruction can, if used strategically, engender powerful conversations around timely, if controversial, issues (Boyd & Dyches, 2017; Dyches, 2017). To that end, this case study investigates how Lainey,[1] a first year teacher at a public arts school, opened up and relied on the intertextual connections between canonical literature, social resistance movements, and multimodal graphics to develop her students' sociopolitical consciousness.

The investigation follows Lainey's teaching of Langston Hughes' (1945) "I, Too," a poem that illustrates the hegemonic ways in which African Americans have been treated due to the social stratification and endemic racism of U.S. society. Lainey's students made intertextual connections between the poem and the social resistance movements, #BlackLivesMatter (BLM) and #WeAreNotThis. Protestors created the second hashtag to oppose North Carolina's Public Facilities Privacy & Security Act of 2016, more commonly referred to as House Bill 2 (HB2), or the "Bathroom Bill." Finally, students engaged their penchant for artistry along with their knowledge of "I, Too" and current events/policies to generate multimodal graphics (Jewitt & Kress, 2003) intended to bring awareness to a particular social injustice. In examining the case, this study asks:

1. What possibilities exist for teaching canonical literature in tandem with social resistance movements?
2. How might multimodal graphics help students synthesize and apply their knowledge of the ways in which canonical literature and social resistance movements speak to each other intertextually?
3. What factors promote teachers' willingness to engage social justice issues?
4. What factors inhibit teachers' willingness to engage social justice issues?

This study opens up conversations around social justice by exploring the links between teachers' dispositions, lived experiences, and contextual realities, and how they shape teachers' instructional decisions—both those pedagogical and curricular in nature (Dyches & Boyd, 2017). Moreover, this study holds that equity relies on teachers' understanding that teaching for social justice is undeniably political (Cochran-Smith & Lytle, 1999) and requires them to embrace that charge, particularly in their attempts to develop students' sociopolitical consciousness— that is, helping them identify issues salient to their own lives and equipping them with the knowledges and skills necessary to solve problems and ultimately disrupt hegemonic conditions (Ladson-Billings, 1995).

THEORETICAL FRAMEWORK

While pedagogical content knowledge (PCK) (Shulman, 1986, 1987) has long been lauded in both teacher education and in-service classrooms, the framework incompletely articulates the ways in which teachers' social justice orientations impact their PCK practices. To more fully nuance teachers' PCK choices, the *Social Justice Pedagogical and Content Knowledge* (SJPACK) theoretical framework advances that all PCK choices are political in nature (Dyches & Boyd, 2017). SJPACK holds that teachers' *social justice knowledge* serves as the foundational domain that shapes the entirety of their instructional choices; as such, the framework offers *social justice pedagogical knowledge* and *social justice content knowledge* as its second and third knowledge domains.

SJPACK considers teachers' social justice knowledge to be bound to their understanding and ability to perform particular Discourses (that is, behaviors that reflect one's social roles, values, beliefs, and attitudes—their "ways of being in the world" (Gee, 2014, p. 3)); their understanding of salient theories (including critical race and feminist theories); recognition of competing histories (both "traditional" and counter-narratives); and ability and willingness to act as change agents. Secondly, SJPACK holds that because teachers' social justice knowledges osmose their instructional choices, *social justice pedagogical knowledge* serves as a more apt description of the teaching practices that occur (or do not occur) in teachers' classrooms. Pedagogies falling under this domain include culturally accessing pedagogies (pedagogies that utilize students' cultures as vehicles for teaching—e.g., Villegas & Lucas, 2002); critical pedagogies (pedagogies that position students to identify aspects of hegemony and ideology by developing their critical consciousness—e.g., Freire, 1968/1970); and agency-inciting pedagogies (pedagogies that leverage teachers' sense of personal agency and invite students to action—e.g., Kumashiro, 2001). Lastly, SJPACK advances *social justice content knowledge*, which suggests that while teachers must have basic knowledge of their traditionally taught content (e.g., understanding the particulars of iambic pentameter or the themes of *The Great Gatsby*), so too should they have critical content knowledge, a particularized form of disciplinary knowledge and awareness that allows teachers to deliver their content in transformative, equity-oriented ways (e.g., using *Macbeth* to open up conversations around the oppressive traits of whiteness—e.g., Dyches, 2017). Here, I rely on the SJPACK model to distill the ways in which Lainey's instructional practices make manifest her own orientation to social justice, and show the ways in which she applies various pedagogical and curricular approaches to open up these conversations.

METHODOLOGY

Research Design

Bounded by time, persons, and other constraints, this study assumed the case study design (Merriam, 1998) in that it sought to understand the particulars of one teacher's instructional maneuvers. A first year teacher, Lainey Davis recently completed a traditional teacher education program at a small, private university. At 22, Lainey was a dynamic teacher with a reputation for indomitable energy and a voracious desire to hone her craft. Having worked with Lainey during various professional development encounters throughout the year, and knowing that she self-identified passionately as a social justice-oriented teacher, I asked Lainey if she would be willing to participate in the study. Important to Lainey's case is the context in which she worked. Nestled in the downtown area of a large urban city, Roman High School served approximately 300 students in grades 9–12. With a focus on the performing arts, the public charter school attracted students from across the county who had a gift for artistry—from music to dance to visual arts, the latter emerging as the focus on this work.

Significantly, when the study took place two social movements were sweeping the national landscape. Founded by Patrisse Cullors, Opal Tometi, and Alicia

Garza, the 21st-century civil rights movement #BlackLivesMatter (BLM) seeks to shed light on and oppose the disproportionate number of violent acts committed against people of Color across the United States (Day, 2015). With its genesis rooted in a Facebook message in which Garza decried George Zimmerman's 2013 acquittal of killing Trayvon Martin, others began to share and elaborate on her post, using the hashtag #BlackLivesMatter to connect their writings. Garza's original Facebook post has been called "the hashtag that launched a thousand protests" (Day, 2015, para. 63). The movement's official website reads that #BlackLivesMatter intends to "build connections between Black people and our allies to fight anti-Black racism, to spark dialogue among Black people, and to facilitate the types of connections necessary to encourage social action and engagement" (Black Lives Matter Official Website, para. 2). At the time of writing, the movement had over 240,000 followers on Facebook and another 28,000 followers on Twitter; nationwide, the movement had over 38 local chapters.

Signed into law March 23, 2016, North Carolina's General Assembly passed the Public Facilities Privacy & Security Act—House Bill 2 (HB2). "The Bathroom Bill," nicknamed for the segment of the legislation that drew the most attention—both ire and support—marginalized thousands of NC citizens by removing protections that had previously permitted persons to use the restrooms of their choice based on their gender identity rather than their birth-assigned sex. Additionally, the bill replaced existing city non-discrimination laws with a statewide nondiscrimination law that purposefully left out protections for sexual orientation, gender identity, or gender expression. After the bill was hurriedly passed just hours after its introduction, dissenters created the #WeAreNotThis hashtag to show their disapproval of the measure, which impacted over 336,000 LBGTQIA+ (lesbian, bisexual, gay, transgender, queer, intersex, asexual, and people with other non-heterosexual identities) NC citizens. In addition to its infringement on citizens' civil liberties, HB2 deeply wounded NC's economic climate: a 2016 report from the Williams Institute at UCLA School of Law projected that the bill would cost NC approximately $500 billion annually, the majority stemming from a loss of federal funding, given that, according to the U.S. government, HB2 violated both the U.S. Civil Rights Act and Title IX (Peralta, 2016). While the movements maintain differences in their aims, #BlackLivesMatter and #WeAreNotThis share two commonalities: they represent a manifestation of collective strength and resistance to the oppressive ways in which marginalized people are treated, and they rely on social media to both assemble and project the voices of those who advocate for equality.

Data Collection and Analysis

During the course of the three week study, I collected various forms of data which included written teacher reflections, one classroom observation, student work samples, and a post-lesson interview with Lainey. Lainey completed three teacher reflections; the first asked her to unpack her various teaching identities (including her understanding of herself as a social justice-oriented teacher). After I observed her lesson on "I, Too," Lainey completed a second reflection that explained the technical motivations of her lesson—that is, the elements of her lesson consistent with traditional elements of instructional planning, such as teaching figurative devices and pacing—and explored the social justice-oriented goals that inspired her motivations. In a third reflection, Lainey discussed the challenges and success of the lesson, and offered insight into her instructional decisions. Following the observation and completion of her reflections, we convened a semi-structured interview in which I asked Lainey questions related to both my observation and her reflections. Lastly, I collected digital examples of her students' multimodal projects to demonstrate the ways in which students applied their knowledge of "I, Too," #BlackLivesMatter, and #WeAreNotThis to create multimodal representations indicative of their developing sociopolitical consciousness. Across reflections, observation notes, interview data and student work samples, I triangulated findings to make sense of the ways Lainey and her students were able to understand and make intertextual connections between canonical literature and social resistance movements.

Analysis involved first openly coding all data sources (Strauss & Corbin, 1998). Subsequent readings involved writing analytic memos and collapsing various codes to identify the most salient themes of Lainey's case. Ultimately, data were deductively analyzed (Gilgun, 2010) to elucidate the ways in which Lainey's lesson promoted more socially just realities as encapsulated by the SJPACK framework—that is, her social justice knowledge, social justice pedagogical knowledge, and social justice content knowledge. To make sense of the factors outside of SJPACK that both nourished and hindered her positionality, I applied inductive coding (Glaser & Strauss, 1967) which allowed me to locate, extend, and offer themes specific to Lainey's case and untethered to any particular set of theoretical a priori codes.

TEACHING CANONICAL LITERATURE IN TANDEM WITH RESISTANCE MOVEMENTS

Teaching "I, Too"

Leaders in Lainey's school crafted a list of required readings for each grade level—something akin to a curricular "sampler," according to Lainey. Teachers were expected to teach their students basic literary elements such as rhyme, theme, and repetition while reading the various assigned texts. Lainey shared that while she met her school's requirements, she also made her own curricular choices, stating that "to me, a 'sampler' means covering poetry from all time periods and all structures." Lainey's decision to teach "I, Too"—a poem not explicitly required by her school's curriculum—was based on her own sense of her students' need to discuss the pressing issues happening around them. "I could tell that they had a lot of thoughts on some of these deeper subjects like HB2 and Black Lives Matter," Lainey shared. "I wanted to give them an opportunity to talk about them through poetry. I ran across 'I, Too' and thought, 'That's perfect … I've got to do something with this.'"

Lainey taught "I, Too" in tandem with Hansberry's (1994) *A Raisin in the Sun*. For homework, students independently read the poem, looking for rhyme, repetition, dialect, and other salient figurative devices. In class, students listened to a recording of Hughes reading the poem. Lainey then asked students to work in teams to identify important figurative devices and note themes. Following the discussion, students were asked to complete a graphic representation of the poem. As Lainey said, "The goal is to show 'I, Too' is still relevant today and to demonstrate, via your art, that equality is something to be given to everyone."

Applying the SJPACK theoretical model helps make sense of the nuances of Lainey's lesson. Firstly, the political context of the lesson deeply shaped her planning processes—HB2 had recently passed, and her students were frustrated over local events related to #BlackLivesMatter. To help her students process the events, Lainey decided to let her students engage their thoughts through their art. In this way, Lainey applied two approaches of *social justice pedagogical knowledge*. In centralizing students' voices by "allowing students to make connections with real events and the text" Lainey also made use of culturally accessing pedagogies. Her willingness to incorporate art into her assignment likewise showed an intent to honor students' cultural assets. Secondly, Lainey moved her students into a critical pedagogical space when she worked to equip her students with skills to critically evaluate and critique the contexts in which they lived (Dyches & Boyd, 2017).

Lainey's delivery of *social justice content knowledge* also merits scrutiny. While Lainey positioned the lesson to cultivate students' understanding of poetry as a technical text—that is, the traditional content knowledge of SJPACK—Lainey also used the poem "to give [students] an outlet for their anger toward HB2." In this way, she applied critical content knowledge in order to open up a conversation around social injustice.

Intertexual Connections: Melding "I, Too," #BlackLivesMatter, and #WeAreNotThis

Lainey articulated that linking #BlackLivesMatter to "I, Too" provided students with an "entrance" into both conversations—a type of intertextual connection that deepened their reading of the texts. Barthes (1977/1988) argued that a text's meaning is not inherent, singular and confined to the text itself, but rather rests on the intersection of the text within a web of texts the new reading conjures; to that end, all texts represent and invoke a plural, collective array of meanings. Intertextuality improves student access to difficult, complex texts by providing them with a "way-in" (Bintz, 2011, p. 34). Lainey and her students relied on these intertextual connections to open up and extend important classroom dialogues. After reading "I, Too," Lainey's students discussed, "That the [same othering] happens now. They said, 'When it comes to Black Lives Matter, we just want to be treated the same way as everyone else and that's all Black Lives Matter is about.'" During our post-observation interview, she shared that "pairing 'I, Too' with [conversations around BLM and HB2] helped the students not only understand each idea more fully, but also see how all three are connected."

Pairing conversations of "I, Too" with social resistance movements HB2 and BLM benefited students more reticent to engage in the conversation. She shared:

> Putting it inside the content gives it a cushion and so students are more willing to [talk and listen] ... Especially when it's a very subtle connection. They say, "Oh. Well. I never really thought of it like that," and so as they see those connections occurring they feel a lot better about being more aware of other events.

Lainey noted that even students resistant to the topics benefited from the class conversations, even if they did not actively contribute. She mused that class conversations "helped [resistant students] see ['I, Too'] through the lens of the HB2, #WeAreNotThis, #BlackLivesMatter, so they were sort of forced, in a sense, to look at these new ideas, just by listening." In this way, students' exposure to "hot lava" topics (Glazier, 2003)—those conversations often avoided in lieu of safer dialogic terrain—was achieved.

Intertextuality, Multimodal Art and Sociopolitical Consciousness Development

Lainey's idea to have students create a multimodal representation of their understanding of "I, Too" and its relevance to #BLM and #WeAreNotThis showed her belief in the capaciousness of the notion of literacy. As noted by Cope and Kalantzis (2000), "multimodality implies that meaning-making occurs through a variety of communicative channels in which written linguistic modes of meaning are part and parcel of visual, audio, and spatial patterns of meaning" (p. 5). Multimodality distances itself from traditional forms of academic literacies, which largely see literacy as print based. Her students' responses to the art prompt pleased Lainey. While engaged in conversation, students worked for over an hour to create their multimodal graphics.

Lainey's project married the traditional academic literacies of reading and writing with art and activism; this amalgamation of literacies provided a multimodal approach to fostering students' sociopolitical consciousness. The graphics showed how students came to understand the thematic links between "I, Too" and the social resistance movements. In one graphic, overlaying the language of the poem against images of bathrooms, students sought to show how bathrooms have long been sociopolitically contested spaces for both African Americans who were forced to use separate bathrooms, and also more recently for people who do not identify with the sex assigned to them at birth. Another image revealed White and Black hands outstretched with an apple bearing the United States flag between them. For this group, the image indicated that all groups deserved the same educative rights, access privileges, and supports. Lainey found too that this outlet was helpful because it allowed students to express their feelings without the potential fallout a heated classroom conversation might incite.

FACTORS PROMOTING LAINEY'S SOCIAL JUSTICE INSTRUCTION

Sociocultural Awareness

Lainey unequivocally owned her zeal for social justice, an orientation deeply rooted in her own lived experiences. "I grew up in a southern family; a family who is not shy in sharing their (not so positive) thoughts on gender, race, sexuality, faith." Her family's disdain for non-mainstream groups particularly complicated Lainey's situation given her identification as a lesbian. For example, Lainey shared that, when HB2 passed, "they literally were cheering … If I even try to talk to them about [issues of social justice], it's just like, 'Nope.'" But growing up in a less accepting household had a surprising effect on Lainey. She shared:

> Because those [oppressive] beliefs were pushed on me, maybe it started as I'm pushing back, I don't want to be a part of it, but as I opened my mind up to everything else there is in the world, I realized, "Oh my goodness, there's so much more to me than just what my parents wanted."

Lainey's intimate understanding of marginalization made her especially attuned to the needs of her students. "As a lesbian," Lainey reflected, "I recognize the frustrations and struggles of LGBT students more than other groups. Those are experiences I have had, so I push myself to keep an eye on those students." But Lainey also understood the complicated ways in which intersectionality (Crenshaw, 1991) functions, and that while she experienced marginalization due her sexuality, her race afforded her certain privileges. She mused:

> As a White woman, I recognize that I have privilege that some of my students will never have. That being said, I make sure that all students—White, Black, ethnic, gay, straight, male, female, intersex, genderfluid, transgender, atheist, Christian, conservative, liberal— have equal opportunities to participate and learn.

Lainey's handle of her own sociocultural awareness—her biographical experiences, lived realities, and sense of self—positioned her to be mindful of creating a classroom space and delivering instruction that was affirming of her culturally diverse students. Moreover, they reveal her understanding of her own Discourses, and in particular, how these Discourses shape her sense of agency—all elements of the *social justice knowledge* domain of SJPACK.

INHIBITING FACTORS

First-Year Teacher

Despite these elements that positioned her social justice teaching practices, Lainey experienced certain obstructions to her efforts. One of the most prominent was the limitations she felt as a first year teacher. She shared:

> Because I am a first year teacher, I know I am hindering myself from having more direct discussions about social justice issues. I am perfectly comfortable allowing students to write about these topics, because I know the writings won't spark a debate. My first experience with a seminar led to the discussion of heavy subjects … and students in tears. I think I am worried that I won't be able to control a discussion where students voice opposing beliefs.

Lainey communicated that while she wished to open up conversations around "hot lava topics" (Glazier, 2003), she felt unsure of how to do so without the conversation spiraling out of control. Even when she opened up provocative conversations that allowed students to grapple with important issues, "that underlying fear for me, as a beginning teacher, is always there." Lainey attributed some of her fear to her teacher preparation. Talking about her teacher education program, Lainey mused:

> [The program] instills this idea like, "You have to follow every rule. You cannot go outside the box. You have to be A+ all the time." Maybe they were just feeling that way because they wanted to make sure that we all understood that there are limits to what we can do, but to some degree it sort of scared me into confining myself from going outside the box and taking more risks with the students and the discussions.

Thusly was Lainey mindful of the ways in which she could—and couldn't—broach certain conversations. Even when her instruction was strong, Lainey admitted feeling "scared that maybe one day I'll take it too far and it will cost me my job and my career," a sentiment that hindered the depth of the conversations—as well as the mode of the instruction—she was willing to engage. To overcome this trepidation, Lainey found comfort in asking students to engage the issues in less public, vocal ways, such as through writing and other forms of art.

Dissenting Students and Parents

More than any other factor, Lainey cited student resistance as the most difficult obstacle to overcome when she wished to promote social justice conversations in her classroom. Lainey shared that some students complained of feeling "targeted" in a class that was "one-sided." She reflected, "perhaps my own liberal views keep me oblivious to the views of others. However, I do my best to be aware of all belief systems that students may have." When dissenting students clashed, Lainey tried "to steer conversations away from getting too heated." Lainey mused that, "I can read a room … If I sense that maybe now's not a good time to bring that up because of the tension that's already brewing in the room, then I know not to bring it up." Thus, while Lainey wished to promote these conversations, students who vocally opposed the conversation stymied her attempts.

Relatedly, Lainey found that her students' parents also played a role in the types of instructional practices she felt self-efficacious performing. She shared that sometimes, students balked against conversations around equity and social justice, a tension she attributed to their upbringing:

> It's difficult to get them to open their minds when their minds are being filled with their parents' beliefs because, unfortunately, especially with freshmen, they haven't reached that point yet where they're like, "Oh, there is more to belief systems than just my parents".

Lainey also felt fear that a parent might take issue with her identification as a lesbian. She stated:

> I don't go around with gay pride flags waving, "Hey, look at me," but if the students ask, of course I'm not going to lie to them. If the wrong parent gets ahold of that information and they don't want me working at the school, they're going to use whatever it takes to get me out of here.

Lainey was mindful of her instruction becoming too provocative and in turn, casting light on her sexual orientation.

DISCUSSION AND CONCLUSION

Lainey's lesson shows the propensity for marrying traditional literature with conversations around social resistance movements; her work reveals that coupling these conversations and encouraging students to make intertextual connections can lead to a deepening of students' sociopolitical consciousness. Lainey's handle of her traditional content knowledge—here, the Hughes' poem—acted as a conduit through which she could extend the conversation in more critical ways. Said differently, her traditional content knowledge acted somewhat subversively by allowing her to move into more social justice-oriented curricular spaces. However, it bears mentioning that students' orientations to social justice conversations were not static—some were monocultural, and others more ready to engage more deeply with the topics (Nieto, 2006). Accordingly, the conversations addressed various needs and provided various supports for students depending on their positioning. Allowing students to combine and respond to the texts multimodally allowed a differentiated way to explore their own understanding of the content. Likewise, it allowed them to leverage their own cultural assets—their artistry—to more deeply engage with the materials. But for Lainey, it also provided a "safer" space to have students grapple with the pressing social justice issues the lesson presented—in a way that did not intimidate her in the same way that a class-wide discussion might have.

Lainey's case also shows that a teacher's own sociocultural positioning can both nourish and hinder her ability and willingness to deliver social justice-oriented instruction. Lainey recognized that growing up in a less tolerant household helped her to "always acknowledge that there are going to be people like my family in the classroom, so it teaches me to know the boundaries between preaching my beliefs to the students and pushing those beliefs on them." While she wanted to move all students into developing a deeper sense of their sociopolitical consciousness, Lainey considered it a success if she could help certain students "just share different viewpoints and get them to open their minds." Lainey felt at once compelled and stymied by her identification as a lesbian—her experiences made her want to discuss issues of social justice, but also made her worry that her forthright approach might ultimately end with her losing her job. These fears were only exacerbated by the fact that as a first year teacher, Lainey felt little job security and struggled to maintain her classroom composure. This study thus finds that teaching career status may also impact the depth of the agency a teacher may experience in their classroom.

Here, Lainey has shown the complexities that arise when a self-identifying social justice teacher works to realize social justice in her English classroom. Hers is an approach at once intentional and careful. Yet, Lainey understands that social justice requires a constant revisitation of self and practice, a reflexivity she continues to engage even now.

NOTE

1. All references to people and places are pseudonyms.

REFERENCES

Barthes, R. (1977/1988). *Image, music, text* (S. Heath, Trans.). New York, NY: The Noonday Press. (Original work published 1977.)

Bintz, W. P. (2011). "Way-In" books encourage exploration in middle grades classrooms. *The Middle School Journal, 42*(3), 34–45.

Bissonnette, J. D. (2016). *Privileged pages: Contextualizing the realities, challenges, and successes of teaching canonical British literature in culturally responsive ways* (Doctoral dissertation). Retrieved from Proquest Dissertations & Theses Global. (Order No. 10119821).

Bissonnette, J. D., & Glazier, J. (2015). A counterstory of one's own: Using counterstorytelling to engage students with the British canon. *Journal of Adolescent and Adult Literacy, 59*(6), 1–10.

Black Lives Matter Official Webpage. (n.d.) Retrieved from http://blacklivesmatter.com/

Boyd, A. & Dyches, J. (2017). Taking down walls: Countering dominant narratives of the immigrant experience through the teaching of *Enrique's Journey. Assembly for Literature on Adolescents of the National Council of Teachers of English (ALAN) Review, 44*(2), 31–42.

Carter, S. P. (2007). "Reading all that crazy White stuff": Black young women unpacking Whiteness in a high school British literature classroom. *Journal of Classroom Interaction, 41*(2), 42–54.

Cochran-Smith, M., & Lytle, S. L. (1999). Relationships of knowledge and practice: Teacher learning in communities. *Review of Research in Education, 24*, 249–305.

Cope, B., & Kalantzis, M. (2000). *Multiliteracies: Literacy learning and the design of social futures.* London: Routledge.

Crenshaw, K. (1991). Mapping the margins: Intersectionality, identity politics, and violence against women of color. *Stanford Law Review, 43*(6), 1241–1299.

Day, E. (2015, July 19). #BlackLivesMatter: The birth of a new civil rights movement. *The Guardian.* Retrieved from https://www.theguardian.com/world/2015/jul/19/blacklivesmatter-birth-civil-rights-movement

Dyches, J. (2017). Shaking off Shakespeare: A White teacher, urban students, and the mediating powers of a canonical counter-curriculum. *The Urban Review, 45*(3), 1–26.

Dyches, J., & Boyd, A. (2017). Foregrounding equity in teacher education: Toward a model of Social Justice Pedagogical and Content Knowledge (SJPACK). *Journal of Teacher Education, 68*(4).

Freire, P. (1968/1970). *Pedagogy of the oppressed.* (M. B. Ramos, Trans.). New York, NY: Bloomsbury. (Original work published 1968.)

Gee, J. P. (2014). *An introduction to discourse analysis: Theory and method.* New York, NY: Routledge.

Gilgun, J. F. (2010). A primer on deductive qualitative analysis theory testing & theory development. *Current Issues in Qualitative Research, 1*(3), 1–10.

Glaser B. G., & Strauss A. (1967). *Discovery of grounded theory: Strategies for qualitative research.* New Brunswick, NJ: Aldine Transaction.

Glazier, J. A. (2003). Moving closer to speaking the unspeakable: White teachers talking about race. *Teacher Education Quarterly, 30*(1), 73–94.

Hansberry, L. (1994). *A Raisin in the Sun.* New York, NY: Vintage. (Original work published 1959.)

Jewitt, C., & Kress, G. (Eds.). (2003). *Multimodal literacy.* New York, NY: Peter Lang.

Kumashiro, K. (2001). "Posts" perspectives on anti-oppressive education in social studies, English, mathematics, and science classrooms. *Educational Researcher, 30*(3), 3–12.

Ladson-Billings, G. (1995). Toward a theory of culturally relevant pedagogy. *American Educational Research Journal, 32*(3), 465–491.

Merriam, S. B. (1998). *Qualitative research and case study applications in education: Revised and expanded from Case study research in education.* San Francisco, CA: Jossey-Bass.

Nieto, S. (2006). Affirmation, solidarity and critique: Moving beyond tolerance in education. In E. Lee, D. Menkart, & M. Okazawa-Rey (Eds.), *Beyond heroes and holidays: A practical guide to K-12 anti-racist, multicultural education and staff development* (pp. 18–29). Washington, DC: Teaching for Change.

Peralta, K. (2016, May 11). House Bill 2 could cost N.C. $5 billion a year, report says. *The Charlotte Observer.* Retrieved from http://www.charlotteobserver.com/news/business/article76997927.html

Public Facilities Privacy & Security Act, NC Assemb. 2.2, Chapters 115, 143, & 158 (NC Stat. 2016).

Shulman, L. (1986). Those who understand: Knowledge growth in teaching. *Educational Researcher, 15*(2), 4–14.

Shulman, L. (1987). Knowledge and teaching: Foundations of the new reform. *Harvard Educational Review, 57*(1), 1–23.

Strauss, A., & Corbin, J. (1998). Basics of qualitative research: Grounded theory, procedures and techniques. Newbury Park, CA: Sage.

Villegas, A. M., & Lucas, T. (2002). Preparing culturally responsive teachers: Rethinking the curriculum. *Journal of Teacher Education, 53*(20), 20–32.

CHAPTER SIXTEEN

Teaching Columbus TO Newcomer Students

Social Justice in the Classroom and Across the Urban Landscape
9th–10th Grade

JAY M. SHUTTLEWORTH AND JOSEF DONNELLY

In 2016, on the second Monday in October, about 35,000 people marched up Fifth Avenue in New York City. Nearly 500,000 gathered along the route to watch, and millions more joined as the audience of a globally televised event. In previous years, attentive observers would have glimpsed Grand Marshals like Joe DiMaggio, Frank Sinatra, Sophia Loren, and Antonin Scalia. It is a grand affair where the governor and mayor march, too. If you are lucky, you will see popular musical groups and representatives of professional sport teams. Such is Columbus Day in America's largest city.

If for some reason you missed seeing the actor portraying Columbus marching along in his billowy outfit (complete with sword and plush hat), do not worry; one can see him any other time in the city, typically in enduring bronze. K–12 students around the country are likely to register at least an acknowledgement of him when school closes in his honor: out of America's ten federal holidays, Columbus is one of three people to adorn such a day. Only Martin Luther King, Jr. and George Washington, the most famous Americans identified by young people (Wineburg & Monte-Sano, 2008), have also received this Congressional nod.

While Columbus's position as a murderer, enslaver, and abuser of women is well-established by historians (Kasum, 2015; Loewen, 1995; Taylor, 2002; Zinn, 2003)—and can be considered a "closed" controversial issue (Hess, 2009)—public perception of his role remains unsettled. For example, people remain uncomfortable talking about genocide, especially as it pertains to Columbus's landfall in Hispaniola (Daniels, Ferrannini, & Padilla, 2015), and many choose to sidestep the issue altogether. Additionally, Columbus is so embedded in America's cultural consciousness that few prominent politicians are willing to jeopardize their careers by challenging a figure so lauded by Congress and millions of parade-goers around the country (Mai-Due, 2015). Thus the gap between reality and perception persists.

The social studies classroom is an appropriate venue to address this problematic gulf, especially given the field's historic role in addressing matters involving democratic social justice (Bickmore, 2008). In fact, because of the inconsistencies between his troubling history and his public adulation, education researchers elevate Columbus's legacy as a starting point for addressing systemic oppression through transformational learning objectives (Bickford & Wilton, 2012). Loewen (2014) offered a concurring assessment, as he noted that 22 of the most widely used middle and high school history texts put forth a "wrong" narrative of Columbus (p. 1).

Instruction centered on Columbus's conflicting legacy takes on greater significance for the most recently arrived English Learner. A social justice approach to teaching about Columbus acknowledges that many newcomers may not have had educational experiences that encourage challenging the status quo, thus making critiques of icons in their new country all the more difficult (Cruz & Thornton, 2009). And like most other students, they may be unclear about how "official knowledge" is formed (Apple, 2000), and they may be reluctant to challenge their own stigmatized status as a recently arrived person.

Social justice instruction about Columbus assists newcomers in building the civic skills necessary for development as informed and participatory adults. Yet, the need to fit in may impede nonconformist thinking for many of them (Eckert, 1989). Teachers can counterbalance such pressures by posing social justice as a way to enhance self-perception and civic identity-making (Flanagan, 2013). Thus, empowering newcomers to challenge de facto icons goes beyond an opportunity to transform the Columbian-monument landscape and what Loewen (2014) identified as a "simple-minded form of patriotism" (p. 45). Here, a social justice approach to teaching about the United States' founding can influence newcomers' perceptions of the nation and their membership within it.

THEORETICAL FRAMEWORK

Social Justice

A social justice approach aims for students to critically analyze the world around them and disrupt oppressions they uncover. Bell (2007) described such an objective in two parts. She said that students first need to "develop the critical analytical tools necessary to understand oppression and their own socialization within oppressive systems" (p. 2). Thus, before students can deconstruct the legacy of Columbus, they must first construct an understanding of his historical context. Second, students need to become actors "to interrupt and change oppressive patterns" (p. 2). How students recognize and disrupt such patterns requires scaffolded instruction.

When students are first developing the skills necessary to recognize oppression, they will benefit from instruction that clarifies what to look for. Indeed, oppression can be overtly discriminatory, violent, and readily apparent; however, a more pervasive form of oppression, and perhaps a much more difficult type for adolescents to decipher, is one that defines reality from a singular perspective. For example, oppression can be an assumption by a majority group that their identity or perspective is normal or correct, thereby subjugating others to a sort of second-class identity (Hardiman, Jackson, & Griffin, 2007). Therefore, an observer unfamiliar with Columbus needs guidance in deciphering how celebrating his memory may actually be oppressive to the people and the perspectives omitted from this narrative.

Examining subtle oppressions can assist newcomers in developing other needed skills, like recognizing similarly problematic assumptions about American identity. Indeed, all newcomers encounter normative assumptions about such ideals, particularly when it comes to national icons (Bell, Joshi, & Zúñiga, 2007). Therefore, a purpose of social justice instruction about Columbus is to challenge an assimilationist notion of civic membership. Banks (2007) cited "nonreflective and unexamined cultural attachments" (p. 157) and "blind nationalism" as obstacles to self-reflection and cultural identity development. Here, social justice teaching is as much, if not more so, about developing the students' understanding about themselves than it is about recognizing oppressive ideals. This means that newcomer students can simultaneously seek ways to retain their own cultural aspects while incorporating new ones from their adopted community.

The next step in a social justice approach to teaching about Columbus is to mitigate or eliminate the oppressive manifestations of his exaltation. This action-oriented approach of social justice education usually falls into two categories: in "intimate relations," like among friends or within the bounds of a classroom or school, or in larger institutional or community settings (Adams, 2007, p. 30).

Problem-posing, Issues-centered Education

An effective way to prompt students to act upon a social-justice issue is to adopt a problem-posing stance. Problem-posing methods may suggest that the gap between Columbus's historical and public context is best settled by a well-informed student and not "the-one-who-teaches" (Freire, 1970/2007, p. 80). This kind of constructivist instruction insists that students assume primary responsibility for how they shall transform his legacy (Brooks & Brooks, 1993). A problem-posing approach relies upon the idea that effective social justice action is guided by an open-ended, issues-centered question in which well-informed students are likely to disagree (Ochoa-Becker, 1996). Such instruction challenges students to use evidence to defend their claims. Social studies historians explain it as such:

> The purpose of issues-centered education is not just to raise the questions and expose students to them, but to teach students to offer defensible and intellectually well-grounded answers to those questions ... ultimately, an issues-centered approach to social studies aims at empowering the learner. (Evans, Newmann, & Saxe, 1996, p. 2)

For example, the issues-centered question guiding a summative assessment (which will be elaborated on later in this chapter) was, "How should Columbus be memorialized?" Here, the learning objective takes on a distinctive social justice orientation. Students may organically discover the existing contradictions about his public and historic depictions and then think of ways to challenge and transform such official knowledge and its cultural implications (Apple, 2000; Banks, 2007). Importantly, the instructional timing of an issues-centered question is key. For example, such a question is often best introduced *after* the investigatory phase, after students have contemplated preliminary questions like "Who was the historical Columbus?" Withholding a question like "Are the representations of Columbus through memorial and monuments an accurate depiction?" allows students unfamiliar with Columbus to avoid premature characterizations.

RESEARCH METHODS: CASE STUDY APPROACH

Analysis of the instructional unit outlined in the next section used case study as the organizational approach and relied on qualitative methods for data collection and analysis. This perspective is appropriate because we sought to describe instruction in a natural setting and account for its contextual complexities (Denzin & Lincoln, 2005). Additionally, a qualitative case study enhances the "vividness" (Marshall & Rossman, 2011, p. 267) of detail ordinarily obscured by more quantitatively-situated studies. Yet, the case presented does not represent a best practice in teaching, nor do we believe that this distinction is attainable or even recommended, given the innumerable forms that good teaching can take (e. g., Daniels & Bizar, 1998; Daniels & Zemelman, 2004; Gutstein & Peterson, 2013; Marzano, 2007).

The context for this study is a social studies classroom located in a high school for recently immigrated students (referred to by its pseudonym, Newcomer School). The school is located in a highly urbanized section of a large, east coast city. The teacher, Josef Donnelly (second author) has been teaching at this school for five of his eight years in the profession. He previously taught social studies in Micronesia as a Peace Corps Fellow.

The instructional context of this study is a 9th and 10th grade social studies class, with the primary focus a six-week unit on the legacy of Christopher Columbus. All of the students in this course were designated English Learners (EL). Many also identified as Students with Interrupted Formal Education (SIFE). Most students' primary language was Spanish, but for some students, it was French or Arabic.

Data collection involved the gathering of instructional artifacts like lesson plans, student assignments, and informal reflections recorded from semi-monthly dialogues between the co-authors. While some of the findings were co-constructed, Mr. Donnelly is responsible for the creative vision of this unit, the creation of all instructional materials and learning objectives for this study, and curricular implementations in 9th and 10th grade courses at his school setting.

SOCIAL JUSTICE TEACHING ON COLUMBUS

Broadly speaking, teaching the history of Christopher Columbus is fraught with difficulties. Global history standards often feel less globalized and more of an introduction to the traditions that America invokes (e. g., Greek democracy, revolution, and freedom). In 9th and 10th grade global history courses at other schools, students often participate in a mock trial of Columbus, which asks students to deliver a verdict—was Columbus good or evil? Yet, a debate of this kind usually leaves more important questions unanswered. For example, one might wonder why so many memorials are dedicated to Columbus at all. Such a question takes on even greater significance if students concur that his legacy is primarily negative. Why would a historical villain be so publicly lauded in the present?

Mr. Donnelly's Columbus Unit

The inspiration for developing this social justice unit came from the omnipresent Columbian tributes in Mr. Donnelly's home city. For example, one granite likeness of Columbus projects 70 feet into the air, and even a life-sized bronze of Columbus stands near Mr. Donnelly's home. These images prompted him to inquire if his students might be outraged to know that prominent landmarks in the city and elsewhere present history contrary to fact. He described some of his past teaching experiences as "teaching the past and not teaching history." He previously taught what Columbus did, but he did not explore why Columbus is still so prevalent in society, or what we, as citizens, can, or should, do about it (if anything). He also wanted to address why the historic Columbus is a global figure but largely memorialized as an American. He wanted to teach students to question why current historical portrayals are ineffective at depicting historical realities. Providing an endless amount of historical content was not helping his students question the numerous Columbus memorials or become aware of the social justice issues surrounding him.

Mr. Donnelly pondered his questioning strategies with this predicament in mind. For example, after a walk one day, he mused, "What is the message of the statue of Columbus in a nearby park? Why does the statue exist?" This question influenced his decision to avoid a unit that put Christopher Columbus on trial in favor of a more existential approach about historical memory and public perceptions of the man. After all, if teachers tell students that the final project is to put Columbus on trial, the teacher inevitably creates two unintended consequences that diminish the potential for social justice thinking: (1) students receive the message that Columbus has been indicted and therefore, he presumably was involved in some wrongdoing, and (2) the student defense and prosecution of such a trial may be affected by confirmation bias when they look through evidence. Students might suppress or ignore information that refutes their arguments. Thus, putting Columbus on trial seemed to be a sort of ahistorical, manufactured inquiry. After all, if a class trial finds Columbus is guilty of some charge, then a substantial question remains: So what? The students have not grappled with why much historical reasoning about Columbus misaligns with popular public perception. Therefore, analyzing this discontinuity remains an important application of social justice thinking.

All students in this history class were recent immigrants from countries around the world. Mr. Donnelly utilized this context by centering initial instruction on Columbus memorials from the students' native countries (like those in West Africa) as well as from around the United States. At the beginning of the six-week unit, Mr. Donnelly posed initial learning objectives around two questions: "Who was the historical Christopher Columbus?" and "Are the representations of Columbus through memorials and monuments an accurate depiction?" Once students established this baseline of knowledge, they then proceeded to deconstruct Christopher Columbus's public mythology.

For the summative project, Mr. Donnelly asked students to create a memorial/monument to Columbus based on the information they acquired throughout the unit. He posed the following social justice-oriented question to guide this inquiry: "How should we remember Christopher Columbus?" This inquiry, however, created several pedagogical dilemmas for Mr. Donnelly. The first was he could not begin the unit by introducing this question or the objective of reimagining memorials to Columbus. He reasoned that implicitly suggesting anything wrong about the memorials would bias the students from the start. He wanted students to discover the tension between Columbus's historical context and his public portrayal on their own. Even hinting at this problem might diminish students' ability to discover it independently. Therefore, Mr. Donnelly waited to introduce the final project after a few weeks of instruction. The initial objective would be to develop several understandings: (a) broadly, what purpose memorials serve, and (b) how memorials and both primary and secondary sources portray Columbus.

To spur an analytical lesson at the beginning of the unit, Mr. Donnelly sought to first validate the richness of the students' cultures and to activate their knowledge about why societies make memorials and statues. He selected images of memorials from students' countries of origin like the African Renaissance Monument outside Dakar, Senegal; the Ghoree Dakur Statue, also in Dakar; and the Memorial to the Jewish Holocaust in San Juan, Puerto Rico. He supplemented these images with local memorials, like a painting on the side of a building that honored a local young man who had died.

Once students developed schemas about memorials as a construct, Mr. Donnelly then introduced images of statues dedicated to Columbus in their current city and around the country, like the granite likeness of Columbus standing atop a pedestal in Pittsburgh, PA. Mr. Donnelly asked students how his symbolic portrayal seemed to echo the idea of Columbus as a great man who innovated, protected, and acted as a savior. Students said that such portrayals intentionally put Columbus into dashing, physically idealized poses.

Mr. Donnelly surveyed the students to see what they knew about Columbus, and many had a basic knowledge of him. Many students from the Dominican Republic said that Columbus was an explorer who traded items like a mirror for gold. No students knew that Columbus completed four separate journeys or that he was eventually arrested and taken back to Spain. This gap in knowledge helped emphasize the importance of focusing instruction on Columbus and on how society represents his legacy. Thus, the next learning objective for students would be to practice questioning official knowledge in their world and the messages that are reinforced through such depictions.

After asking students what they knew about Columbus, Mr. Donnelly had students analyze the dozen or so monuments dedicated to Columbus in their city. Visiting these memorials as part of a field trip would be time prohibitive. Therefore he took personal pictures with several of the memorials to use as a virtual fieldtrip. He selected a range of depictions: one memorial (the one near Mr. Donnelly's bus stop) shows a broad-chested and handsome Columbus with a sword. Two others show him with a staff or holding a replica of the world. Another mysteriously locates him on the top of a museum for Native American culture and history. All the monuments are celebratory in tone. This characteristic relates to a question Mr. Donnelly regularly asked all of his students: "Why do monuments rarely show tragedy or present an argument or controversy?" For example, in a later instructional unit on the world wars, Mr. Donnelly's students analyzed the Katyn Massacre memorial statue in Jersey City, New Jersey, which diverged from other bronze tributes in that this one depicted a lone soldier striking a tragic and decidedly un-heroic pose.

After the students constructed a conceptualization of how Columbus is depicted through memorials, Mr. Donnelly then introduced a series of lessons dedicated to analyzing his legacy through primary and secondary documents. While public depictions are also secondary sources, included here were perspectives of trained historians, like William D. Phillips, Jr. and Carla Rahn Phillips, authors of *The Worlds of Christopher Columbus* (1993). His reasoning was to provide information about some of the topics omitted in the primary sources, like slavery and Columbus's familiarity with violent patterns of Spanish colonization. Thus, these readings illustrated that Columbus did not stumble into unfamiliar territory when it came to subjugating indigenous people: he was a product of his time.

Mirroring the previous lesson on memorials around the world, the students worked in groups and recorded their impressions of monuments of Columbus from multiple countries. These monuments included a statue and inscription in San Juan, Puerto Rico; a statue in Columbus Circle, Washington, District of Columbia (and notably, Columbia means "Land of Columbus"); a lighthouse and tomb in Santo Domingo, Dominican Republic; a tomb in Seville, Spain; and a plaque in Indiana. Mr. Donnelly guided the lesson by asking students to write responses to the following questions: (1) What do you notice? (2) What are some similarities between the monuments? (3) What do you think is the artist's message?

Especially for the last question, Mr. Donnelly hoped students were able to notice symbolic details, like how far above the Native Americans Columbus is standing in the Washington, D. C. monument. Before moving to a larger group discussion where he recorded students' responses on a white board, students shared their ideas in triads.

After analyzing public portrayals of Columbus, students took about a week to construct a formal written description of how he was depicted, guided by the prompt, "How was Columbus represented by society?" Mr. Donnelly instructed students to reference specifics from the monuments as evidence. Their final effort came via a collectively-written paragraph produced in small groups of four or five. This kind of literacy objective is known as the Language Experience Approach, and it involves the teacher writing down student statements verbatim in a whole-class meeting and students later returning to the text to correct mistakes. Mr. Donnelly did this so they could more clearly visualize the writing process. Afterwards, students worked in groups to re-read and edit the paragraph. Most students concluded that Columbus was a great explorer, brave, and an Italian (although the students did question if the concept of Italy existed during his lifetime).

Following this activity, students entered the final phase of the unit: the completion of the summative project. This effort asked students to apply their knowledge of how Columbus is depicted in historical documents and public memory and create their own monument (in this case, through a mural) of how Columbus *should* be remembered publicly. Setting forth the prompt, "How should we remember Christopher Columbus?", Mr. Donnelly gave no other suggestions other than that students could represent Columbus in either a metaphorical or literal sense. Students also had to craft an artist's statement, much like one might see alongside artwork in a museum. He directed students' writing responses this way: "After painting your mural, you need to create an artist's statement. Your statement needs to be persuasive and needs to include the following: (1) How are you representing Christopher Columbus? (2) What specific events about Christopher Columbus support your argument (that is reflected in the artwork)? (3) What symbolism are you using, if any, and why are you using it?" Students also had the additional option of writing to their local government representative to express their thoughts and concerns about current memorials and to recommend their own rendition of a Columbian monument (only one student completed this extra task). Mr. Donnelly clarified the purpose of the additional assignment by noting that transforming Columbus's legacy within the classroom boundaries was a limited application of social justice.

The final assessments took shape through oil paint and canvas; many of them offered transformative depictions of Columbus's influence on the settlement of North America. For example, one effort showed Columbus's disembodied head drifting in a dream-like state, perhaps having a nightmare about his actions. He is present in the center of a sort of triptych, with the painting divided horizontally into three equal sections. The upper section shows a Spanish ship on an expansive sea. The center section shows dream bubbles of a severed hand, a skull, and agitated dogs, reminiscent of the animals Columbus and his men set loose on the native people. The final section ominously shows two Spaniards holding a bound Indian while a fire burns nearby. We applauded this effort for its transformational approach to social justice. Nowhere to be found were heroic poses; Columbus remains the central historic figure, but his legacy was now shrouded by the shame his destruction had caused.

A second effort similarly reflected a transformative view of how Columbus should be remembered; in this depiction, students characterized his arrival not as a new beginning but rather as a descent into darkness. In this artwork, students organized their interpretation of his legacy by loosely dividing the scene with a single vertical border. On the right side, the Tainos (the Native American tribe who met Columbus) are displayed in a bright setting. One person canoes in the background, and several Native Americans smile near a fire in the foreground. Moving from right to left, the painting shifts toward a darker background, with most of the figures shrouded by night. Spaniards torturing the Tainos dominate this macabre scene. The message is clear: Columbus's legacy is a dark descent into depraved violence.

SIGNIFICANCE

The students' work signals their ability to transform their own thinking about the unsettled legacy of the Columbian Encounter. Students began this unit with assumptions that Columbus's public image matched reality and finished the unit with a dramatic overhaul of their perceptions. The result was an introduction to social justice thinking: in their own way they had transformed their thinking of Columbus, and by proxy, the official knowledge of their new country's heroic stories.

For future iterations of this instructional unit, Mr. Donnelly wants to expand students' engagement with people outside of school. The summative assessment for future versions of this unit would still include creating a transformed memorial but also be accompanied by a student-designed pamphlet addressing the public and historical disconnect about Columbus's legacy. As a way to strengthen the action portion of the social justice project, Mr. Donnelly envisioned students distributing this leaflet to passers-by around a Christopher Columbus statue in a nearby park. He was hopeful that dialogue might occur in such an exchange, but he acknowledged that engaging with strangers could be unsafe. This project aligns more with his belief that social justice instruction asks students to share their transformative thinking with others, especially those outside their immediate social network. Additionally, Mr. Donnelly wanted to revisit his initial plan to have students advocate their transformation via letters to city council members. This idea needed revision to better address the concerns the students described about publicly sharing their writing. Mr. Donnelly considered the possibilities of creating a whole-class draft that could then be signed on behalf of all students.

For a social studies teacher of ELs, social justice instruction rests between the complementary objectives of culturally relevant and responsive pedagogy (Cruz & Thornton, 2009; Ladson-Billings, 1995; Thornton, 2005), issues-centered education (Ochoa-Becker, 1996; Saxe, 1996), multicultural education (Banks, 2007), and critical pedagogy (Freire, 1970/2007). It is an inclusive and transformative approach to teaching essential for preparing effective civic actors (Banks, 2007). Recognizing oppression via curriculum about Christopher Columbus may lead students to even more relevant understanding about how they address marginalization in everyday living. If students can understand the significance of social justice thinking and action-taking based in the social studies classroom, they may become more prepared to engage in broader dialogues about oppression in the world they encounter every day.

REFERENCES

Adams, M. (2007). Pedagogical frameworks for social justice education. In M. Adams, L. A. Bell, & P. Griffin (Eds.), *Teaching for diversity and social justice* (pp. 15–33). New York, NY: Routledge.

Apple, M. W. (2000). *Official knowledge: Democratic education in a conservative age.* New York, NY: Routledge.

Banks, J. A. (2007). *Educating citizens in a multicultural society.* New York, NY: Teachers College Press.

Bell, L. A. (2007). Theoretical foundations for social justice education. In M. Adams, L. A. Bell, & P. Griffin (Eds.), *Teaching for diversity and social justice* (pp. 1–14). New York, NY: Routledge.

Bell, L. A., Joshi, K. Y., & Zúñiga, X. (2007). Racism, immigration, and globalization curriculum design. In M. Adams, L. A. Bell, & P. Griffin (Eds.), *Teaching for diversity and social justice* (pp. 145–172). New York, NY: Routledge.

Bickford, J. H., & Wilton, M. (2012). Historicizing Christopher Columbus for elementary and secondary students. *World history connected, 9*(2), 1–36.

Bickmore, K. (2008). Social justice and the social studies. In L. S. Levstik & C. A. Tyson (Eds.), *Handbook of research in social studies education* (pp. 155–171). New York, NY: Routledge.

Brooks, J. G., & Brooks, M. G. (1993). *The case for constructivist classrooms.* Alexandria, VA: Association for Supervision and Curriculum Development.

Cruz, B. C., & Thornton, S. J. (2009). *Teaching social studies to English language learners.* New York, NY: Routledge.

Daniels, H., & Bizar, M. (1998). *Methods that matter: Six structures for best practice classrooms.* Portland, ME: Stenhouse Publishers.

Daniels, H., & Zemelman, S. (2004). *Subjects matter. Every teacher's guide to content-area reading.* Portsmouth, NH: Heinemann.

Daniels, J., Ferrannini, J., & Padilla, J. (2015, October 12). Debate: How should Columbus Day be commemorated? *The American River Current.* Retrieved from http://www.arcurrent.com/. opinion/2015/10/12/debate-how-should-columbus-day-be-commemorated/

Denzin, N. K., & Lincoln, Y. S. (Eds.). (2005). *The SAGE handbook of qualitative research* (3rd ed.). Thousand Oaks, CA: Sage.

Eckert, P. (1989). *Jocks and burnouts: Social categories and identity in the high school.* New York, NY: Teachers College Press.

Evans, R. W., Newmann, F. M., & Saxe, D. W. (1996). Defining issues-centered education. In R. W. Evans & D. W. Saxe (Eds.), *Handbook on teaching social issues* (pp. 2–5). Washington, DC: National Council for the Social Studies.

Flanagan, C. A. (2013). *Teenage citizens: The political theories of the young.* Cambridge, MA: Harvard University Press.

Freire, P. (1970/2007). *The pedagogy of the oppressed.* London: The Continuum International Publishing Group. (Original work published 1970.)

Gutstein, E., & Peterson, B. (Eds.). (2013). *Rethinking mathematics: Teaching social justice by the numbers.* Milwaukee, WI: Rethinking Schools.

Hardiman, R., Jackson, B., & Griffin, P. (2007). Conceptual foundations for social justice education. In M. Adams, L. A. Bell, & P. Griffin (Eds.), *Teaching for diversity and social justice* (pp. 35–66). New York, NY: Routledge.

Hess, D. E. (2009). *Controversy in the classroom: The democratic power of discussion.* New York, NY: Routledge.

Kasum, E. (2015, October 15). Columbus Day? True legacy: Cruelty and slavery. *The Huffington Post*. Retrieved from http://www.huffingtonpost.com./eric-kasum/columbus-day-a-bad-idea_b_742708.html

Ladson-Billings, G. (1995). But that's just good teaching! The case for culturally-relevant pedagogy. *Theory into Practice, 34*(3), 159–165.

Loewen, J. W. (1995). *Lies my teacher told me: Everything your American history textbook got wrong*. New York, NY: Touchstone.

Loewen, J. W. (2014). *Lies my teacher told me about Columbus: What your history books got wrong*. New York, NY: The New Press.

Mai-Due, C. (2015, October 12). This is why we still have Columbus Day. *Los Angeles Times*. Retrieved from http://www.latimes.com/nation/nationnow/la-na-nn-columbus-day-why-do-we-still-celebrate-20151012-htmlstory.html

Marshall, C., & Rossman, G. (2011). *Designing qualitative research*. Thousand Oaks, CA: Sage.

Marzano, R. J. (2007). *The art and science of teaching: A comprehensive framework for effective instruction*. Alexandria, VA: Association for Supervision and Curriculum Development.

Ochoa-Becker, A. S. (1996). Building a rationale for issues-centered education. In R. W. Evans & D. W. Saxe (Eds.), *Handbook on teaching social issues* (pp. 6–13). Washington, DC: National Council for the Social Studies.

Phillips, W. D., & Phillips, C. R. (1993). *The worlds of Christopher Columbus*. Cambridge: Cambridge University Press.

Saxe, D. W. (1996). Using issues in the teaching of American history. In R. W. Evans & D. W. Saxe (Eds.), *Handbook on teaching social issues* (pp. 142–151). Washington, DC: National Council for the Social Studies.

Taylor, A. S. (2002). *American colonies*. New York, NY: Penguin.

Thornton, S. J. (2005). *Teaching social studies that matters: Curriculum for active learning*. New York, NY: Teachers College Press.

Wineburg, S., & Monte-Sano, C. (2008). "Famous Americans": The changing pantheon of American heroes. *The Journal of American History, 94*(4), 1186–1202.

Zinn, H. (2003). *A people's history of the United States, 1492-present*. New York, NY: Harper Perennial.

CHAPTER SEVENTEEN

"Couch the Oppression IN Resistance"

Teaching Strategies for Social Change Through U.S. History
11th grade

HILLARY PARKHOUSE

I mean there's a risk of asking students to be critical, and it's cynicism. I worry all the time that my students are going to reach this saturation point for learning about past atrocities or injustice, where they're just going to believe that things have always been bad and will always be bad. And there's nothing they can do. And basically by oversaturating them with examples, take away their agency and feeling of hope about the possibility for things to be better. I think a lot about whether the critical way that I teach history makes students preconditioned to want to disengage or feel disconnected from the government.

—Ms. Ray[1]

Actually her class makes me love America more because people like her is what make America better.
—AMINA, 11TH GRADE STUDENT

U.S. History classes, with their focus on contextualizing history and understanding the antecedents to current social conditions, are well-suited for social justice teaching. One of the central goals of social studies education, in fact, is to develop democratic citizenship skills (Parker, 1996; Ross, 2006), skills which—like those emphasized in social justice teaching—involve engagement in the community and working collaboratively to effect change. However, one of the major concerns about teaching U.S. History from a social justice perspective is that if students learn about injustices such as racism, sexism, and heterosexism, they may become *dis*engaged or even cynical and hopeless. Typically, one function of social studies education has been to help students appreciate the strengths of American democratic systems—an aim that seems to be in conflict with supporting students' critiques of America's shortcomings. However, these two aims are not mutually incompatible, as the classroom described in this chapter illustrates. It is possible to both condemn some aspects of American society while also recognizing elements to appreciate. We can appreciate, for example, the freedom to make these types of criticisms without incurring retribution.

Some researchers have actually found the opposite—that highlighting America's strengths without acknowledging its weaknesses can lead students to feel cynical, particularly for those who are already aware of the weaknesses through their own firsthand exposure to inequities. These students perceive a disjuncture between their experiences and the "cleansed, idealized, and fairy-tale like" (Abowitz & Harnish, 2006, p. 681) version of American citizenship that is presented to them in the curriculum (Rubin, 2007). Thus when teachers avoid controversial aspects of society, either out of their own discomfort or out of a desire to instill patriotism and prevent cynicism, students perceive these lessons as dishonest. As a result, they are even more likely to become cynical, as they realize that social institutions such as schools are contributing to the problem rather than to the solution. Even for students who see the idealized narrative as congruent with their own experiences, curriculum that confronts injustices helps them to become aware, rather than complacent (Rubin, 2007).

The next question, then, is how can one balance these two aims well? How can a teacher help students to develop critical consciousness while also taking precautions that this does not lead students to view society as beyond repair? At the same time, how does a teacher help students appreciate the privileges of living in America while not minimizing contemporary social inequities such as growing income inequality and racialized poverty? There are very thin lines here, but this study provides a detailed example of one teacher who was able to enhance her students' critical consciousness without compromising their beliefs that American ideals such as equality and democracy may one day be truly realized.

TOWARD A GROUNDED THEORY OF CRITICAL PEDAGOGY IN SOCIAL STUDIES CLASSROOMS

Critical pedagogy is one of the many foundations of social justice teaching. Both share a commitment to liberating people from oppressive social structures and a belief that students are active producers of knowledge, rather than passive recipients of it. This perspective on students' roles emerged in part from Paulo Freire's (1970/2000) critique of traditional education and its reliance on what he called the *banking model*. In this common model, students are perceived as empty vessels, waiting for the teacher to deposit knowledge into them. In contrast, critical pedagogy theorists, as well as social justice teachers, recognize that students construct knowledge themselves and therefore the teachers' role is to nurture this process, and even learn from their students, rather than *deliver* knowledge to them.

Another important concept within critical pedagogy is *conscientization* or critical consciousness development. This is the increased awareness of inequitable distribution of power and resources across various groups in society, as well as the processes that produce and maintain these distributions. Many of these processes are hidden from the view of most people, and therefore a level of critical consciousness is needed to see them. For example, most people have a commonsense understanding that the United States is a meritocracy in which hard work is economically rewarded. Through the process of conscientization, a person can begin to see how this ideology rests on the assumption that everyone begins with equal access to schools and career options that offer opportunities for upward economic mobility. Even though personal experience, or what critical theorist Antonio Gramsci (1971) called *good sense*, might contradict such common sense misconceptions about how the world operates, ideologies such as meritocracy are so powerful and appealing that conscientization is required to see through these myths.

One reason critical pedagogy has not been more widely seen in social justice education literature is that the language of its theorists is too abstract and dense to be easily accessible to practitioners (Hytten & Bettez, 2011). Recognizing this problem, Duncan-Andrade and Morrell (2008) developed a grounded theory of critical pedagogy based on their work in urban high school English classrooms and extra-curricular groups. This study attempts to build upon their work by developing a grounded theory of critical pedagogy in social studies education classrooms. Whereas English teachers typically have some freedom to determine which texts to read and what types of projects to assign, standards for social studies courses such as U.S. History often include requirements to teach specific factual information, limiting the options for projects and texts. This does not mean critical pedagogy is more possible in English classrooms than history ones, however. Rather, it may just take a different form.

RESEARCH METHODS

Context: Ms. Ray's Classroom

Ms. Ray embodies critical pedagogy. Although at the time of data collection she was only in her second year of teaching, her mastery of both content and pedagogy was exceptional. As a white teacher in a predominantly black school, her candor about racism and anti-racist pedagogy went a long way in establishing rapport with her students. I chose Ms. Ray for this study after observing her critical pedagogy practices in a free college-access program for low-income students where we both worked. In that program, she developed and taught curriculum on critical media literacy, anti-sexist education, and the city's history in the African American Civil Rights Movement.

Ms. Ray taught at a small, public magnet school with a focus on health careers. The class I observed (her 4th period U.S. History class) consisted of 22 females and 6 males; 22 black, 3 Latina, and 3 white students. At the time of the study, about 55% of students in the school qualified for free or reduced-priced lunch. Ms. Ray described her 4th period class as opinionated and chatty, but in a good way, as they were typically chatting about the material being learned.

Data Collection and Analysis

I observed the 90-minute class for ten weeks, four to five days per week. I audio-recorded all classes and transcribed the portions that were relevant to this study. I also interviewed seven students on their opinions about American society and how their U.S. History class influenced these opinions, if at all. I conducted two in-depth interviews with Ms. Ray and collected instructional materials and anonymized student artifacts. Ms. Ray helped me analyze the student interview data by reading and commenting on their anonymized transcripts and co-analyzed the class observation data by giving me her impressions of students' comments and written work each day after my observation. I also independently analyzed all data both inductively, to seek emergent themes, and deductively, to identify data that related to a priori codes derived from critical pedagogy literature.

Researcher Positionality

Throughout the data collection, analysis, and representation process, I attempted to interrogate my own positioning, actions, and interpretations. I am a white, middle-class, heterosexual, cisgender woman who taught high school social studies and English as a Second Language in a public New York City high school serving predominantly Dominican students. After observing hundreds of my intelligent students finish high school with fewer opportunities than I had upon graduation, I became interested in critical pedagogy as a means of preparing the next generations to transform society.

TEACHING PRACTICES

The four practices Ms. Ray used to balance growing critical consciousness with critical hope were: (1) describe how every historical oppression has been met with resistance; (2) show how ordinary people—not just Martin Luther King Jr. and other famous activists—effected social change through communal efforts; (3) debunk common misperceptions and simplifications, such as that the Civil Rights Movement started in the 1950s; and (4) explain the specific and varied strategies these movements relied upon in order to succeed.

Oppression as Always Met with Resistance

Ms. Ray expressed concern that teaching critically may lead some students to feel disillusioned or cynical. While reading her students' interview transcripts, however, she did not find evidence that this had occurred. When I asked why she thought that might be, she answered,

> I *hope*—because this is a thing I'm purposefully implementing to try to avoid it—I *hope* it's because I'm always trying to couch the oppression in resistance. And not tell about anything without showing how someone was pushing back against it. And so making it almost like cause and effect. Like … "this happened, but here's the way that people used activism to push back. Or used violence, or whatever. To push back."

Indeed, every time she taught about oppression in class, she paired it with how people resisted it. She did this for the topics that typically get covered in U.S. history, such as antebellum slave rebellions, abolitionist movements, sit-ins and boycotts during the African American Civil Rights Movement, Native American resistance to perpetual U.S. encroachment, and labor union strikes for better treatment of workers, but also for less well-known examples of resistance. For example, while teaching about discrimination in the hiring of black Americans during World War II, Ms. Ray asked the class, "Because of what we know about the history of African Americans—when they face discrimination, do they usually just accept it?" Several students shouted enthusiastically, "No!" Ms. Ray went on to describe how A. Phillip Randolph, as leader of the Brotherhood of Sleeping Car Porters labor union threatened President Franklin Roosevelt (FDR) with a march on Washington unless he acted against this. As a result, FDR did in fact issue an executive order prohibiting wartime employment discrimination.

By pointing to less well-known examples, Ms. Ray showed that opposition to oppression is not just a phenomenon that periodically occurs with the right conditions, such as a charismatic leader and a group that has been pushed to the breaking point. Rather, opposition of oppression has occurred continually throughout history, in *every* instance of oppression. She made sure this lesson stuck by repeating throughout the year, "Every time that there has been injustice, there has been someone fighting against it." In one interview, Ms. Ray told me that she would say this "20 times a year. At least. I say them in videos [made for students], and I say them in class, and I say them one-on-one." She hoped that by doing so, students would see that although we can probably expect oppression to persist since it has been a pervasive theme throughout history, we can also expect resistance to persist, as it has been equally pervasive.

The Power of Ordinary People

Another social justice teaching strategy Ms. Ray used was emphasizing that change has not only come through famous and incomparable figures like Dr. Martin Luther King, Jr. and Abraham Lincoln. In fact, these leaders would not have been able to accomplish what they did without the help of ordinary people. To teach this lesson, Ms. Ray consistently highlighted "unsung heroes" in her lessons, regular people with flaws like anyone else. For example, people like Claudette Colvin, who was the first person to commit the civil disobedience act of refusing to give up her bus seat to a white person but was passed over as a symbol of the movement for Rosa Parks, on account of her being pregnant by a married man while a teenager. Others included the many Freedom Riders and participants of sit-ins and boycotts who risked injury and even death without future history students even learning their names. To debunk the notion that Martin Luther King Jr. and Malcolm X (and perhaps Angela Davis and Huey Newton in more progressive schools) were the only black agents of social change in the mid-20th century, Ms. Ray assigned a project in which students had to research a lesser-known figure from the 1960s. They could choose from a list of people that included Kathleen Cleaver of the Black Power movement, Frank Kameny of the Gay Liberation Movement, Dolores Huerta of the Farmworkers Movement, and many lesser-known figures in the Civil Rights Movement such as Bayard Rustin, Fannie Lou Hamer, Anne Moody, Diane Nash, and Pauli Murray.

When I asked students in interviews whether they believed ordinary people had the power to create change, most said yes. Even though the content of U.S. History curriculum consists largely of political leaders, famous figures, and other topics that may lead students to view power as wielded only by a select few, the emphasis on organized resistance in these classes helped students to also see power as possessed by ordinary individuals. One student, Josephine, cited Ms. Ray's lesson about Malala Yousafzai as helping her to realize the power of individuals and even youth. Melony mentioned that people can exert power through writing letters to representatives and Amina said that social media can be used to raise awareness: "Even though you might not think maybe one retweet or something isn't important, it really is. Because the more people that see it, the more it will be out there."

Misconceptions about Social Movements

A third strategy Ms. Ray used to help develop students' critical consciousness was debunking myths about how progress happens. For instance, typical U.S. History curriculum supports a *march of progress* belief that history has a way of correcting itself. In this view, the gradual triumph of rationality over baser instincts, such as intolerance, has led to an expansion of freedom and equity—an expansion that we should expect will continue. Ms. Ray, on the other hand, emphasized that progress is not inevitable, but rather occurs only because ordinary people fight hard for it.

She led students to debunk many other myths about specific social movements, such as the African American Civil Rights Movement. In a lesson she called "Mythbusters" students analyzed primary sources to uncover the truth behind common misconceptions such as the following:

1. The Civil Rights Movement was an unplanned, spontaneous uprising of exceptional individuals who acted without organization or premeditated strategy.
2. President Kennedy and his administration were unconditionally supportive of the Civil Rights Movement.
3. The landmark Supreme Court decision *Brown vs. Board of Education* resulted in the immediate and permanent desegregation of schools across the U.S.
4. The Civil Rights Movement happened only in the South because there was no racial discrimination in other parts of the country.
5. Although women did help out a little bit behind the scenes, the most effective organizers and leaders of the Civil Rights Movement were men.

Through reading primary sources, students began to learn information such as just how many years of careful planning went into the movement, and that people actually went to trainings to learn how to picket and conduct sit-ins, among other protest strategies. They learned that "everyday college students" and other "everyday people" made up the movement. This is particularly important, given that textbooks (Alridge, 2006) and instruction (Woodson, 2016) portray civil rights leaders as superhuman, Messianic figures, leading students to underestimate their own civic agency.

The Necessity of Multiple Organizations and Strategies

A final strategy Ms. Ray used was teaching students that social movements like the Civil Rights Movement relied upon multiple viewpoints, approaches, and specific strategies. Most U.S. History curriculum includes the Student Nonviolent Coordinating Committee (SNCC) and their direct acts of civil disobedience such as sit-ins. Some curriculum may present, as foils, Malcolm X and the Black Panthers who advocated for armed self-defense. Less often does curriculum discuss how the primary strategy used by the National Association for the Advancement of Colored People (NAACP) was litigation, nor the importance of grassroots, door-to-door work in propelling the movement. Ms. Ray, on the other hand, explained how these differing strategies were used by the Southern Christian Leadership Conference (SCLC) and SNCC, as well as the NAACP. In this way, students could understand the complexity of social movements and specifically that the presence of opposing viewpoints can actually enhance, rather than hinder, a movement. This is important for students, who are developing civic agency, to see how there may be multiple paths to the same endpoint and the pursuit of these simultaneously may actually help achieve social transformation. Or to put it negatively, dismissing viewpoints that differ from one's own may push away collaborators and weaken the movement. In other words, multiple types of work, on multiple fronts (e.g., in courts, in public spaces, in places of employment, through door-to-door recruitment) is necessary. As Ms. Ray said, "It doesn't just magically happen" as simplified textbook narratives may imply, further contributing to the inevitable *march of progress* misconception about social change.

STUDENT RESPONSES: CRITICAL HOPE, NOT CYNICISM

What effects did the above teaching strategies have on students' opinions about the United States, racism, and the likelihood of achieving social justice? Based on their comments in both class and one-on-one interviews, the students were able to critique both past and present injustices without becoming cynical, disillusioned, or hopeless about the future. Most were happy to live in the United States and appreciated the freedoms protected here, even while they also criticized racial injustice, mistreatment of immigrants, and discrimination against same-sex couples, among other things. Josephine expressed this stance well when she explained that she "loved the country" but that she would not risk her life for it:

> I think the country itself doesn't really protect its people enough for me to want to go out and put myself in a predicament ... If police brutality and other things like—you're not ensuring my safety here, so what would make you think I would feel safe outside of here [in another country]?

Similarly, Amina stated,

> Just because you love your country doesn't mean—like if you love something, you can say you know, "that was wrong" or "this was wrong." ... Just because you love it doesn't mean it didn't do something wrong in the past. Or won't do something wrong in the future.

Amina said that Ms. Ray pointed out what was or is wrong, while still showing her love for the country.

When I asked Amina if she thought some students might lose patriotism when the teacher points out flaws in the country, she replied,

I don't think so because actually her class makes me love America more, because people like her is what make America better. Because if there was nobody in America saying segregation is wrong, we would still be segregated. I would be sitting in the back of the bus, or you know just different things like that. Because if she teaches her students to stand up, or if she teaches her students to look at sexist ads and say, "Oh that's definitely sexist" when they might've just scrolled through the TV before her class, then I think she's making America a better place. And eventually if someone isn't patriotic, they will begin to love America because there are people saying, "this is wrong," and then, "We're changing it to fix it and make it better."

Another student decided to write a thank-you letter at the end of the year in which she thanked Ms. Ray for teaching her about black history, helping her see the world differently, and become more aware of things. Ms. Ray was delighted by the letter because, as she described it, she and this student "had butted heads" at the beginning of the year. She attributed the change of heart to the student starting to "recognize what I was doing" in terms of emphasizing resistance and the African American perspective of history much more than the U.S. History curriculum typically does. Overall, the students' comments in class and interviews demonstrated a critical hope (Freire, 1992) and awareness that, while there are injustices that need addressing, American democracy provides avenues for doing so.

CONCLUSION

As James Loewen pointed out in his widely read book, *Lies My Teacher Told Me* (1995), the version of U.S. history commonly taught in schools omits many of the shameful moments in the country's past in an effort to ensure students identify with their nation and feel compelled to engage in civic and political life. Teachers, too, may wish to avoid conversations about the historical antecedents of contemporary injustices to protect students from difficult knowledge and potential frustration or despair. On the other hand, research with marginalized youth has suggested that they perceive this cleansed version of history as dishonest and that they may actually be more likely to participate as they become increasingly conscious of contemporary social inequities. The question then is how to be honest and encourage critical consciousness, while minimizing the risk of despair.

This chapter presents four strategies one social justice-oriented teacher used to achieve these two goals. Although Ms. Ray was honest about the atrocities committed throughout the history of the United States, she modeled critical hope by continually reminding students of the ways people have fought back against these atrocities. In particular, she taught about the power of ordinary people, and the various strategies that they have used successfully, and sometimes in combination, in order to achieve social change. As a result, her students expressed a belief that ordinary individuals, including themselves, do have the power to improve society. Moreover, they explained that just because they can critique the United States, this does not mean that they want to distance themselves from the country. In fact, some even said that seeing their teacher candidly critique some elements of American society made them love the country even more, because they could appreciate how people like themselves or their teachers are free to fight for a better future.

At the time of writing, Donald Trump's presidency has spurred protests against his actions on immigration, health care, education, climate change, foreign policy, and other issues. Although this reflects a welcomed general increase in political participation, we have also seen a backlash against public demonstrations of resistance (Agrawal, 2017; Cheney, Dawsey, & Morin, 2017). This has underscored the need for social justice educators to teach constitutionally-protected resistance strategies, in particular the strategies that may be most effective in a polarized society in which each side seems increasingly unable to understand the other (McAvoy & Hess, 2013).

NOTE

1. All names are pseudonyms.

REFERENCES

Abowitz, K. K., & Harnish, J. (2006). Contemporary discourses of citizenship. *Review of Educational Research, 76*(4), 653–690.

Agrawal, N. (2017, February 3). In North Dakota, it could become legal to hit a protester with your car. *Los Angeles Times.* Retrieved from http://www.latimes.com/nation/la-na-bills-protest-criminal-20170201-story.html

Alridge, D. (2006). The limits of master narratives in history textbooks: An analysis of representations of Martin Luther King, Jr. *Teachers College Record, 108*(4), 662–686. doi:10.1111/tcre.2006.108. issue-4

Cheney K., Dawsey J., & Morin R. (2017, January 14). Trump rips John Lewis as Democrats boycott inauguration. *Politico.* Retrieved from http://www.politico.com/story/2017/01/trump-john-lewis-233630

Duncan-Andrade, J., & Morrell, E. (2008). *The art of critical pedagogy: Possibilities for moving from theory to practice in urban schools.* New York, NY: Peter Lang.

Freire, P. (1970/2000). *Pedagogy of the oppressed, 30th anniversary edition* (M. B. Ramos, Trans.). New York, NY: Continuum. (Original work published 1970.)

Freire, P. (1992). *Pedagogy of hope.* London: Continuum.

Gramsci, A. (1971). *Selections from the prison notebooks* (Q. Hoare & G. N. Smith, Trans. and Eds.). New York, NY: International Press.

Hytten, K., & Bettez, S. C. (2011). Understanding education for social justice. *Educational Foundations*, *25*(Winter-Spring), 7–24.

Loewen, J. W. (1995). *Lies my teacher told me: Everything your American history textbook got wrong*. New York, NY: The New Press.

McAvoy, P., & Hess, D. (2013). Classroom deliberation in an era of political polarization. *Curriculum Inquiry*, *43*(1), 14–47.

Parker, W. (1996). "Advanced" ideas about democracy: Toward a pluralist conception of citizenship education. *The Teachers College Record*, *98*(1), 104–125.

Ross, E. W. (Ed.). (2006). *The social studies curriculum: Purposes, problems, and possibilities* (3rd ed.). Albany, NY: State University of New York Press.

Rubin, B. (2007). "There's still not justice": Youth civic identity development amid distinct school and community contexts. *The Teachers College Record*, *109*(2), 449–481.

Woodson, A. N. (2016). We're just ordinary people: Messianic master narratives and Black Youths' civic agency. *Theory & Research in Social Education*, *44*(2), 184–211.

CHAPTER EIGHTEEN

"It's Like We Were Slow-Roasted ... BUT IN A Really Good Way"

Embedded Y-PAR in a U.S. History Course
11th Grade

BRIAN GIBBS

Mr. Aguayo[1] is in his tenth year of teaching social studies at a large urban high school in a historically economically-stressed and primarily Latinx area of Southern California. He has taught World and U.S. History, American Government, Economics, International Law, an advisory for young men, and Ethnic Studies, though he indicated that all of his courses are "ethnic studies and social justice infused." For six of his ten years, he has received a pink slip from the district stating that he may be displaced from his current teaching position or he may lose his position within the district altogether due to the district's response to the economic slowdown. The high school in which he teaches has also undergone many changes during his tenure, each in the name of educational reform. The overpopulated campus went through a transformation process shifting from one large to several small schools on the same campus, a complex model (Cuban, Lichtenstein, Evenchik, Tombari, & Pozzoboni, 2010; Hantzopolous & Tyner-Mullings, 2012), then reverting back again to a comprehensive high school model. All of this was done at the direction of the quasi-mayoral takeover organization described as a partnership between the mayor's office and two local school "families."[2] During that time Mr. Aguayo was on the design team and a member of four different small schools, all of which were shuttered for various reasons.

Mr. Aguayo's ability to survive the turmoil is largely due to the pedagogical power and teacher activist community surrounding Y-PAR (Youth Participatory

Action Research). Through an association with an activist group, he was invited to participate with students in a summer program offered by a local university that trained students and teachers to become quantitative and qualitative researchers. The program, which consisted of two weeks in the summer along with follow-up meetings, allowed Mr. Aguayo to guide and support his 11th grade U.S. History students in researching the inequities and problems in their school and local neighborhood and presenting their research and recommendations to the community. This provided Mr. Aguayo with a clear way to not only have students investigate injustice but to grow student empowerment, sharpen agency (Anderson, 2010; Gillen, 2014), and help students become "dangerous citizens" (Ross, 2015) by offering them ways to interrupt systemic injustice. The organization also provided him with a network of like-minded educators in similar school situations from which to learn, grow, and process, while also being inspired.

Since Mr. Aguayo's first summer and year engaging students in Y-PAR, he has made it a significant part of his U.S. History course. Initially adding Y-PAR to the last few weeks of the school year, he found that students struggled, the product was wanting, and Y-PAR skills went unlearned. He came to the understanding that research is complicated and difficult to do for college-educated adults much less high school students. As a result, he now begins teaching his students what research is and how to do it slowly over the entire year by embedding it in historical content. This culminates in student-engaged research on a community problem, which is presented to the school community with a solution-driven action plan. Mr. Aguayo forms his instructional units around profound justice-oriented essential questions and problems, through which he teaches the discrete skills of Y-PAR. What follows is a description of how Mr. Aguayo does this using three vignettes, two from his unit on the Vietnam War and a third describing an "analysis day" during the community-based Y-PAR project cycle.

THEORETICAL FRAMEWORK

The theoretical framework for this study is critical civic literacy. Critical civic literacy grew out of arguments over what the intent and expectation of civic education is. During the Common School era, civic education was a pillar of the curriculum (DeVitis, 2011), but was largely code for assimilation. Critical civic literacy instead builds from critical pedagogy, and advocates a thorough examining of texts to identify, challenge, and interrupt social constructs, assumptions, and ideologies (Mulcahy, 2011). Expanding on this, critical civic literacy uses reading, writing, listening, and speaking to create critical democratic citizens who question what is deemed official and legitimate knowledge (Teitelbaum, 2011). Praxis, reflection and action (Freire, 1970) are crucial parts of critical civic literacy, as they push to advocate for societal transformation to disrupt social inequalities. Ross (2016) may have the clearest vision of critical civic literacy with his notion of dangerous citizenship. Dangerous citizenship calls for a reimagining of teachers' roles as the pursuit of creating meaningful ways for students to "develop understandings of the world" (p. 8). It involves risk and engaging "certain necessary dangers" and involves more than "voting and signing petitions" (p. 8). It is in essence dangerous not only to the participants but to the hierarchical power structures. Through awareness, participation, and intentional action the society that so many want can be created.

A NOTE ON METHOD AND POSITIONALITY

The data for this chapter emerged from a previous multi-case study (Stake, 1995) that investigated how U.S. History teachers conceive of and enact the concept of instructional rigor, in which Mr. Aquayo was a participant. Over the course of one semester—the second semester of that school year—he was interviewed four times for between 90 and 120 minutes each; instruction was observed 17 times, recorded in a running record format; and all class assignments, readings, and assessments for the semester were collected and analyzed. The semi-structured interviews (Merriman, 1998; Yin, 1989) were designed to allow him to theorize about his teaching (Lather, 1986) and steps were taken to make the interviews more interactive and conversational (Holstein & Gubrium, 1995; Segall, 2002).

I was a classroom teacher in East Los Angeles, California for 16 years and wrote my own inquiry- and discussion-based curriculum steeped in critical pedagogy. I worked hard at engaging a justice-oriented pedagogy within a large urban school system. As a university professor and researcher, my struggles and interests are the same as when I was a classroom teacher: how can we be fully-engaged, justice-oriented teachers within the system as it presently exists? It was this ongoing interest that led me to the work of Mr. Aguayo.

TEACHING VIETNAM

Mr. Aguayo was hovering a bit, pacing back and forth and then hovering again, a Cheshire cat grin on his face, his hands and arms in motion, circling and waving, revealing his intense energy and enthusiasm for students, teaching, and the topic. Thirty-two students or so—the children of immigrants primarily from Mexico but also a smattering of other Latin American countries—looked on. In jeans, sweat pants, hoodies and one huipil top with matching skirt, most with still-wet hair, the students sat subdued by both the early morning hour and the weight of Mr. Aguayo's question. The students had just unanimously declared the Vietnam

War to be unjust, "a little too unceremoniously and easily," Mr. Aguayo, shared later, "I don't think they had really struggled with it yet."

Sensing the heavy silence, Mr. Aguayo, asked the question again, "So you're saying nothing is worth fighting for?" The class had been investigating the question, "What is a just war?" using the war in Vietnam as a case study. The students began the unit by examining all the wars America had been involved with up to the war in Vietnam and had grown increasingly distressed as they began to identify "power," "land acquisition," and "feigned wounded party" as some of the reasons for war. Mr. Aguayo had made it intentionally and incredibly personal for students. When the unit began, he asked students, "For what reasons would you send a family member to war?" explaining, "Every time we send a soldier into combat, it's someone's daughter, son, friend, husband, wife ... so why not ours?" The students had struggled, their internal gears grinding and pushing against each other as if they were free of oil. Like the current question, it had given them pause.

"No ... there are," a female student answered defiantly, then faded as she started to argue that things were worth fighting for, but did not have the words to express her feelings. "Yes they are, but not in the way that you're saying," a male student interjected. "Like with blockades, protests, economic sanctions and stuff", his voice trailing off, "fighting isn't always death and violence, soldiers and stuff ..." Mr. Aguayo paused for a moment to see if anything else would surface, then asked a question, "So even though the people of Vietnam asked 'us' to help it's not worth fighting for?" Two students began talking simultaneously, with one relenting. A female student continued, "The people didn't ask did they? It was what's his name ... the so-called president ... Diem, yeah he asked, but I think it was to maintain power." A male student continued, "Yeah, and then the Free Fire Zones ... Operation Rolling Thunder ... that war was not fought justly. I mean maybe war is necessary sometimes, but I don't think it's ever just." The students went on to collectively list their critiques of American military policy during the Vietnam War. The critiques included the disputed "attack" in the Gulf of Tonkin, a war by attrition, carpet-bombing, the use of napalm, agent orange, and the abandoning of those who helped as the American embassy fell. Students critiqued military strategy, the foreign policy leading up to and continuing after the war (specifically the Domino Theory and the Containment Policy) alongside the racism and classism they saw in the draft and college deferment system.

The discussion was brought to a close by a female student who said, "Yeah Mr., I mean what was it 3 million Vietnamese people and 58,000 Americans ... and for what?" This is what Mr. Aguayo wanted. He wanted the discussion to be difficult, complicated, thoughtful, searching, and engaged. Social justice, he argued, was not just saying this is wrong and that is wrong, it is really looking at the history in all its complexity, which can be very difficult, and then making an argument. After the female student spoke, Mr. Aguayo smiled again and then said,

"Ok, now what are you going to do about it?" There was a loud moment of silence, a collective releasing of breath, then one brave female student said, a bit hesitantly, "You mean Y-PAR don't you? Ahhh ... man ... It's like we were slow-roasted ... but in a really good way."

YOUTH PARTICIPATION ACTION RESEARCH (Y-PAR) AND SOCIAL JUSTICE EDUCATION

Mr. Aguayo's students explored Youth Participatory Action Research (Y-PAR) all year and, by the beginning of the second semester, the students had already begun to recognize the signs warranting Y-PAR, which is research that is focused on community problems, engaged in by community members, and presented to the community publicly (Cammarota, Berta-Avila, Ayala, Rivera, & Rodriguez, 2016; Cammarota & Fine, 2008; Mirra, Garcia, & Morrell, 2015). Y-PAR is the process of helping students speak out and speak back by teaching them to investigate real problems, develop real solutions, and learn how to use their many voices (oral, written, and visual) to cause change. Many social justice teachers examine problems of race class, gender, power, and issues related to LGBTQ people. Far fewer offer concrete steps and practice in how to speak back to power and engage in resistance. Y-PAR does that. Y-PAR is a democratic practice and engagement in its purest form.

Mr. Aguayo stretched this definition to fit it into the thematic and justice-oriented curriculum he designed. Rather than teaching U.S. History chronologically, Mr. Aguayo designed units that were thematic in nature and organized around essential questions that were critically-oriented and open to multiple interpretations. He pushed students to apply the content and process skills they learned to formulate an answer. Mr. Aguayo took elements of Y-PAR and blended them into units throughout the school year. He understood that Y-PAR is complicated and challenging and that to learn how to do it well, students were going to have to engage in it multiple times. Students identified a research problem from course content; formulated research questions; investigated and evaluated available resources; discussed the merits of quantitative, qualitative, and mixed research methods; learned how to function as a team; practiced argumentative writing; and presented in front of a critical audience.

These skills grew over time, culminating in the Y-PAR final project teams. For Mr. Aguayo, the Y-PAR project was the pinnacle of social justice and critical teaching (North, 2009; Swalwell, 2013). He believes that to teach social studies is to teach controversy. If not, he indicated, "you're doing it wrong." Social justice teaching is discussing uncomfortable history, analyzing topics that challenge student perceptions of content and self, and focusing on issues of power and the stories that are often left out of traditional history courses. In the classroom, this means examining and critiquing the dominant narrative, as Mr. Aguayo did with teaching the Vietnam War by focusing on two essential questions: *What is a just war?* and, *How do we end an unjust war?*

Mr. Aguayo taught differently, critically, some might say radically, but no one would accuse him of teaching traditionally. Mr. Aguayo's class did not begin with the first chapter of the textbook; they did not use a textbook. He was not alone in these choices, but he did stick out. Like someone locked in the jailhouse who is largely powerless, he explored and memorized the rules and guidelines in order to mount a defense of his teaching. To this end, he had read the state content standards from cover to cover. Mr. Aguayo spoke of the standards often, displaying them prominently on the walls of his well-decorated (mostly with student work and justice-oriented posters) walls and connected lessons and units of instruction to them, explaining the rationale to his students. He volunteered to be his school's Common Core State Standards (CCSS) coordinator, knowing that how the CCSS was interpreted on the school level was going to impact his ability to teach critically, thematically, and with Y-PAR. He explained that to teach for social justice meant more than teaching; it meant, as he put it, "being involved." This involvement included the lives of students, colleagues, teachers, and community members active in social movements. It was not, he argued, for the faint of heart or as he concluded with a wry smile, "the easily exhausted."

THE ANTI-WAR MOVEMENT

The anti-war movement that developed in response to the war in Vietnam is mentioned lightly, if at all, in most textbooks and curriculum guides. However, Mr. Aguayo spends a fair amount of time on it for several reasons. First, the United States has been in perpetual war since the invasions of Afghanistan and Iraq in the early 2000s, so the Vietnam War serves as a model for students to examine, critique, and learn from. It is also an example of modified Y-PAR. The various actors in the anti-Vietnam War movement researched the war in Vietnam, investigated various resistance strategies, and then presented their ideas in front of many critical audiences in their attempt to end the war. As Bill Ayers indicated in his memoir *Fugitive Days* (2001), it takes a lot of strong research to be a good activist.

Mr. Aguayo transitioned into the second essential question of the unit with a writing activity. The majority of the students became convinced that the war in Vietnam was unjust, and he asked all students to assume this position. He then asked them to respond to the following prompt: "You are convinced that the war in Vietnam is unjust. How do you end it?" Immediately students hissed and guffawed verbally, demonstrating the difficulty of the question. You could almost hear the sounds of the gears grinding inside students' heads. Pushing and pulling, the students struggled to figure out how individuals—namely, themselves—could end the war in Vietnam.

"You can't," a student finally muttered in frustration after several minutes of staring at the ceiling lights and flipping his pencil in search of inspiration. "The government started it ... they gotta stop it," he continued. "Congress right?", another student chimed in, seeming a little lighter from the forward motion of the conversation. "No, not Congress ... it's an illegal war right Mr. Aguayo?", another student added. "Right, right," another student continued, "it was the President ... LBJ right?". "Right," Mr. Aguayo chimed in, "Many folks argue Vietnam was an illegal war. Why?" Several students went on to explain that constitutionally a President asks for a Declaration of War from Congress and, though none had been asked or given, the President had sent soldiers. Students countered that the president has the right to send troops. The students argued until a female student, exasperated, asked, "But how does this end the war?". "We can't!", another student said loudly. "The government has to," he continued.

Mr. Aguayo, who hovered in the background smiling as the discussion was happening, stepped forward with a question. "What did Emma Goldman teach us?". "Free love," a male student said quickly and for a laugh. "Yes ... and?", Mr. Aguayo added, staring the student down, so that he and all the students would take it seriously. "Organize?", a female student asked. "Governments do stuff because people demand, right?", another student added. "Right," Mr. Aguayo added.

He counted students off into teams of three or four and assigned each a historical character and group that resisted the war in Vietnam. The groups included the Students for a Democratic Society (SDS), the Youth International Party (Yippies), the Weather Underground, the Vietnam Veterans Against War (VVAW), the Berrigan Brothers (Philip and Daniel), Daniel Ellsberg, and a group labeled *musicians*, who represented various musical acts during this time. In teams, students analyzed the perspective of their group, what types of research and information they used, and how they used their voices to resist. As a class or in teams, students watched films, read primary and secondary source documents, and analyzed what their assigned anti-war group and other groups did to end the war in Vietnam. Mr. Aguayo went to great lengths to connect the content they were processing to Y-PAR skills. The students engaged in activities like *walk-and-talk*, in which they interviewed one another, gathering information about each anti-war group as an anticipatory set and pre-reading activity. They engaged in a document analysis to analyze the writings and speeches of the anti-war groups and were also asked to evaluate the Y-PAR skills each used, or how closely to Y-PAR each group aligned.

This section of the unit culminated in a historical simulation (Wright-Maley, 2015), or as Mr. Aguayo called it, a Character Driven Seminar (CDS).

A CDS is a discussion utilizing Socratic Seminar rules (Roberts & Billings, 1999), where the lives, philosophies, and arguments of the characters serve as the text. In this case, student teams represented and argued in favor of the point of view, philosophy, and tactics of their assigned anti-war group. Students wrote testimonies or speeches, developed critical questions to ask the other groups, and prepared to defend and explain their group's tactics while attacking other groups' tactics to end the war in Vietnam.

HEADING TOWARDS THE FINAL Y-PAR PROJECT

The students were huddled together, leaning in close, speaking agitatedly in small teams, some with stricken looks on their faces. Occasionally an admonishment was shouted, "I told you!" or a regretful, "I wish we would have …". "It's analysis day," said Mr. Aguayo by way of explanation. As the end of second semester approached, the students shifted away from the historical content and in teams identified problems in the school community to be researched and examined. The students designed projects, formed research questions, and decided how best to collect and analyze data on their problem. During each stage (problem, research question, data collection strategies) student teams had to briefly present to Mr. Aguayo so that he could give students direct and immediate feedback. The topics included: examinations of the (un)healthiness of school-based food, why students skipped classes, whether or not sports teams' field assignments were sexist, gender access to advanced coursework, the environmental health of the neighborhood, what could be learned from the activist history of the neighborhood and school, and if school could be less boring and more relevant, among other topics. After the Vietnam unit and several others Mr. Aguayo began to assign the final Y-PAR project incrementally. Mr. Aguayo, his student teacher, and a graduate student from a local university who had worked with Y-PAR as a classroom teacher were making the rounds, problem-solving, pushing, questioning, and supporting. Mr. Aguayo, always ebullient, was teasing and making fun of the students as well. It lightened students' moods. They were asked to complete a difficult and complicated task and were looking at the real and sometimes less than satisfactory results of their labor.

"I think we were asking the wrong questions," a female student was saying as she hunched over their interview protocol. "Students just didn't see the sexism … I mean come on it's kind of obvious." They were researching whether or not sports teams on campus, specifically field use, was sexist. A male student in her team leaned back, hands resting on the top of his head, took a deep breath, then said, "Maybe they're just what's the word … misogynist, right?". "That's what the evidence is saying," chimed in the third member of their team, a female who was looking bleary-eyed and weary. "I know they are … I assumed they would be … but for real have you seen the girls softball field? Have you seen the boys [field]? They bus them over there!". "Did you read what some boy players have said in the interviews? They say it's reverse sexism that they have to get bused. They should have a field here," the male student adds. The conversation continued, as the students tried to understand what their data revealed, whether they had asked incorrect or incoherent questions, or whether the results revealed what the school community clearly believed. They analyzed their survey data next, which revealed similar trends. The team eventually decided to design a follow-up interview instrument targeted at particular people, realizing that the solution they had planned to present, an updated women's softball field, was not going to be as strongly supported as they hoped.

A few feet over, across a mangle of backpacks, chairs, and strewn papers, Mr. Aguayo was speaking to another team of students. A young man was leaning back in his chair trying not to laugh while he spoke. "Come on Mr. Aguayo, I'm an expert, you know that. But my opinion can't stand alone ... that's not research, you taught me that." One member of his research team was laughing while the third member was looking on, horrified. He was a known ditcher, skipping class with abandon. "I know you're king of the ditchers" Mr. Aguayo began, "Well royalty for sure," the young man interjected, "But the point is to figure out why it's a problem and to solve it, right?" The team laughed and agreed. Their data revealed some disturbing trends to explain why students skipped class including disinterested teachers, too much teacher talk, no student engagement, and negative student image. The team talked about dividing the work in two: one team doing a small follow-up study with a few more interviews to confirm the results and possibly narrow them down, while the other team would begin to work on realistic school-based solutions.

DISCUSSION AND CONCLUSION

Three weeks later, the students presented their research, methodology, and recommendations over a series of days and before a series of audiences. Students, parents, teachers, and administrators attended. They presented their research using a PowerPoint and each team member spoke and answered audience questions. Students were formal and well-rehearsed. It was not the students' first time speaking publicly, making arguments, using evidence, or answering questions; it had been built into every unit the entire year. There were special clothes for the occasion. There was laughter and there were tears, a few stutters and start-overs, nervous energy, but mostly feelings of success. The strongest feelings may have been of having just done something important, something that had the possibility of making a difference. The looks on their faces, whispered congratulations, hugs and high-fives as they left the stage said it all. The adults took the students' inquiries seriously; for example, the principal took notes furiously and always asked a question, sometimes two. The problems were not solved that day, nor the next. In the long run, this was a very good thing. True problems take time, effort, resolve, planning, re-planning, and a shoulder to the wheel. The students knew that going in.

As one student said in the conclusion of his team's presentation, "What we're supposed to talk about now are the solutions the school community should enact to cause change … but that's not what we're going to talk about. We're going to talk about … I'm going to talk about what I'm going to do." Y-PAR does not offer easy solutions; it offers reality. It provides students with a pathway to engage in the difficult but necessary act of struggling towards change. When it is well-embedded in a justice oriented classroom, Y-PAR can help create the next generation of dangerous citizens (Ross, 2015), with the awareness and skill to build new possibilities.

NOTES

1. Pseudonym.
2. The school communities were given a vote between two possibilities and plans. One offered by the superintendent looked appeared to be restrictive in relation to pedagogy and curriculum, while the other was a partnership with the Mayor's office that seemed to offer the possibilities of some teaching freedom and the possibilities of gaining financial support as a non-profit entity. School "families" included were two large high schools with all of the feeder elementary and middle schools.

REFERENCES

Anderson, L. (2010). Embedded, emboldened, and (net)working for change: Support-seeking and teacher agency in urban, high-needs schools. *Harvard Educational Review, 80*(4), 541–573.

Ayers, W. (2001). *Fugitive days.* Boston, MA: Beacon Press.

Cammarota, J., Berta-Avila, M., Ayala, J., Rivera, M., & Rodriguez, L. (2016). PAR Entremundos: A practitioner guide. In A. Valenzuela (Ed.), *Growing critically conscious teachers: A social justice curriculum for educators of Latino/a youth* (pp. 67–90). New York, NY: Teachers College Press.

Cammarota, J., & Fine, M. (Eds.). (2008). *Revolutionizing education: Youth participatory action research in motion.* New York, NY: Routledge.

Cuban, L., Lichtenstein, G., Evenchik, A., Tombari, M., & Pozzoboni, K. (Eds.). (2010). *Against the odds: Insights from one district's small school reform.* Cambridge, MA: Harvard Education Press.

DeVitis, J. (2011). Introduction. In J. DeVitis (Ed.), *Critical civic literacy: A reader* (pp. XI-XII). New York, NY: Peter Lang Publishing.

Freire, P. (1970). *Pedagogy of the oppressed.* New York, NY: Continuum Publishing.

Gillen, J. (2014). *Educating for insurgency: The roles of young people in schools of poverty.* Oakland, CA: AK Press.

Hantzopolous, M., & Tyner-Mullings, A. R. (Eds.). (2012). *Critical small schools: Beyond privatization in New York City urban educational reform.* Charlotte, NC: Information Age Publishing.

Holstein, J. A., & Gubrium, J. F. (1995). *The active interview.* Thousand Oaks, CA: Sage.

Lather, P. (1986). Research as praxis. *Harvard Educational Review, 56*(3), 257–278.

Merriman, S. (1998). *Qualitative research and case study applications in education.* San Francisco, CA: Jossey-Bass.

Mirra, N., Garcia, A., & Morrell, E. (2015). *Doing youth participatory action research: Transforming inquiry with researchers, educators, and students.* New York, NY: Routledge.

Mulcahy, C. M. (2011). The tangled web we weave: Critical literacy and critical thinking. In J. DeVitis (Ed.), *Critical civic literacy: A reader* (pp. 1–11). New York, NY: Peter Lang Publishing.

North, C. (2009). *Teaching for social justice?: Voices from the front lines.* Boulder, CO: Paradigm Publishing.

Roberts, T., & Billings, L. (1999). *The paideia classroom.* New York, NY: Taylor and Francis.

Ross, E. W. (2015). Dr. Dewey, or: How I learned to stop worrying about where ideas come from and love critical pedagogy. In B. Porfilio & D. R. Ford (Eds.), *Leaders in critical pedagogy: Narratives for understanding and solidarity* (pp. 141–157). Boston, MA: Sense Publishing.

Ross, E. W. (2016). The courage of hopelessness: Creative disruption of everyday life in the classroom. In W. Journell (Ed.), *Reassessing the social studies curriculum: Preparing students for a post-9/11 world* (pp. 1–27). New York, NY: Rowman & Littlefield.

Segall, A. (2002). *Disturbing practice: Reading teacher education as text.* New York, NY: Peter Lang Publishing.

Stake, R. (1995). *The art of case study research.* Thousand Oaks, CA: Sage Publishing.

Swalwell, K. (2013). *Educating activist allies: Social justice pedagogy with the suburban and urban elite.* New York, NY: Routledge.

Teitelbaum, K. (2011). Critical civic literacy in schools: Adolescents seeking to understand and improve the(ir) world. In J. DeVitis (Ed.), *Critical civic literacy: A reader.* New York, (pp. 11–217). NY: Peter Lang Publishing.

Wright-Maley, C. (2015). On "Stepping back and letting go": The role of control in the success or failure of social studies simulations. *Theory and Research in Social Education, 4*(2), 206–243.

Yin, R. (1989). *Case study research: Design and methods* (Rev. ed.). Newbury Park, CA: Sage Publications.

CHAPTER NINETEEN

Students AS Researchers

A Co-teaching Narrative from a Social Justice-Oriented U.S. Government Class
12th Grade

LINSAY DEMARTINO AND SARA RUSK

JOSÉ'S[1] TRIUMPH

For one particular student it began with a poem describing the issues he saw in his community. Refusing to stand up in front of his peers, he read it haltingly from his desk, seeming to hold his breath the entire time. Rather than relief at finishing, he looked angry and agitated. Then he heard the responses from his classmates: support, connections, a "You did it!" This clearly surprised him, and his reaction moved the whole group. From that moment on, José came to class more, smiled at his peers, and even joked around. He had struggled throughout high school and had expressed to his special education caseworker that he hated most of his teachers and just being in a school environment.

The course was titled American[2] Government Social Justice Education Project, and this was our first year teaching it together. Linsay served as the special education teacher, and Sara was the mainstream teacher. Linsay's skills working predominantly in resource classes were crucial and proved that this collaborative class was an important model to better support students with disabilities and to build sensitivity for learning differences. José had been in few mainstream classes and had a school-wide reputation as a troublemaker with alleged gang ties and violent outbursts. His special education label further alienated and angered him.

At the end of the school year when José got up to present his participant action research project with his peers in a high school/community *Encuentro* at the university, our school's special education department head cried. She told us she did not recognize this young man whom she had met four years earlier. As in many documented cases of ethnic studies courses, it was this particular class and the peers within it that kept José coming to school and motivated him to graduate.

INTRODUCTION

The demographic composition of the United States population continues to change, becoming increasingly more diverse. Unfortunately, the U.S. education system too often fails to reach all students. Students from groups that have been historically marginalized based on race, ethnicity, class, gender, language, ability, and/or sexual orientation are excluded from the mainstream school community. Since the backgrounds and interests of these students may not match those of the historically dominant group, their stories and needs are largely ignored. In the name of educational progress, the trend in schools is to adopt "light" multicultural curriculums, such as incorporating the historical contributions of different racial and ethnic groups during their designated month (Castagno, 2009). Through dominant society's perpetuation of cultural stereotypes and prejudices, schools fail to provide integral educational equity through the use of culturally-based, social justice-centered curriculum.

RESEARCH FOCUS

As we collaborated on this chapter, our main focus was to highlight the ways in which the use of culturally responsive practices within our U.S. Government class challenged dominant classroom hierarchical structures and traditional pedagogical approaches. Following a review of empirical and theoretical literature, this book chapter will detail the methodology and site description. Next, the findings section will describe the practices used in our course as well as implications for practitioners.

Funds of Knowledge

Providing a space for the unique voices of communities of color by exploring the connection between education and culture is fundamental to the academic success of students. Funds of knowledge (Moll, Amanti, Neff, & Gonzalez, 1992) are best described as the belief that students come from culturally rich households.

Moll et al. (1992) claimed "that by capitalizing on household and other community resources, we can organize classroom instruction that far exceeds the rote-like instruction ... children commonly encounter in schools" (p. 132). By using funds of knowledge in the classroom, the student becomes more connected to the curriculum and, in turn, makes educational gains.

Through qualitative inquiry, the funds of knowledge possessed by historically marginalized communities are brought to the pedagogical forefront. Moll et al. (1992) utilized a combination of observations, interviewing, life-histories, and case studies to accurately portray "the complex functions of households within socio-historical contexts" (p. 132). Through analysis of these data, Moll et al. (1992) argued, "funds of knowledge represent a positive (and, we argue, realistic) view of households as containing ample cultural and cognitive resources with great potential utility for classroom instruction" (p. 134). In sum, funds of knowledge successfully combat the cultural deficit model by embracing and legitimizing students' home cultures and resources.

Cultural Responsiveness

Similar to the use of funds of knowledge within the classroom, the use of culturally responsive pedagogy is a fundamental part of providing educational equity through culturally-based, social justice-centered curriculum. Since "connecting with students and responding to their cultural identities are at the heart of cultural responsive pedagogy," culturally responsive teachers are influenced by diverse cultures and learning styles present within the same classroom (Irizarry, 2007, p. 21). As educators validate their students' fluid cultures, the students become connected to the classroom and student achievement rises.

Since culture is ever-changing, educators must seek to enrich not only their curriculum but themselves and their students. According to Irizarry (2007), "culturally responsive pedagogy is about more than what teachers need to know about a specific group of students; it also involves who they need to be and who they need to continuously become" (p. 27). In this way, "culturally responsive teachers help students to understand that knowledge has moral and political elements and consequences, which obligate them to take social action to promote freedom, equality, and justice for everyone" (Gay, 2002, p. 110). As a result of culturally responsive pedagogy, the students become linked to the classroom and the world around them.

Racism and Education

Racism comes in many forms. It can manifest overtly or covertly, symbolically or literally, and privately or publicly. Since our student population is becoming increasingly diverse, it is essential for educational institutions to consider the implications and effects of race on education and society.

According to Bonilla-Silva and Forman (2000), "color-blind racism allows whites to appear 'not racist', ... preserve their privileged status, ... blame Blacks for their lower status, ... and criticize any institutional approach ... that attempts to ameliorate racial inequality" (p. 78). In this way, racism—especially systemic racism—is widely ignored. Bell (1992) expressed this ignorance of racial consciousness through the voice of his character, Jesse B. Semple. Semple stated, "the white ones really think racism is over, despite anything we tell them" (Bell, 1992, p. 30). He continued, "I don't ever see white people getting smart about race ... unless there is a crisis, they learn nothing" (Bell, 1992, p. 28). In addition to colorblindness, this particular narrative alludes to insidious racism: racism affects all aspects of life, including education, jobs, power, prestige, and wealth accumulation for people of color. Examples of contemporary insidious racism range from overt—a state condemns ethnic studies in the K-12 classroom—to covert—an instructor continuously corrects the grammar of a student of color and ignores the grammar of a white student. As such, different levels of consciousness contribute to overt and covert forms of racism.

Freire's Levels of Consciousness and Models for Education

Freire's (1970) levels of consciousness, including magical, naïve, and critical, are stages of people becoming aware of their individual and collective power to overcome oppression. Magical consciousness is the idea that things are just the way they are. To a person with a magical consciousness, God wills it to be this way. There is total acceptance and no questioning. Naïve consciousness is self- and community-blaming. A person with naïve consciousness believes they are not successful because they are not as smart or do not work as hard as others. Critical consciousness, or the idea of reading the world, acknowledges that oppression exists and looks at its roots with the goal of transformation.

As a result of colonization, legitimate knowledge is determined by the predominant group of people in power, or the white middle class. As such, the former struggle for power and control is discussed through the dichotomy of oppressors and the oppressed (Freire, 1970). According to Freire, "the more the oppressors control the oppressed, the more they change them into inanimate things" (p. 59). In other words, when educators reinforce the normative hierarchical structure within the classroom, they do not see their students as a viable part of the broader local community. Furthermore, Freire's argument is twofold: first, the oppressed must self-recognize their oppression; then, they must proactively fight to emancipate themselves from the oppressor. However, through critical consciousness, or the realization of and emancipation from oppression, the oppressed must not in turn become the oppressor and reinforce the existing status quo (Freire, 1970). The status quo in education is the banking model, which places teachers in the sole position of power and control over knowledge within the classroom.

Typically, when the teacher uses methods associated with banking education, the teacher uses narration and does not empower their students to become educational collaborators; rather, their "words are emptied of their concreteness and become hollow and alienating" to the students (Freire, 1970, p. 71). In fact, the narrator follows "the banking notion of consciousness that the educator's role is to regulate the way the world 'enters into' the students" (Freire, 1970, p. 76). Banking education identifies the teacher as the depositor of knowledge. Then, the teacher makes intentional daily deposits of information, requiring minimal analysis, into the minds of students. The students become passive learners. Their interests, culture, and curriculum connections are lost.

On the other hand, the critically conscious educator uses problem-posing education. Through dialogue, "the teacher-of-the-students and the students-of-the-teacher cease to exist and a new term emerges: teacher-student with students-teachers" (Freire, 1970, p. 80). In other words, as the students contribute to the teaching and learning in the classroom, the educator is no longer the depositor of knowledge. Through reflective and critical dialogue, each member of the learning community is an educational leader as all become jointly responsible for academic and personal growth. All members of a problem-posing learning environment "are now critical co-investigators in dialogue with the teacher" (Freire, 1970, pp. 80–81). The barrier ceases to exist between educators and students. Thus, they arrive at clear, authentic, and ethical critical knowledge.

CRITICAL RACE THEORY AS A METHODOLOGY

As classroom teachers become conscious educators, they become well versed in the historical presence of marginalization and work to dismantle this within their classrooms. Accordingly, Solórzano and Yosso (2002) argue "critical race theory recognizes that the experiential knowledge of people of color is legitimate, appropriate, and critical to understanding, analyzing, and teaching about racial subordination" (p. 26). Critical race theorists appropriately utilize counter-storytelling to re-tell the lived experiences of historically marginalized populations by including storytelling, family histories, biographies, scenarios, parables, *cuentos, testimonios*, chronicles, and narratives (Bell, 1992; Solórzano & Yosso, 2002). As such, we used narratives to counter dominant classroom practices and curriculum "to reframe the tale, to flip the script" (Leonardo, 2013, p. 20) in order to acknowledge our students' lived experiences.

Site Description

Our high school is located roughly 70 miles from the U.S.-Mexican border. The school is identified as a Title I school. The demographics of the student population are: 90.1% Latino/a, 4.0% Native American, 3.8% white, 1.3% African American, 0.6% Multi-Racial, and 0.3% Asian American/Pacific Islander. Many students are identified as first-generation, English Language Learners (ELLs). In addition, 14.6% of the students are identified as students with IEPs (Individualized Education Plans). This 12th-grade course was open to all students and each year had students from all racial and ethnic groups, as well as ELL and mainstreamed special education students. The class size ranged from 30–36 students per year, and this particular group had 31 students.

OUR NARRATIVE

The 2010–2011 school year for ethnic studies classes in the Tucson Unified School District (T.U.S.D.) began with some stress because of the recently-passed Arizona law banning ethnic studies courses.[3] *U.S. History: Mexican American Perspectives* and *U.S. Government/Social Justice Education Project* were two classes at our school deemed "dangerous." The attack on culturally-based, social justice-centered curriculum was mind-boggling. It was incomprehensible to the students and teachers involved in the T.U.S.D. Mexican American/Raza Studies Department (M.A.S.), as well as to other teachers whose focus was on students' lives and critical consciousness. In this context of heightened scrutiny and Arizona Department of Education's random visits, we began our year.

Preparation and Course Focus

Teacher team-building was essential in our preparation for the school year. Prior to teaching the government course, we shared our philosophies, methodologies, strengths and fears. We recognized the value of being vulnerable with each other, as well as the importance of consistent reflection. This helped us be more connected and authentic in working together with our students.

Both of us were committed to education as liberation with the central focus on decolonization and the development of critical consciousness. From the beginning, we established that we were facilitators and that all of us would learn from each other and explore, with a constructivist approach, issues of concern in our communities. Committed to encouraging our students' agency and active citizenship, the course centered around what mattered to them and how they were impacted by society and governmental institutions. We created an ongoing list of resources and activities that would highlight and acknowledge their experiences and ensure that their voices dominated the classroom. Too often our students do not see themselves in the predominant curriculum, so we sought out materials that provided voices of those with whom they connected culturally.

We introduced the course by discussing the fact that education is political—in what we include, do not include, and how the class is organized. The syllabus was based on the state standards (Foundations of Government; Structure of Government; Functions of Government; Rights, Responsibilities, and Roles of Citizenship; and Government Systems of the World), but the focus was on the students, their experiences, and those of their ancestors. And, as a class fostering conscientization, we analyzed topics such as white supremacy, capitalism, sexism, heterosexism, gentrification, ageism, classicism, neoliberalism, and immigration. By discussing and researching these issues, we provided opportunities for students to write counter narratives, critique hegemony, and problematize systems of oppression.

Though much of the course dealt with the social construction of race, institutional racism, and systems of oppression, we also highlighted progress and hope with different case studies and a final community project. Students learned the cycle of praxis, researched an issue affecting their community, and proposed solutions.

The syllabus requested input from the home, and parents and guardians were welcomed to attend and participate in classroom activities and field trips. Each semester we planned community *Encuentros*, meetings where students presented their research and projects. Held in our library, a classroom, and a nearby park, these were celebratory family and community meetings that included dinner and other entertainment.

Mexican American/Raza Studies Principles

Our teaching philosophy embraced the indigenous epistemology of our school district's M.A.S. Department and Freire's (1970) levels of consciousness. *In lak ech* and *panche be* are Mayan guides that are fundamental to our pedagogy, as is the *Mexica Nahui Ollin*, which promotes self-connection, reflection, and transformation.

In lak ech, translated as "you are my other me," speaks to our seeing ourselves in others. Embracing this phrase helps to re-humanize and cultivate a safe environment for sharing and growing. The necessary attitude is that we are in this struggle together and responsible to each other. The idea is beautifully expressed in an excerpt of a poem entitled *Pensamiento Serpentino* written by Luis Valdez (1990) and presented to students at the beginning of the year.

IN LAK ECH

Tú eres mi otro yo.	You are my other me.
Si te hago daño a ti,	If I do harm to you,
Me hago daño a mi mismo.	I do harm to myself.
Si te amo y respeto,	If I love and respect you,
Me amo y respeto yo.	I love and respect myself.

Panche be, translated as "seeking the root of the truth," encourages us to look at historical events and present-day issues from all sides, analyzing context and perspective. We connected *panche be* to the College Board analysis tool SOAPS (Subject, Occasion, Audience, Purpose, and Speaker) to delve into primary documents and newspaper and magazine articles. Invariably in questioning data or attitudes, students would say, "*panche be,*" and the discussion went deeper, the unpacking further. They were inspired to question.

We introduced the *Nahui Ollin* (Four Energies or Reflections) from the Aztec Sunstone, a historical record and cyclical calendar still used today, by giving a lesson on how the Mexica Calendar has been misinterpreted and misrepresented since the arrival of Europeans to the Americas. This supported the goal of countering how people's histories are too often told by the colonial culture and the brainwashing impact that has. The *Nahui Ollin* is made up of *Quetzalcoatl* (precious, beautiful knowledge, our students' cultural knowledge and what they bring from home), *Tezcatlipoca* (self-reflection), *Huitzilopochtli* (the will), and *Xipe Totec* (transformation). We transform when we embrace our precious beautiful knowledge, when we reflect on our thoughts and actions, when we have the will to make change, to support our community, and to take action for a better world.

Community Building

We spent a substantial amount of time throughout the year developing our class community. Community-building activities can easily be adapted for use throughout the year. Activities such as inside-outside circles, dyads, connecting stories, and voting with your feet, are great ways to introduce, explore and review concepts. In addition, they often incorporate movement, which can re-energize the classroom. Many students' previous experiences of marginalization required that we take time to build trust and establish our focus. The first icebreaker activities centered on the M.A.S. principles to create a humanizing environment with precepts that inspired reflection and helped the group connect on a deeper level. We all felt responsible to each other. At the end of the year students commented on the class being like a second family.

Levels of Consciousness

Freire's (1970) levels of consciousness were useful in analysis and provided a structure to help students reflect on their own thinking as they developed critical consciousness. As we dialogued, debated, and researched, we asked ourselves what level of thinking was happening. This was a powerful tool that facilitated our understanding of socialization and hegemony. It motivated us to confront blaming situations often heard in our own school, such as the claim that "our parents don't care about education" because they were not at parents' night, rather than looking into the reasons they may not have been able to attend.

We introduced the levels of consciousness by providing statistics on topics like graduation and incarceration rates, racial profiling, and controversial legislation in Arizona, such as SB1070, the anti-immigration law, and HB2281, the anti-ethnic studies law. We documented responses from the group. After reviewing the levels, we asked students to evaluate their thinking. Which levels were represented? This activity facilitated our "reading the world."

The process of becoming critically conscious is frustrating, but that distress, even if it serves to shut down some students for a while (and it is important to acknowledge this), eventually leads to agency. Whereas the state lawmakers who pushed to ban ethnic studies in our state believed we were teaching our students to feel oppressed by these readings, Freire's work promotes the opposite. The idea that we can actually make a difference in the world is transforming, so the process of conscientization is connected back to *Huitzilopochtli* and *Xipe Totec*.

Student Voice and Autonomy

Students' voices dominated the classroom. All students were constantly provided opportunities to present to their classmates with the understanding that this was *their* class and *their* voices mattered. At first they were invited to share and then expected to present assignments, such as the poem José read to the group. For students who struggled with social anxiety, we accommodated their needs by reading or having others read aloud, with permission, their thought-provoking, poignant journal entries and parts of essays. The class was scaffolded so as to encourage those reluctant to participate to gain confidence in a supportive environment.

Students had a choice in different types of activities and with whom they preferred to work. This helped to support the varying skill levels and strengths within our classroom. They were also encouraged to bring in resources to support our learning. They met regularly in small discussion groups and research teams and came to determine how much time they needed for particular activities. One lesson we used several times was a group analysis of an article or editorial on an issue in the news. Each group was given a different piece with basic instructions: read, comment, connect it to the cycle of praxis, and present. They were given time to figure out how to organize and complete the assignment. Then, they presented to the whole group. The students determined the process and product. Some groups chose one speaker and others took turns. Some groups created and presented a poster. These assignments helped guide students in framing arguments with peers and in developing skills to fulfill other class projects.

Tezcatlipoca (Reflection) Through Journals

One way we valued student voice was through journals. Though journals took time to read regularly, they were an excellent tool to support students in their learning. Regular journal writing assignments were one of the best gauges of student understanding, engagement, and growth. They provided a forum for individual student-teacher discussions, helped to build relationships, and extended critical thinking.

Journals were a safe medium for students to engage the roots of their thoughts. We asked them to write their stream of consciousness ("pencil to the paper, pedal to the metal") to deal with the self-defeating filter and to build confidence in their thought processes. Being able to articulate a stance and reflect on that stance was transformative. They grappled with difficult ideas and could experiment with different voices. Volunteers shared what they wrote, and this served to inspire emerging writers. Through their journals students got to see how their views changed and how their critical analysis skills grew over the course of the year.

Group Work

Groups changed relatively often the first semester in order for students to get to know each other and to build relationships across peer groups with varying skills. They assisted each other with note-taking, in supporting absent teammates, and in discussions and debates. To create a supportive space for all learners, students practiced different roles at their own pace within the groups—note-takers, discussion leaders, and presenters. The support and interdependence were *in lak ech*-oriented and helped them appreciate each other's strengths and intelligences.

We used an excellent dyad activity from Professor Antwi Akom of San Francisco State University (Akom, 2008). Students sat across from each other in pairs and were instructed to answer a question or respond to a prompt one at a time without interrupting. The facilitator gave each person (A or B) time to answer. Using his presentation as a model, we gave A more time to answer a couple of questions. We also asked the As or Bs to describe their partners' answers, rather than allowing them to tell their own stories. The partner could not correct or add to the telling of their perspective. This was a way to initiate a discussion on privilege and delegitimization. After a few rounds, the participants formed a circle and shared, unpacking the experience and responses. We posed the following questions: Did anyone notice the discrepancy in the times allotted for each speaker? How did you feel when your partner was telling your story and you could not respond? Whose voice counts? Whose story is "legitimate"?

Guest Speakers

Guest speakers provided different lenses, new perspectives, and helped change the class dynamic. There were many people willing to take the time to come into our classroom. We appreciated regular visits from former students who had taken the class in years past. One lovely aspect of our district M.A.S. Department was that graduating students were encouraged to work as paid support staff to facilitate presentations and activities with our current students. One young man attended periodically and assisted in discussion activities. He also mentored a number of students who benefitted from his shared experiences and support.

Our guest speakers were family members and other community leaders who were involved in different struggles or in community organizing. One visitor was a local *calpolli* (Mexica community) leader who provided beautiful lessons on indigenous Mexican culture, focusing on reading the Aztec Sunstone, or *Tonalmachiotl*. This reinforced the M.A.S. precepts and the connection to other communities.

We invited tribal leaders, one from the Yaqui community and one from the Tohono O'odham community to discuss the structure of their governments and relationship to the state and federal systems. If potential speakers could not come during the school day, they were invited to present to students, staff, and teachers after school through our school's Movimiento Estudiantil Chican@ de Aztlan (MEChA) group.

Field Trips

Another way to promote school-community connections was through field trips. We wanted to relate what we were learning in the classroom with what was going on in the community, culturally and politically. We had an ongoing collaboration with an ethnic studies professor in the Anthropology Department at the local university. Each year, students from her class came to our school to learn about what our students were studying. In turn, we visited the university and attended one of her classes with break-out sessions. Our students developed relationships with college students, and this supported many in seeing themselves continuing with their education after high school.

An activity in mapping community assets helped us connect with organizations close to our school that we could visit. One such collective welcomed us to a presentation on water harvesting and sustainable farming. The community mapping helped provide a list of places students could go to fulfill an "outside event" assignment. Posted in the classroom was an ongoing list of activities, such as school board meetings, plays, community meetings, and movies. Students could earn additional credit for participation and analysis by documenting the experience and connecting it to some aspect of the course.

Students as Researchers

For the culminating project, students researched an issue in the community that they were passionate about with the goal of proposing viable solutions. Since we had a variety of skill levels, we took additional time to develop students' understanding of the cycle of praxis: identify the problem, analyze the problem, plan action to address the problem, implement the plan, evaluate how it went, and continue/start again. This helped organize their research project. Our students memorized the cycle earlier as one of the steps of the Definite Dozen (Summitt, 1998), a guide for revolutionary struggle for social justice by San Francisco State Professor Jeff Duncan-Andrade.

To initiate the process of naming problems (identifying) we used several activities, as well as simply brainstorming. The "isms" or the different types of oppression discussed in the unit introducing critical consciousness got students thinking about problems they saw daily in our communities. Two of our assignments, the "I Am" poem and an analysis of a current popular song, generated multiple issues important to the students. After student presentations, the themes were pulled out and discussed.

Groups were formed by interest. Students created a topic poster with everything they knew, their questions, and visuals. This served as a basis for their research focus. They presented the poster to the class and solicited additional information and questions. After an introduction to the research assignment, they discussed what exactly their problem was and why it was important, as well as its causes and effects. As students were starting their initial investigations, we found and distributed academic articles for each topic to expand their critical thinking and to use as models for the process of analysis.

As a class we brainstormed different sources for their research and then did short lessons on field notes, surveys, and interviews, focusing on effective questioning and note-taking strategies. We also discussed conceptual terms to denote patterns in their data. Reviewing Freire's (1970) concepts, such as banking education and false generosity, helped students come up with creative categories to use in their analysis.

Students had an outline of steps to complete the research paper and a presentation that included a reflection on the process and recommendations for responses to the problem. We spent most of the class time at the end of the year in preparation for their presenting at the district conference at our local university. We invited other students, faculty, and staff to support and critique practice sessions. The camaraderie and commitment team members exhibited in these sessions was particularly moving. Students had become educational leaders, responsible to each other in their academic and personal growth.

IMPLICATIONS FOR PRACTICE

Historical marginalization based on race and ethnicity is abundant in our educational institutions, as is the unsanctioned sidelining of special education students who are often denied access to mainstream, enhanced-learning courses. Our students with disabilities brought unique strengths into the classroom. We all benefitted from their diverse perspectives and assets, which we incorporated into our curriculum. This pedagogical approach of building sensitivity for learning differences strengthened teacher and student conscientization.

When teachers truly embrace that they are also students in the classroom and recognize that they must reflect on who they need to be and continuously become, they leave behind the traditional banking education paradigm and model the process of reading the world with their students. This makes the experience more effective for all involved.

Our class was successful because a safe and authentic environment was created by the educators and students. Through culturally responsive curriculum, problem-posing strategies, student agency, and community involvement, we transformed the classroom and ourselves. We share our experience as a model for incorporating activities that support the development of a critical consciousness, a necessary endeavor in social-justice-oriented education.

NOTES

1. A pseudonym.
2. We discussed the issues of "American" and preferred the use of U.S. instead because the U.S. is only one of the countries in the Americas.
3. HB2281 banned courses that promote the overthrow of the United States Government, promote resentment toward a race or class of people, are designed primarily for pupils of a particular ethnic group, and advocate ethnic solidarity instead of the treatment of pupils as individuals. Presently, it is in litigation in the 9th Circuit.

REFERENCES

Akom, A. A. (2008, July). *Untitled*. Presentation at The Mexican American/Raza Studies Institute for Transformative Education, Tucson, AZ.

Bell, D. (1992). *Faces at the bottom of the well: The permanence of racism*. New York, NY: Basic Books.

Bonilla-Silva, E., & Forman T. E. (2000). "I am not a racist but ...": Mapping white college students' racial ideology in the USA. *Discourse & Society, 11*(1), 50–85.

Castagno, A. E. (2009). Making sense of multicultural education: A synthesis of the various typologies found in the literature. *Multicultural Perspectives, 11*(1), 43–48.

Freire, P. (1970). *Pedagogy of the oppressed*. New York, NY: The Continuum International Publishing Group.

Gay, G. (2002). Preparing for culturally responsive teaching. *Journal of Teacher Education, 53*(2), 106–116.

Irizarry, J. G. (2007). Ethnic and urban intersections in the classroom: Latino students, hybrid identities, and culturally responsive pedagogy. *Multicultural Perspectives, 9*(3), 21–28.

Leonardo, Z. (2013). *Race frameworks: A multidimensional theory of racism and education*. New York, NY: Teachers College Press.

Moll, L. C., Amanti, C., Neff, D., & Gonzalez, N. (1992). Funds of knowledge for teaching: Using a qualitative approach to connect homes and classrooms. *Theory into Practice, 31*(2), 132–141.

Solórzano, D. G., & Yosso, T. J. (2002). Critical race methodology: Counter-storytelling as an analytical framework for educational research. *Qualitative Inquiry, 8*(1), 23–44.

Summitt, P. (1998). *Reach for the summit: The definite dozen system for succeeding at whatever you do*. New York, NY: Broadway Books.

Valdez, L. (1990). Pensamiento serpentino. *Early works: Actos, Bernabé and pensameinto serpentino*. Houston, TX: Arte Público Press.

Notes ON Contributors

Janice L. Anderson received her Ph.D. in Curriculum and Instruction with an emphasis in Science Education and Technology from the Lynch School of Education at Boston College in 2008. She is currently an Associate Professor of Science Education at the University of North Carolina at Chapel Hill.

Alyssa Bauermeister is a secondary English Language Arts teacher at Hanford High School in Richland, Washington. She is a graduate of Washington State University from the Master in Teaching program (2016) and additionally attained a Bachelor's degree in English Literature from WSU (2013).

Stef Bernal-Martinez, an elementary teacher, was born in Southern California and grew up in the West Texas borderlands. She received a degree in Political Science at The University of Texas at El Paso and her master's degree in Early Childhood Education at Sarah Lawrence College.

Beverly Milner (Lee) Bisland is an Associate Professor of Social Studies Education in the Elementary and Early Childhood Education Department at Queens College of the City University of New York. She has made numerous presentations and published scholarly articles in a variety of research journals.

Marissa Bivona holds a BA in English with a Minor in Black Studies from Pomona College and is working towards a Masters in Psychology from

Southern Connecticut State University. She has six years of teaching experience and completed the Harris Fellowship in Early Childhood Education.

Laura Bower-Phipps holds a Ph.D. in Curriculum and Instruction from the University of Nevada, Las Vegas. She is currently an associate professor of Curriculum and Learning at Southern Connecticut State University. Dr. Bower-Phipps publishes in the areas of sexual and gender diversity in teacher education.

Ashley S. Boyd is Assistant Professor of English Education at Washington State University where she teaches courses on critical theory, English Methods, and Young Adult Literature. She earned her BA in English, MAT in Secondary English, and PhD in Education from UNC-Chapel Hill.

Daniel Kelvin Bullock is a graduate of UNC Chapel Hill (Bachelors and Masters) and NC State University (Doctorate). Currently, he is the Executive Director for Equity Affairs for Durham Public Schools in NC. He has worked in education for over 12 years.

Ronda Taylor Bullock is a third-year doctoral student in the Policy, Leadership, and School Improvement Program at UNC Chapel Hill. Using a critical race theory lens, she studies white elementary students' racial identity construction. She's the Director of we are (working to extend anti-racist education).

Courtney B. Cook is a former high school English teacher and is currently a doctoral student in the Cultural Studies in Education Department at the University of Texas at Austin. She is interested in art's potential to inspire humanizing dialogue around systemic injustice, cultural trauma, and contemporary violence.

Linsay DeMartino is a researcher, educator, and active community member. After completing her doctoral degree in Educational Leadership at the University of Arizona, her work and publications are grounded in transformative leadership practices, tempered radicalism, and social justice.

Josef Donnelly is a high school history teacher in New York City. He currently teaches global history and an ethics course for freshmen. He is a former ambassador for the Teacher Powered Schools movement. Before teaching, Josef was a Peace Corps Volunteer in Micronesia.

Jeanne Dyches is an assistant professor of literacy education at Iowa State University. She earned her Ph.D from the University of North Carolina-Chapel Hill; her master's and bachelor's degrees are from NC State University. Recent publications include Journal of Teacher Education and The Urban Review.

Bryan Fede is a doctoral candidate at the University of North Carolina–Chapel Hill. He is a former high school math instructor and elementary school math coach. Current research interests include teacher training in mathematics and the pedagogy of online learning in the content areas.

Brian Gibbs taught social studies in East Los Angeles, California for 16 years. He is currently an Assistant Professor of education at the University of North Carolina at Chapel Hill.

Jeff A. Greiner, a doctoral student at NC State, received the Martorella Award and teaches social studies at Martin MS in Raleigh, NC. He published Seventh-Grade Social Studies versus Social Meliorism (2016) and Technology and Disciplined Inquiry in the World History Classroom (2016) with Dr. Meghan Manfra.

Rebecca Harmon is pursuing a BS in Elementary and Special Education and a BA in English at Southern Connecticut State University, where she is in the Honors College. She is a preschool teacher at a private childcare center in Wallingford, CT.

Martinette Horner (Ed.D. University of North Carolina at Chapel Hill). Dr. Horner coordinates the MSA programs. As a former NC Teaching Fellow and NC Principal Fellow as well as a National Board Certified Teacher, she brings practitioner experience as a teacher and principal in North Carolina public schools to the courses she teaches about supervisory practices and empowerment. Dr. Horner also facilitates partnership and outreach efforts between the school and P–12 educators.

Alison LaGarry is a Clinical Assistant Professor of Education at the University of North Carolina at Chapel Hill. Her research interests include social justice pedagogy, arts education, educational sociology, and qualitative methodology. Her publications include manuscripts on social justice teaching methods, and arts integration.

Holly Matteson currently attends Washington State University where she is pursuing a degree in English. Her areas of inquiry include critical literacies, English education, and adolescent literature. She recently won a university research award for her work on PROGRESS, an original framework for engaging pre-service teachers' critical literacies.

Lana M. Minshew is a doctoral candidate in the Learning Sciences and Psychological Studies program at the University of North Carolina at Chapel Hill. She earned her M.Ed. in Educational Psychology from the University of Houston in 2013. Prior to beginning her doctoral work Lana was a middle school science teacher in Houston Independent School District.

Deb Morrison earned her Ph.D. in Science Education at the University of Colorado Boulder. She is currently a research associate at the Institute for Science and Math Education at the University of Washington Seattle. For more information on Dr. Morrison see www.debmorrison.me.

Celina Martínez Nichols is a PhD student in the Department of Curriculum and Instruction at the University of Texas at Austin. Her research interests center on neoliberalism and education with a particular interest in "no excuses" charter schools.

Anne Olcott earned an AB from Harvard and an M.Ed. from Tufts University. She started teaching in 1988 and has been in her current position at Westville Community School in New Haven, CT since 2004.

Hillary Parkhouse is an Assistant Professor of Teaching and Learning at Virginia Commonwealth University. Her research interests include critical citizenship education, global education, youth civic empowerment, and critical pedagogy. She has published articles on undocumented immigrant youth activism and teaching culturally and linguistically diverse students.

Alexis Patterson earned her Ph.D. in Curriculum and Teacher Education at Stanford University. She is an assistant professor in the School of Education at the University of California, Davis and a faculty scholar with the Center for the Advancement of Multicultural Perspectives on Science.

Joanne M. Pattison-Meek holds a Ph.D. in Curriculum Studies and Teacher Development from the Ontario Institute for Studies in Education, University of Toronto. She is currently the Instructional Program Leader for Research in the Halton District School Board in Ontario, Canada.

Summer Melody Pennell is an Assistant Professor of English Education at Truman State University. Her research interests include social justice pedagogy, English education, queer theory, Young Adult literature, and qualitative methods. Her publications include manuscripts on her theory of queer cultural capital and teacher education.

Jessica S. Powell holds a Ph.D. in Education from the University of North Carolina-Chapel Hill. She is an Assistant Professor of Education and Co-Director of the Urban Education Fellows program at Southern Connecticut State University. Her recent publications address racial justice.

Sara Rusk taught at the high school level for 25 years, 10 of which included Chican@ Studies classes for the banned Mexican American/Raza Studies Department in Tucson, Arizona. She is grateful to have worked in a district department that supported student and teacher conscientization.

Elizabeth E. Saylor, PhD, is a clinical assistant professor of educational theory and practice in the College of Education at the University of Georgia. She is a former elementary school teacher of ten years and a National Board Certified teacher.

Alexandra Schindel earned her Ph.D. in Curriculum and Instruction, University of Wisconsin-Madison. She is an assistant professor at the University at Buffalo, a recipient of a NAEd/Spencer post-doctoral Fellowship and has published her research in international journals including Science Education and Environmental Education Research.

Sunghee Shin is an Associate Professor of Educational Technology in the Department of Early Childhood and Elementary Education, Queens College, City University of New York. Her research is focused on collaborative learning in web-based learning communities and the impact of technology in global education.

Jay M. Shuttleworth is Assistant Professor and Chair of Adolescent Education at Long Island University, Brooklyn. His research interests include citizenship and sustainable living, issues-centered education, and teacher education. He is a Fulbright Memorial Fellow and was a finalist for California Teacher of the Year honors.

Cherish Williams, a third-year doctoral student studying School Psychology at UNC Chapel Hill, has a master's degree in School and Mental Health Counseling from the University of Pennsylvania. Cherish's training centers cultural sensitivity and promoting the social and emotional well-being of children and adolescents.

Index

Action Research, 28–29, 217, 226, 229–230

Activism, 3, 16, 33, 85, 105, 124, 129, 160, 194, 217, 225–226, 230, 232

African-American, 19–21, 42, 45–47, 50, 71, 85, 111, 136, 139, 154, 164, 187, 194, 217, 221, 242

Afrocentric Education, 19

Agency (student), 17, 83, 107, 108, 155, 162, 189, 195, 197, 213, 219–220, 242, 246

Anti-colonial Education, 15, 20

Anti-Racism, 25–26, 41–52

Arts, 45, 192

    Art Education, 4

    Arts Educators, 88

Asian (ethnicity), 164, 71, 97, 136, 242

Assessment, 56, 137, 227

    Formative, 101, 208

    Summative, 74, 204, 207, 209–210

Autobiography (as reflexive methodology), 88, 194

Care, 110, 138, 140

Case Study, 67, 148, 189, 204–205

Multiple case study approach, 178

Christopher Columbus, 201–202, 205–210

Citizenship, 17, 65–66, 76, 213–214, 227

Citizenship Education, 17, 175–178, 213

    Multicultural Citizenship Education, 176–177

Civic literacy, 18, 202, 226–227

Class discussion (teaching method), 26, 31, 44, 47–50, 58, 60, 73, 95, 125–126, 128, 139, 149, 165, 192, 195, 197, 208, 227–228, 231–232, 244, 247

Co-teaching, 44, 93

Colorism, 45

Community Building, 244

Communities of Care, 109

Community Mapping, 248

Community Research, 26, 53, 55

Conscientization, 5, 20, 243

Counter-story (counter-narrative), 43, 45, 124, 150, 155, 188, 241, 243

Critical Consciousness, 6, 20, 91, 103, 155, 214–216, 218, 221, 242, 245

Critical Conversations, 168–170

Critical Ethnography, 148
Critical Hope, 10, 221
Critical Literacy, 6, 91, 95–97, 156, 163
Critical Mathematics, 95–97, 103
Critical Pedagogy, 3, 5, 15, 20, 22, 108, 122, 149, 189, 214–216
Critical Race Parenting, 42
Critical Race Theory, 19, 42, 241
Critical Theory, 5
Cross Talk, 110
Culturally Accessing Pedagogies, 189
Culturally Responsive Pedagogy, 19–20, 26, 80, 187, 239
Culturally Relevant Pedagogy, 5, 15, 18, 19–20, 80, 134–135, 139–140, 142
Culture of Feeling, 115

Dialogue, 20, 21, 74, 107, 109, 122, 162, 176, 210, 241
Democracy, 15, 17, 66, 75, 108, 159, 214, 221
Democratic Education, 17, 108
Digital Storytelling, 55
Disability, 18, 160
Discourse, 72, 75, 188
Discourse Analysis, 166
Discrimination, 19, 217, 219, 220
Dramatic Play, 32

English Language Arts, 4, 10, 93, 103, 105, 137, 187–197, 159
English Language Learners (ELL), 10, 160, 202, 205, 242
Ethnic Studies, 15, 17, 18, 19, 225, 242, 245

Feminism, 21, 65–67, 75
    Critical Feminist Theory, 66–67
Field Trips, 247
Focus group, 67, 178
Freire, Paulo, 5, 20, 94, 108, 109, 122, 123, 124, 127, 145, 146, 147, 151, 155, 162, 163, 189, 204, 210, 214, 221, 226, 240, 241, 245, 248
Funds of Knowledge, 5, 238–239

Gender, 16, 18, 21–22, 25, 27, 35, 65–67
    Gender Identity Development, 65–66, 68, 71, 74

Globalization, 20, 122
Group Work, 95, 97, 99, 101, 139, 149, 153, 164–165, 167–170, 181–182, 245–248

Homophobia, 168
Human Relations, 176, 187
Human Rights, 17, 122

Identity, 18, 21, 43, 80–81, 146
Immigration, 10, 26, 53–54, 160, 179, 222
Interdisciplinary, 10, 103–104
Intergroup Relations, 181, 183–184
Interpretative Phenomenological Analysis, 111–112
Intersectionality, 21, 43, 194
Interviewing (research method), 67, 80, 82, 97, 112, 137, 148, 178, 231–233
Interviewing (by students), 21, 55, 57–59, 61, 181–182, 184, 191, 193, 216–218, 220, 227, 248
Inquiry Activities or Projects, 56–58, 100, 122, 136

Journaling, 42, 44, 67, 245–246

Knowledge
    Knowledge Production, 26, 214–215
    Official Knowledge, 19, 147, 202, 226

Ladson-Billings, Gloria, 5, 134, 138–140, 150, 188, 210
Latinx (Latina/o), 111, 154, 216, 225, 71, 242
Levels of Consciousness, 240, 245
LGBTQIA, 22, 99–102, 229
    Transgender, 16, 21, 68, 159
Liberating Pedagogy, 163, 214, 242
Literacy, 3, 10, 15, 146, 208
Literacy Practices, 31
Literature, 44, 47, 50, 187, 196–197

Mathematics, 3, 10, 91, 94, 98–99, 101, 137–139
Marriage Equality, 91, 94, 98–103
Mixed Race students, 97
Multicultural Citizenship Pedagogy, 128

Multicultural Education, 15–16, 18, 19, 79, 176–177
Multimodality, 193
Music Education, 4, 26, 80–88
Narrative Inquiry, 26, 81
  Narrative Case Study, 81
  Narrative Analysis, 81

Newcomer Students, 160, 176, 179, 202–203, 206

Observation (as research method), 29, 55–56, 137–140, 142, 148, 166, 168, 178, 19–191, 216

Pedagogical Content Knowledge, 188
  Social Justice Pedagogical and Content Knowledge, 188
Phenomenology, 91, 111
Positionality, 82, 146, 216, 227
Post-critical Ethnography, 95
Power (systems of), 19, 20, 21, 66, 67, 72, 75, 146, 147, 148, 150, 152, 154–155, 164, 215, 218, 222, 227–229
Problem-posing Education, 203–204, 241
Professional Development, 136–137, 139, 141

Queer Pedagogy, 15, 21–22, 28, 33–34, 37, 95–97
Queer Theory, 21–22, 28–29

Race and ethnicity, 5–6, 18–21, 26, 42–45, 49–51, 56–57, 71, 97, 99, 103, 111, 179, 194, 229, 238, 240, 243, 249
Race to the Top, 133–134, 136
Racism, 20, 45, 147, 213, 215, 220, 228, 239
Reading Attitudes, 164, 166
Refugee, 180–181, 17, 129–130
Resistance, 196, 222
Resistance Movements, 193, 217–218, 221
Rigor, 8–9, 104, 227
Rural Community and education, 179

School Culture, 135–136, 140–141
School Reform, 141–142, 146–147
Science Education, 92, 137, 139–140, 146–147

Social Action, 8, 15–16, 159, 209–210, 248
Social Justice Education, 3, 41, 79–80, 121, 188
  Definitions, 5, 15–16, 27, 41, 54, 79–80, 94, 108, 202–203
  Practices, 6–8, 55–61, 97–98, 104–105, 205–210
Social Movements, 10, 21, 65, 67, 157, 217–220, 230–231
Social Studies, 4, 10, 53, 121, 202, 205–206, 213, 214–215, 225, 229, 160
Socioeconomic Status, 5, 25, 30, 68, 71, 92, 123, 133–135, 137, 141, 149, 154, 228, 238, 240, 243
Sociopolitical Consciousness, 20
STEM, 92
Story Circles, 91, 109, 112
Student Engagement, 137–138, 140, 145, 148, 229
Student Voice, 245
Survey Research, 164

Teacher Beliefs, 103–104, 136, 139–142
Technology Integration, 55, 59, 92, 96, 117, 133–136, 153, 170
Tucson Unified School District, 19, 242

Urban Education, 141, 180, 205–206
U. S. Government (course), 160, 225, 238
U. S. History (course), 53, 160–161, 213, 215, 217

Vietnam, 227–229

White (Caucasian), 20, 30, 42–43, 46–48, 50, 68–69, 71–72, 82, 85, 94, 97, 100, 111–112, 117, 136–137, 149, 164, 166, 167, 176–179, 181, 184, 185, 194–195, 215, 216, 218, 240, 242, 252
White Supremacy, 19, 243
Whiteness, 43, 117, 189
World History (global history-course), 92, 121–131, 205

Young Adult Literature, 162
Youth Participatory Action Research, 160, 226, 229–230